SpringerBriefs in Archaeology

For further volumes:
http://www.springer.com/series/10186

Martin Carver • Bisserka Gaydarska
Sandra Montón-Subías
Editors

Field Archaeology from Around the World

Ideas and Approaches

Editors
Martin Carver
University of York
York, UK

Bisserka Gaydarska
Durham University
Durham, UK

Sandra Montón-Subías
Department of Humanities
ICREA/Universitat Pompeu Fabra
Barcelona, Spain

This book consists of slightly modified selections from the Encyclopedia of Global Archaeology edited by Claire Smith, originally published by Springer Science+Business Media New York in 2014.

ISSN 1861-6623 ISSN 2192-4910 (electronic)
ISBN 978-3-319-09818-0
DOI 10.1007/978-3-319-09819-7
Springer Cham Heidelberg New York Dordrecht London

Library of Congress Control Number: 2014948760

Printed on acid-free paper

Springer is part of Springer Science+Business Media (www.springer.com)

Excavation in progress in Nara, Japan (see p. 223)

Preface

Students and academics sometimes allow themselves to express the opinion that "not much has changed in field archaeology over the last twenty years". The reason is easily explained. As the commercial profession was formed, field method became standardised and, due largely to national economic and political pressures, it got stuck in its ways. Standardised practice was where the money was. But elsewhere, under the radar, practitioners realised that the version of the past they generate was under-served by standard procedures; it is our job to respond creatively – not passively – to the great variety of the archaeological resource and the host of questions we put to it.

This book hopes to show that field archaeology is archaeology's liveliest sub-discipline. The last few decades have witnessed a surge of experimentation, on and under the ground – but it is not only in technical method that the advances are seen. Field research procedure is breaking away from the "default systems" of the 1960s to 1990s and adopting ingenious attitudes to project design – the "ideas and approaches" of our title. The giant commercial sector is applying itself to the task of increasing the research dividend of every intervention. Academics are coming to realise that ideas are not confined to theory: what you do is as determinant as what you think.

This brief trip around the world offers an impression of how this is happening. Part 1 is a summary overview of current practices in survey and excavation. In Part 2 we encounter some of the special challenges that are posed by working in peat, caves, permafrost, jungle mines, motorways and modern cities and the variety of approaches, tools, and recording systems that have been assembled to respond to them. In Part 3, our authors offer sketches of the traditions adopted by fieldworkers in several continents, explaining their differences, less through the teaching of great pioneers and more from the character of the terrain and the political framework within which archaeologists work.

We will see a thriving subject, spread across the academic, commercial and public sectors. Here high precision and disciplined practice are married to imagination, adaptability and ingenuity in the service of the mission dear to every scientist – to produce something new.

York, UK Martin Carver
Durham, UK Bisserka Gaydarska
Barcelona, Spain Sandra Montón-Subías

Acknowledgements

The material assembled here was originally prepared for Springer's *Encyclopaedia of Global Archaeology*, edited by Claire Smith and published in 11 volumes in 2014. The editors and authors pay tribute and offer their thanks to the publisher for providing this valuable additional outlet. Our subject is archaeological practice, so the venture will be especially beneficial, we believe, to the many thousands of professional and commercial archaeologists practising worldwide who may have limited access to the whole encyclopaedia. The editors are particular grateful to Teresa Kraus and Hana Nagdimov of Springer who have shepherded the new book into being.

Contents

Part I Methods

Contributors

Margaret E. Beck University of Iowa, Iowa, IA, USA

Josep Bosch Gavà Museum, Barcelona, Spain

David M. Carballo Department of Archaeology, Boston University, Boston, MA, USA

Mike T. Carson Micronesian Area Research Center, University of Guam, Mangilao, GU, USA

Martin Carver Department of Archaeology, University of York, York, UK

Graeme Cavers AOC Archaeology Group, Edinburgh, Scotland, UK

Mauro Cremaschi Dipartimento di Scienze della Terra 'A. Desio', Università degli Studi di Milano, Milan, Italy

Anne Crone AOC Archaeology Group, Edinburgh, Scotland, UK

Timothy Darvill School of Applied Sciences, Bournemouth University, Bournemouth, Dorset, UK

Maryam Dezhamkhooy University of Birjand, Birjand, Iran

Nena Galanidou Department of History and Archaeology, University of Crete, Rethymno, Greece

Omran Garazhian Department of Archaeology, Tehran University, Tehran, Iran

Bisserka Gaydarska Department of Archaeology, Durham University, Durham, UK

Daniela Hofmann Department of Archaeology and Conservation, Cardiff University, Cardiff, UK

Simon Holdaway The University of Auckland, Auckland, New Zealand

Madeleine Hummler Department of Archaeology, University of York, York, UK

Hsiao-chun Hung Department of Archaeology and Natural History, The Australian National University, Acton, ACT, Australia

Roman Křivánek Institute of Archaeology of the Academy of Sciences of the Czech Republic, Prague, Czech Republic

Stefan Larsson Swedish National Heritage Board, Lund, Sweden

Denise Leesch University of Neuchâtel, Neuchâtel, Switzerland

Kylie Lower-Eskelson Department of Archaeology, Flinders University, Adelaide, SA, Australia

Curtis W. Marean Institute of Human Origins, School of Human Evolution and Social Change, Arizona State University, Tempe, AZ, USA

Wendy Matthews Department of Archaeology, School of Human and Environmental Sciences, University of Reading, Reading, UK

Yumiko Nakanishi Osaka Prefectural Government, Osaka, Japan

Johan A.W. Nicolay University of Groningen, Groningen, The Netherlands

Simen Oestmo Institute of Human Origins, School of Human Evolution and Social Change, Arizona State University, Tempe, AZ, USA

Vladimir Pitulko Paleolithic Department, Institute for the History of Material Culture, Russian Academy of Sciences, St. Petersburg, Russia

Gustavo G. Politis Facultad de Ciencias Sociales, CONICET-INCUAPA UNICEN, Buenos Aires, Argentina

Dominic Powlesland The Landscape Research Centre & The McDonald Institute, University of Cambridge, Cambridge, UK

Włodzimierz Rączkowski Institute of Prehistory, Adam Mickiewicz University, Poznań, Poland

Per H. Ramqvist Department of Historical, Philosophical and Religious Studies, Umea University, Umea, Sweden

Cynthia Robin Department of Anthropology, Northwestern University, Evanston, IL, USA

Amrita Sarkar Department of Archaeology, Deccan College Postgraduate & Research Institute, Deemed University, Pune, India

Nathan Schlanger Trajectoires, Maison Archéologie & Ethnologie (MAE), 21 Allée de l'Université, Nanterre, France

Rónán Swan Archaeology, National Roads Authority, Dublin, Ireland

Immo Trinks Ludwig Boltzmann Institute for Archaeological Prospection and Virtual Archaeology, Vienna, Austria

Przemysław Urbańczyk Institute of Archaeology and Ethnology, Polish Academy of Sciences, Warsaw, Poland

Jason Wood Heritage Consultancy Services, Lancaster, UK

Rebecca Yamin John Milner Associates, Inc., West Chester, PA, USA

Leila P. Yazdi Neyshabour University, Neyshabour, Iran

Freie Universität Berlin, Berlin, Germany

Liangren Zhang School of Cultural Heritage, Northwest University, Xi'an City, Shaanxi Province, China

List of Figures

About the Editors

Martin Carver is emeritus Professor of Archaeology at the University of York (UK) and Editor of *Antiquity*. He is the founder of two commercial archaeology companies (FAS-Heritage and Birmingham Archaeology) and two museums (Sutton Hoo and the Tarbat Discovery Centre). He was secretary of the Institute of Field Archaeologists at its foundation and has carried out field research in England, Scotland, France, Italy and Algeria. His research interests are field method and the archaeology of protohistoric Europe.

Martin's books include: *Archaeological Value and Evaluation* (Padova, 2003), *Archaeological Investigation* (Routledge, 2009) and *Making Archaeology Happen: Design versus Dogma* (Left Coast, 2011).

Bisserka Gaydarska is a Post Doctoral Research Assistant at the Department of Archaeology in Durham University. After graduating from Sofia University, she received her Ph.D. in Durham University, which has been fostering her research activities ever since. Apart from her homeland Bulgaria, Bisserka has been involved in various field projects and museum studies in Romania, Greece, Turkey and recently Ukraine. Her main research interests are in landscape archaeology, material culture studies, the archaeology of gender and interdisciplinary studies that combine archeological science or information technology with archaeology.

Bisserka's publications include *Landscape, Material Culture and Society in South East Bulgaria.* (Archaeopress, 2007) and *Parts and Wholes: Fragmentation in Prehistoric Context* (with J. Chapman Oxbow Books, 2006).

Sandra Montón-Subías is ICREA Research Professor at UPF (Universitat Pompeu Fabra), Barcelona, Spain. She is interested in broad issues in social and theoretical archaeology, including conflict, gender, identity and funerary practice. More recently, she has added historical archaeology and the archaeology of Modern Spanish colonialism to her research agenda. She is co-chair of the EAA working party *Archaeology and Gender in Europe*.

Sandra's books include *The Archaeology of Bronze Age Iberia: Argaric Societies* (co-authored with G. Aranda and M. Sánchez Romero, Routledge 2014) and *Guess Who's Coming To Dinner. Feasting Rituals in the Prehistoric Societies of Europe and the Near East* (co-edited with the same authors, Oxbow, 2011).

Part I
Methods

Chapter 1
Field Method in Archaeology: Overview

Martin Carver

Introduction

Archaeological investigation is a science that responds to the needs of research, to the way that information has survived in the ground and to the present ownership and stakeholders of the site or landscape in question. Research objectives, terrain, and the social context therefore have to be matched for every field project in a *project design*. The best known methods of field investigation are *survey*, which reviews large areas on the surface (extensive investigation); *excavation*, which examines a constricted piece of ground by dissecting it (intensive investigation); and *the study of buildings*, which deduces the history of buildings that are still standing. Modern projects use all these methods in combination in rigorously planned programs.

Much of the archaeological resource is vulnerable to disturbance from the exigencies of modern life, and may be destroyed through the construction of roads (motorways) and buildings, especially in towns. Even in open country and desert, the surface is subject to continual attrition without human intervention. In each type of terrain, *natural and cultural formation processes* are continually at work, producing a huge variety of archaeological deposits, and demanding tailor-made approaches.

While much field method is directly applied to research questions, much more effort goes in recording archaeological sites that are likely to be damaged by modern construction or clearance. This work is undertaken by the 'rescue' or commercial profession (said to be engaged in *CRM* or Cultural Resource Management). At the present time, CRM activity greatly outnumbers university activity in both in its staff and their budgets. Given the often unique character of archaeological deposits, investigation needs to be of the highest quality and precision, designed to maximize information while it is still detectable and, wherever possible, to conserve deposits in the ground.

M. Carver (✉)
Department of Archaeology, University of York, York, UK
e-mail: martin.carver@york.ac.uk

M. Carver et al. (eds.), *Field Archaeology from Around the World*,
SpringerBriefs in Archaeology, DOI 10.1007/978-3-319-09819-7_1

Some Definitions

Field archaeologists explore the past at a number of different scales and use a basic vocabulary to designate what they find. The basic unit of past activity is the *object*, which might be an *artifact* (man-made – e.g., a brooch) or an *ecofact* or biota (natural-e.g., a seed). A collection of such objects is an *assemblage*. The earth or mineral *deposit* from which an assemblage is retrieved is a *context* (also called a stratum, a stratigraphic unit, or a cultural layer). Any set of contexts which offers evidence for past activity is a *feature* – a general term of great use in archaeology since it often happens that we find something but do not yet know what it is. Defined anomalies that later turn out to be a wall, a grave or a path are examples of features. A set of features, like four walls, can be designated as a *structure* (e.g., a building). A *site* is the term used for a concentration of features and structures, which imply former human occupation. It is also used to denote any place at which archaeologists have focused their investigations. A *landscape* (or *historic landscape* or *historic environment*), in archaeological terms, is compounded of the detected parts of ancient land use, particularly sites.

Procedures

Field investigation typically takes place in six consecutive stages, each of which deploys a range of different methods, briefly described in the contributions that follow in Part I (see Table 1.1).

1. The object of *RECONNAISSANCE* is to explore ancient landscapes and identify sites. The term *site* is used in this case to denote areas likely to contain concentrated remains of earlier human activity. Methods of finding sites include *aerial archaeology*, using satellites, airplanes, or balloons as platforms to capture images of features that are often only visible or most visible from the air. *Surface investigation* involves walking over the land and recording the artifacts that lie on the surface. Sites are inferred from concentrations of objects as they lie. *Subsurface investigations* use geophysical or geochemical prospection, where anomalies detected in, or under, the surface are mapped to show the traces of now vanished walls, roads, pits, and an increasing variety of other features.
2. An area suspected of containing buried information is designated as a *site* and then subjected to *EVALUATION* to determine the best course of further action. The object of the evaluation is to supply as much information as possible to the *design* (which constitutes the subsequent stage). Predicting what lies under the ground is the first task, the result being reported as *deposit model*, showing the depth and character, and if possible the date, of the strata encountered. The research objectives and the social factors affecting further investigation are also assembled at the evaluation stage. This part of the investigation is intended to inflict as little damage as possible, using the techniques of *subsurface investigation*. But many sites require small-scale digging to give a preview of what lies beneath; these include

Table 1.1 Some examples of Field work design stages, *left* to *right: FRP* Field Research Procedure (Carver 2009), *CRM* Cultural Resource Management (Neumann and Sanford 2001), *MAP* Management of Archaeological Projects (Andrews and Thomas 1995)

FRP	CRM	MAP
Reconnaissance	Background	
Inventory survey	Surface survey (Phase 1)	
Evaluation	Evaluation (Phase 2)	*Appraisal*
Desktop assessment		
Resource modeling		Field evaluation
Research agenda		
Project design	Memorandum of agreement	Project specification
Research programmed	Scope of work/data recovery plan	
Management programmed		
Investigation	Data acquisition (Phase 3)	Fieldwork
Analysis		*Post-excavation assessment*
Programmed design: analyses		
Publication		
Programmed design:		
Reports		
Exhibition		
Site presentation		

shovel testing (small shovel sized pits), *test pits* (square pits, usually 1×1 m in plan), or *test trenches* (cuttings between 1 and 2 m wide) (Hester et al. 1997).

3. *DESIGN* is the principal stage of field procedure, because it is at this point that the future of a site is decided. The importance of design is threefold – first it determines the agreed purpose of research and its outcome; secondly it determines the desired measures for the conservation of the site; and thirdly decisions taken at the design stage are often irreversible, particularly those that involve digging. A *project design* is a comprehensive document that incorporates and justifies a research program, a conservation program, and a program for continuing interaction with the public and stakeholders. The research program includes costed plans for survey, excavation, building recording, their anticipated outcome, the likely program of analyses (see below), and the plans for publication. Within this program are included the sampling strategies, itemizing the number, size, and location of areas to be surveyed and excavated. The conservation program includes measures for the long-term protection and management of the resource. The program of public interaction includes plans for display of the site and for serving the requirements of local ownership.

   The *project design* provides the basis for funding and for permissions as well as the document that shows how the academic research agenda is to be addressed. Since there are many interested parties here, not only local, it follows that in modern professional practice, a project design should be published in advance of its implementation, allowing "multi-vocal" responses from a wide constituency.

These responses will be incorporated into the agreed programs confirmed by the representative and funding bodies.

Since the project design is intended as an agreed contract between the field researcher and society, it is generally not varied until it has run its course, when another agreed program may supersede it. In some parts of the world, the old "seasonal" system still endures, whereby the archaeologist redesigns the project every year. However, this would now be considered as less ethical than conforming to an agreed design-led package. The procedure for reviewing and accepting designs is appropriate to both university research and CRM reactive fieldwork, though there will be some variations between them. For example, while both should have research and management plans, CRM will often omit plans for public display.

4. *IMPLEMENTATION* is the active execution of the agreed programs. Using *survey*, *excavation* and *building recording*, and other bundles of techniques where appropriate, the implementation stage is usually performed in intensive seasons of fieldwork, using a range of crews stretching from two or three professional surveyors to a workforce of 50 or more volunteer excavators. The business of this workforce is to execute the study of the landscape or site on the ground and create records of what was measured, seen, or sensed, together with samples of materials encountered. The strategy for *Recording and Sampling* is laid out in project design, and is determined by the research objectives and terrain (see below). Many countries have laid down standard procedures for surveying, digging, and recording, although these are not helpful when they inhibit innovation, and thus the potential of the fieldwork to generate new knowledge. Site records have evolved over the last 20 years to capture observations at a number of different levels: primary data, agreed in advance and captured on proformae (for example, chemical patterns, context records), interpretative definitions, using common vocabulary to describe interpretations on the ground (for example, using feature records) and metadata, which record the course of the field work, the circumstances of locality and weather, the crew, interim assessments, and numerous other matters; this information is traditionally captured in journals, photographs, and audio and video files.
5. *ANALYSIS*. Records made during fieldwork are examined at the analysis stage, with a view to understanding the results. Both survey and excavation usually generate large assemblages of objects, and detailed spatial records relating to objects, contexts, and features. The three main parts of the analytical program are: assemblage, *space*, and *sequence*, which together result in a narrative of what happened in the area examined.

   The *assemblage* comprises all the objects and materials that are kept for analysis. The yield of an assemblage has been greatly increased by *screening* (sieving) the dirt, which helps to capture small objects that may be missed. Dry granular soil may be dry-sieved, and wet cloddy soil wet-sieved, i.e., broken up with water. The size of the mesh depends on what we want to find, so screens can be stacked in diminishing sizes to capture, potsherds, bones of mammals large small, coins, beads and fish. Microscopic organic matter deriving from plants is extracted by *flotation*. New science is hugely increasing the range of what we can learn from the ground, by examining microscopic remains such as seeds, pollen, insects, and residues in pots (see *nano-excavation*, p. 49). The study of *artifacts* usually requires the determination of its fabric (what it is made of), its form (implying its use), and its style (suggesting its cultural affiliations). Routine study of *stone, metal, ceramic, wood, leather*, and *textile* objects is well developed. The biota (biological fraction of the assemblage) includes the *soil, animal* and human remains, *seeds, pollen, phytoliths*, and other plant remains and insects. Parts of the assemblage are particularly valuable for their indications of date, for example, coins, which are provided with a date of minting and circulation by *numismatics*. The single most important method of scientific dating used routinely by field archaeologists is *radiocarbon dating*, which determines the date at death of organic materials, such as wood or bone.

The *use of space* is fundamental to the understanding of human activity, and is recorded on a wide range of scales – at the level of a landscape, a settlement a cemetery, a house, a room, or a hearth. Much of field archaeology is taken up with measuring location, usually in three dimensions and archaeologists produce some of the most precise and fastidious of all land surveys. The use of space is analyzed by *plotting* objects, and *planning* features and structures. Details of the use of space inside a building may also be determined by chemical and geophysical mapping (Carver 2011, Chap. 2). The many kinds of result include the determination of activities, routeways (paths, tracks), social hierarchies (from room and house size), and sequence (by comparing alignments).

On excavated sites, the *sequence* is worked out by *stratigraphy* – the order that contexts and features succeeded each other in the deposit. Their relationships (which came first, which came after) are recorded on site and drawn up in comprehensive *stratification diagrams*. Archaeologists also record sample sequences by cutting a slice through a deposit and drawing the set of layers seen from the side and shown in *section*. Sequence may also be informed by absolute dates of material in the assemblage and by relationships in space (see above). Spatial analysis also plays a role in determining sequence.

Sequence, space, and assemblage together produce the site model or site narrative – our best archaeological account of events that occurred at a place. There will be more research to come – placing these events alongside others near and far, and making better sense of them in human and historical and environmental terms. In this process, a vital ally is *ethnoarchaeology*, which provides analogies from ancient practice and behavior drawn from observations made in modern communities.

6. *PUBLICATION*. Drawing on the analyses, the results of fieldwork are modeled or synthesized, and are then distributed to the people who need them. The range of users is considerable. CRM archaeologists have to report their findings rapidly clearly and succinctly in Client Reports. Researchers will look to outlets in journals and monographs appropriate to the research community. The public are served by exhibitions and displays supported by popular summaries. And all the records made are deposited in an archive (often digital) for the long-term curation of information for the use of future generations.

Terrain

Practices of survey and excavation are different the world over, since the character of archaeological sites, and what we want to know from them, both vary. The existing geology and topography of the land is referred to as the *terrain*, and the way it has been treated by nature (flooded, baked and frozen) and humans (quarried, cultivated, built on) has been studied under the collective terms geoarchaeology (e.g. Goldberg and Macphail 2006) and site formation processes (p. 43; Schiffer 1987, and see EGA also under *Site Formation Processes*). In general, the terrain is the greatest influence on the way archaeological information has been captured, and thus how it can be accessed and understood through investigation. Broad flat sites with little stratification in open country can be best examined in wide areas, and their rewards are to offer comprehensive plans of a settlement or cemetery (p. 44). In contrast, deeply stacked strata under a modern town is much less accessible but offers excellent accounts of historical sequence using stratification (p. 44). At each site, local events will have influenced the way that archaeological strata have built up and survived. Frost or flood may crack or disperse strata. Organic materials may decay, so that structures of wood become barely visible. A waterlogged site, on the other hand, preserves wood; but if the water flows, objects may migrate out of their original layers and be redeposited in much earlier (or later) contexts.

A number of case studies are given here to illustrate responses to the different challenges of terrain the world over (Part II). From England, we have an example of *landscape mapping* applied to a favorable terrain, using surface collection and geophysics deployed as far as possible to give total coverage. *Motorway construction* in Ireland gives an example where very comprehensive coverage was again achieved, both in survey and excavation, in advance of motorway construction. Stark contrasts in terrain are provided by the struggle to investigate *permafrost sites* in Siberia and sites embraced by *jungle* in Belize (Chan). Particular site types also provoke certain kinds of practice. *Klithi* (Greece) shows an exemplary approach to rockshelters from the 1980s, while the *Pinnacle Point* cave site is deploying advanced methods of remote sensing. Three examples show how information can be won by careful excavation from sites where stratified layers are sparse: an *upper palaeolithic floor* in Switzerland, a *Lapita settlement* in the Mariana Islands (Pacific Ocean), and a Neolithic, *linearbandkeramik settlement* in Germany.

Specially revealing sites demanding particular approaches are the well-preserved wetland *crannog*, a type of artificial island in Scotland; the *tell*, a large mound created by the decay of a long sequence of mud-brick structures (the example is from Syria); and a *terp*, artificially raised settlement mounds in the Netherlands. An alluvial site in Italy Terramara and hillforts in the *Czech Republic* likewise require their own procedure. *Human burials* are rich sources of demographic information, and need to be dug with an enhanced care. A pioneering example of a *burial mound dissection* from central Sweden included the lifting of the entire burial chamber for study in the laboratory. A *mining site in Spain* and an *urban site in New York City* show something of the ingenuity required from excavators wishing to profit to the maximum from what terrain and opportunity offer.

An example of a project mainly dedicated to building recording is seen at *Bam* in Iran, where an archaeological team was faced with the challenge of recording of the buildings of a famous historic town severely damaged and destabilized by an earthquake. Our last example is of *ethnoarchaeology* in action: a record of the Gilund potters, themselves now under threat of economic extinction.

Agendas

There is archaeology in every country and every country's archaeology is of equal value to the world as a whole. As well as a world agenda, which seeks to understand the stories of every land and draw general conclusions from them, there are local agendas in which the public appreciation of heritage is primary. These tensions between the values of scientific research and the values of cultural property result in different political attitudes toward the past and the application of different national strategies to archaeology - and thus the kind of funding available. The values may change through time and sometimes look outward to international goals and sometimes inward to the national social mission. The development of procedures in field research, such as sampling, area excavation, context definition and increasingly ambitious schemes for extracting scientific data are often credited to particular pioneering individuals. Talented individuals certainly move the subject forward, but they do so in a social, political and economic context that is often resistant to change. Field practice is notoriously conservative, but it also varies between continents, apparently due to national traditions adopted in the distant past. In Part III, the American, Polish, British, Scandinavian, French, Australian, Chinese, and Japanese experience is explored in a number of brief contributions. These show that the roots of the traditions lie mostly in the local terrain, the national politics and economic priorities. The techniques of archaeological investigation have developed mightily, but these traditions inhibit their application. It is hoped that these examples, and the book as a whole, will give archaeologists a platform for the more creative exploration of our planet.

NOTE: Additional Information relevant to Field Method will be found in other entries in the Encyclopaedia of Global Archaeology (*Springer 2014, henceforward EGA*) *under Cultural Heritage Management; Archaeological Science; Prospection methods in Archaeology; Chemical Survey of Archaeological Sites; Landscape Archaeology; Floors and Occupation Surface Analysis in Archaeology; Heritage sites: Economic incentives, impacts and commercialization; Environmental archaeology; Taphonomy, Regional; Stratigraphy in archaeology: a brief history; underwater ad maritime archaeology. Appropriate links to EGA will be noted in the sections that follow.*

Chapter 2
Natural and Cultural Formation Processes

Margaret E. Beck

Introduction

One of the best-known archaeological sites in the world is Pompeii, a Roman town buried by the eruption of Mount Vesuvius in CE 79. The disaster stopped daily life in its tracks, felling residents who were unable to escape and covering everything with a thick layer of ash. Millions of modern tourists visit Pompeii each year, now able to walk its streets, inspect its art (and graffiti), and peer into shops and homes. The casual observer might therefore imagine that *most* places of past human activity remain as they were in use, perhaps simply buried under a thick layer of dirt or volcanic ash. In this view, an archaeological site – much like the abandoned home described by Philip Larkin in his poem "Home is So Sad" – "stays as it was left,/ Shaped to the comfort of the last to go."

Of course, nothing stays exactly as it was left. All archaeological sites suffer the effects of time, climate, and organisms (including people). Organic materials at Pompeii that were not burnt, subsequently decayed. Remains of the unfortunate residents trapped in the town decayed and could only be reconstructed by pouring plaster into the voids in the ash left by their bodies. Some of those who escaped later attempted to salvage what they could find and remove it from the site. After the rediscovery of the site, the material record at Pompeii was heavily affected by both looting and archaeological investigation.

M.E. Beck (✉)
University of Iowa, Iowa, IA, USA
e-mail: margaret-beck@uiowa.edu

M. Carver et al. (eds.), *Field Archaeology from Around the World*,
SpringerBriefs in Archaeology, DOI 10.1007/978-3-319-09819-7_2

Looting, decay, disturbance, and other natural and cultural processes affect the archaeological record (Schiffer 1987 for the best overview). These processes do not render it meaningless, but they must be recognized so that we can consider their impact on our sample of sites and artifacts, spatial patterning, and other matters so crucial for interpretation.

Natural Processes of Decay (and Preservation in Different Environments)

Some materials survive the vagaries of time better than others (Sease 1994 for an overview). *Highly perishable organic materials* include skin and soft tissue as well as wood and other plant remains. In most cases, these are very vulnerable to decay and hence do not survive in the archaeological record except under unusual conditions. As a result, at most sites we are unlikely to find baskets, textiles, wooden artifacts, leather, and any remains of people or animals other than bones or teeth.

The exceptions generally occur in arid, frozen, or waterlogged environments, such as deserts, glaciers, and peat bogs, which prevent decomposition and are favorable for preservation. Famous examples of organic preservation come from desert sites such as White Dog Cave (a Basketmaker site in northern Arizona), with conditions that naturally mummified burials, and Cahuachi (a Nazca site in coastal Peru), with cotton and wool textiles; the frozen body of the "Iceman" in the Italian Alps; the waterlogged site of Ozette in Washington state, United States, with wooden houses and artifacts; and peat bogs, including sites from northwestern Europe with Iron Age "bog bodies." Burial by volcanic ash may also seal the environment and prevent decomposition, such as in some contexts at the Cerén site in El Salvador. Decomposition may also be retarded by associated materials; copper, salt, or oil around organic items has been observed to preserve the organic remains.

Organic materials may also be preserved through burning. Charcoal (carbonized wood) and other carbonized plant remains are crucial sources of information about diet and other plant uses. Whole loaves of bread have been recovered from Pompeii because they were completely carbonized and therefore could not decay. Carbonized organic material preserves well in a variety of environments, but it is physically fragile. *Less perishable organic materials* include bone, ivory, and teeth, all of which have both a calcium-rich mineral component and an organic component. (We may also include shell here because it is made of calcium carbonate, although shell has no organic component and does not decay.) All of these materials preserve best in soils with neutral or slightly alkaline pH, as acidic environments break down the calcium-rich mineral component. For example, almost no bone was preserved at the Sloan site, a cemetery in the southeastern United States dating to around 10,000 years ago on acidic terrain. As a result, burial locations could only be inferred through calcium concentrations (into which the bone had disintegrated) and artifact clusters. Bones are also damaged and altered during processing and consumption of the carcass. Damage from human butchery provides important cultural information, but it may also result from carnivore and scavenger activity (Binford 1987).

Nonorganic materials include ceramic, glass, metal, and stone artifacts. Porosity is one factor affecting the survival of these materials, because greater porosity increases vulnerability to wet-dry cycles, freeze-thaw cycles, and accumulation of salts in the burial environment – all of which will lead to periodic expansion and stresses within the body of the piece. For ceramics, firing temperature and temper type can significantly affect porosity and other attributes related to survival. Fiber-tempered pottery, which is the earliest pottery used in North America, is especially vulnerable to freeze-thaw action because of its high porosity. Calcareous temper, such as shell or limestone, will dissolve in acidic environments, leading to voids in the fabric. Such environments also cause acid leaching, or leaching of iron, lightening the color of the ceramic (Rye 1981).

The survival of glass and metal depends considerably upon its composition as well as the burial environment. Acidic soils are favorable for glass, but alkaline soils will cause leaching of the glass matrix. Pure gold resists corrosion from moisture and oxygen, but other metals (including those added to gold as part of the alloy) do not. Iron corrodes easily, producing reddish rust. Copper corrosion leads to a variety of colors, including green, and the chlorides in saline soils dramatically speed copper corrosion.

Stone generally survives well, but as with other material types, the structure and porosity is important. Mica, with its many thin sheets, is especially fragile physically. Limestone will erode or dissolve in acidic environments, as do other calcareous materials; this soft and porous rock may also suffer from erosion from wind, water, and crystallization of salts. Some combination of these factors probably caused the damage visible on the famous limestone monumental sculpture in Egypt, the Great Sphinx of Giza. Salts are of special concern in arid regions, because if not removed, they may continue to damage artifacts, even during curation (Fig. 2.1).

Natural Processes That Move and Damage Artifacts

Natural processes can move artifacts and disturb features, sometimes so much so that the archaeological site is no longer a "primary" site (where the cultural deposition originally occurred) but a "secondary" site (where materials were redeposited). The effects of gravity seem obvious – for example, materials on slopes often move downhill – but materials deposited on level ground may also move around, up, and down. All of the processes that deposit, remove, and churn soils and sediments also affect soil within that matrix. Such processes include deposition and erosion from wind and water as well as the movement of particles by animals (faunal turbation; Fig. 2.2), plants (floral turbation; Fig. 2.3), freeze-thaw action (cryoturbation), and the shrinking and swelling of clay (argilliturbation). These natural processes, and their effects on archaeological sites, are also studied by geoarchaeology (e.g., Goldberg and Macphail 2006).

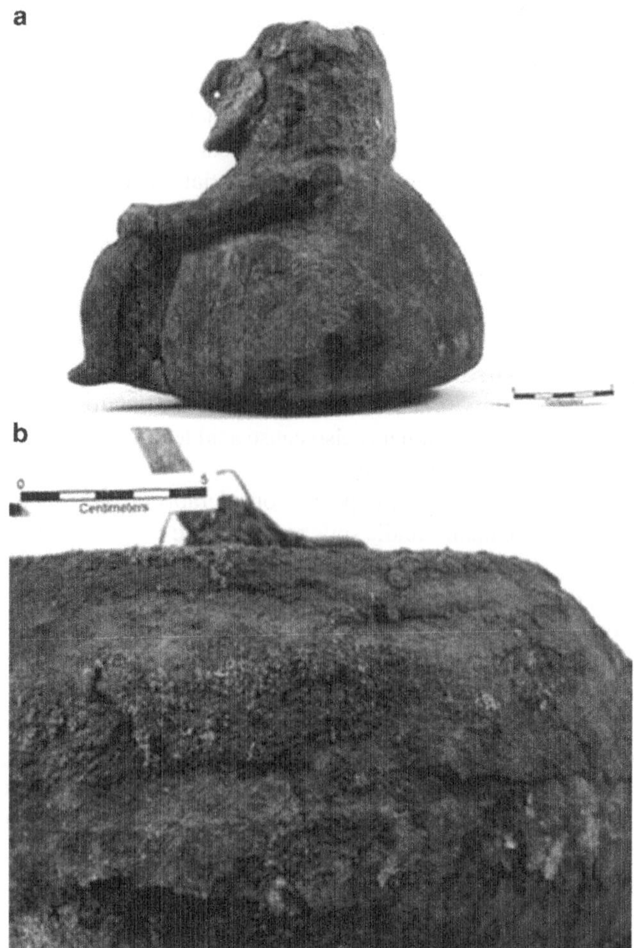

Fig. 2.1 Damage from accumulated salts in (**a**) a prehistoric Hohokam effigy vessel from Arizona and (**b**) a modern flowerpot from Arizona. The modern flowerpot displays active growth of salt crystals (Photos taken by the author)

Fig. 2.2 Mottling indicating movement of soil through animal burrows (Photo courtesy of E. Arthur Bettis, Department of Geoscience, University of Iowa)

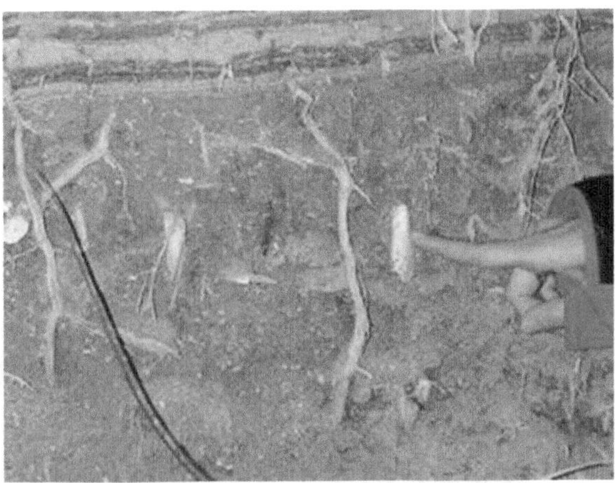

Fig. 2.3 Root disturbance (Photo courtesy of E. Arthur Bettis, Department of Geoscience, University of Iowa)

Cultural Processes of Site Destruction: Scavenging, Looting, and Site Reuse

People frequently interact with material left by past activities, changing the nature of the evidence archaeologists will find. They may remove or alter traces of human behavior, soon after or long after the fact. This happens in a wide variety of ways at all stages of archaeological site formation, often motivated by a desire for the objects previously deposited or for the space these deposits occupy.

The process of reclaiming discarded or abandoned artifacts happens all the time in all societies, although it plays out differently in rich industrialized nations than in poorer ones. In the United States, the regular discard of usable, edible materials directly into the trash has spawned an entire movement known as "freeganism," in which adherents feed, dress, and entertain themselves from garbage deposits to protest against rampant consumerism and reduce environmental impact. In contrast, rural villagers such as Maya groups in Guatemala and the Kalinga of northern Luzon, Philippines, extensively reuse and recycle items before sending unusable scraps to a midden.

But these middens too may subsequently be modified: many are close to paths and activity areas, and may be dispersed by human and animal foot traffic at least along the margins. Children also collect things from middens for their play, and animals wander in to eat vegetable matter left over from food processing (Fig. 2.4). If trash deposits start to interfere with village needs (e.g., if they become too large or too smelly, or if they sit on land now desired for another purpose), they will be moved.

Abandoned residential sites may have more to offer in terms of reuse. Building materials are routinely scavenged from old dwellings for the new ones, either in the same community or a nearby one. If a dwelling or community was abandoned quickly or destroyed catastrophically, residents might have been forced to leave many items there, materials worth scavenging later. Some discarded items prove to

Fig. 2.4 Disturbance of a modern village midden by domestic animals in northern Luzon, Philippines (Photo taken by the author)

be useful later for new reasons; for example, Hopi potters in the US Southwest are among those known to collect both sherds and pots to serve as models for designs and to grind up as temper.

Some collectors are looking for wealth, things of beauty, or souvenirs, and this type of collection – like other processes of cultural disturbance – happened thousands of years ago just as it does today. The tombs of Egyptian pharaohs were targeted by robbers long before excavators such as *Belzoni* arrived in the early nineteenth century. Early visitors to archaeological sites often brought a shovel for souvenirs, a pattern common to many places including the eighteenth-century Spanish *presidio* in Tucson, Arizona, and nineteenth-century ghost towns in the western USA. Once materials have spent a certain amount of time in the archaeological record, many modern societies now have laws regulating their collection, although these laws are not always adequately policed. The illicit trade in antiquities continues, linking looters who dig up the items for sale to the museums who buy them (Watson and Todeschini 2007).

Archaeological sites are frequently reoccupied, reused, or affected by redevelopment and renewal. Boston's Central Artery/Tunnel Project or the "Big Dig" of the late twentieth century, while rerouting Interstate 93, displaced existing structures in use and also encountered abundant archaeological deposits. In the mid-twentieth century, Tucson, Arizona, demolished portions of the city from the nineteenth century, including the Spanish Convento and San Agustín chapel as well as its Chinatown, to make way for a convention center. Needs and values concerning the past change over time, and communities sometimes regret such land-use decisions. In awareness of the potential losses, the *Cultural Heritage Management* profession records sites before they are altered or destroyed to make way for the needs of modern living.

Conclusions

All archaeological sites have been altered in some way since their creation. The question is, how can we identify the types of disturbance and take account of them in interpretation? An understanding of decay processes, and of what we are unlikely to find in certain environments, is crucial for evaluating our sample of the material record. Geoarchaeology can be very helpful for assessing formation of natural and cultural strata, as can the study of artifact damage, fragmentation, and its *spatial analysis*. *Ethnoarchaeological* observations of historical and ongoing site formation processes provide invaluable clues about the range of possibilities we should consider. These alterations do not diminish the value of the archaeological record but add to its richness and complexity.

More information on this topic will be found in EGA under Site Formation Processes; Taphonomy; Anaerobic conditions; Floors and Occupation Surface Analysis in Archaeology; Anthropogenic sediments and soils; archaeological soil micromorphology; deflation, archaeological.

Chapter 3
Aerial Archaeology

Włodzimierz Rączkowski

Introduction and Definition

Aerial archaeology (AA) uses photographs, and other kinds of image acquisition, in archaeological field research. It involves taking photographs of the land from above, examining them for pertinent information, interpreting the images seen there and making the resulting data available in a variety of forms to develop archaeological knowledge about past people and the conservation of archaeological sites and landscapes (Bewley and Rączkowski 2002).

Why Can We See a Variety of Types of Sites?

Since people first learnt to fly, it has been appreciated that traces of early human activity can be observed from the air, recognized from their curved or linear shapes. Humans have always exploited and adapted the environment to their own needs. The surface of the ground has been disturbed and altered by generations of previous occupants, who have dug into it to create foundations, ditches, and pits, and raised structures upon it, in the form of stone buildings or earth ramparts. All this activity has caused "injury" to the land. Much of it has been subsequently covered over or leveled by later exploitation, particularly agriculture. Today, in the majority of such places, there is little sign of this past human activity on the surface, but the "scars" remain beneath and these may show up from the air (Wilson 1982).

W. Rączkowski (✉)
Institute of Prehistory, Adam Mickiewicz University, Poznań, Poland
e-mail: wlodekra@amu.edu.pl

M. Carver et al. (eds.), *Field Archaeology from Around the World*,
SpringerBriefs in Archaeology, DOI 10.1007/978-3-319-09819-7_3

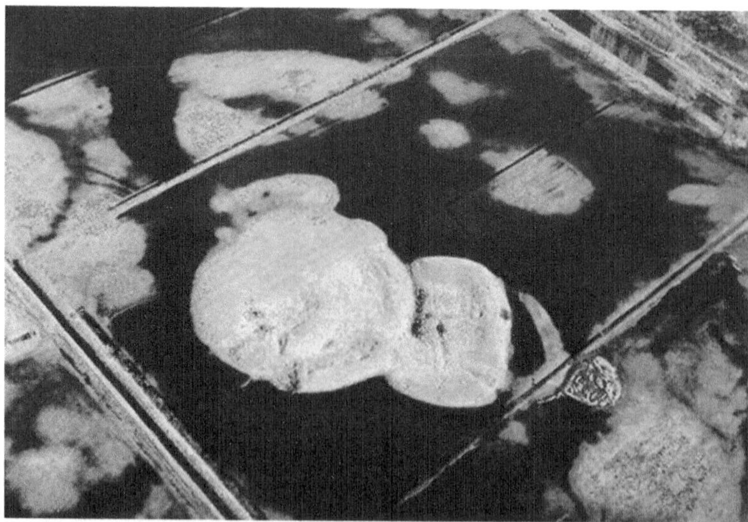

Fig. 3.1 Bonikowo, Wielkopolska Region, Poland. Early Medieval stronghold clearly visible due to flooded bottom of valley (Photo: W. Rączkowski, March 1999)

Some ancient earth, stone, and timber structures are still just visible above ground level as *earthworks*. Most frequently encountered are the remains of barrows, ramparts, walls, banks, and ditches. These can be photographed by exploiting the contrast of the shadows by a sun low on the horizon. The way snow settles and melts may also reveal the presence of archaeological features, as can widespread flooding (mainly on low-lying ground) for it exposes all the topographic elements which are above water level (Fig. 3.1). The new technique of LiDAR (see below) now records low-lying earthworks by measuring their topography directly.

The remains of human activity beneath the topsoil determine growth conditions and cause difference in growth, causing *cropmarks* (Fig. 3.2). Subsurface hollows, foundation trenches, ditches, and pits retain water and nourishment, prompting the plants that grow immediately above them to be taller or greener for longer than others in the immediate vicinity (*positive cropmarks*). Plants growing over stones, bricks, or roads are deprived of moisture, so may be more stunted in growth and more pallid in color (*negative cropmarks*). Cropmarks can also be photographed, thanks to the shadows thrown by taller plants, disclosing the archaeological features beneath. Not all plants are equally "sensitive" to variable soil conditions – some "display" what is beneath the topsoil while others do not react to local conditions. Wheat and barley best show the presence of archaeological remains well, especially late in the growing season, while potatoes, cabbage, or corn are less demonstrative of what lies beneath.

Plowing may disturb the uppermost layer of an archaeological feature and bring it to the surface as a *soilmark*, recognizable by its different color to the topsoil. Soilmarks can be most readily observed when there is no vegetation growing – from late autumn through to early spring (Fig. 3.3).

Fig. 3.2 Mutowo, Wielkopolska Region, Poland. Cropmarks show up archaeological remains of a medieval town (thirteenth century) of Szamotuły (Photo: W. Rączkowski, July 2011)

Fig. 3.3 Rębowo, Wielkopolska Region, Poland. Color of soil differentiation shows up the remains of a plowed rampart of an early medieval stronghold (Photo: W. Rączkowski, March 1999)

Development of Techniques: History

The first known aerial photographs in archaeology used hot air balloons to take aerial photographs of archaeological sites between 1899 and 1911 (Forum Romanum, Tiber delta, Pompei, Ostia) and in 1906 (Stonehenge). The First World War advanced the development of both aeroplanes and cameras. The number of pioneers using aerial photographs to search, identify, and document archaeological sites increased (T. Wiegand, L. Rey, G. Beazeley, A. Poidebard, C. Schuchhardt). O.G.S. Crawford (1923) made a significant contribution to the methodology and its application in research. In the 1920s and 1930s, photographs were taken of archaeological sites (e.g., hillforts) across Europe, excavation work in progress was documented from aircraft (e.g., Biskupin in Poland), and aerial surveys led to the discovery of new sites (e.g., Woodhenge – UK, Ipf near Bopfingen – Germany). Similar surveys were also successful in the USA (C. A. Lindbergh, N. Judd), Mexico (A. V. Kidder, P. C. Madeira Jr.), and Peru (G. Johnson).

Developments in both technology and the interpretation of aerial photographs (e.g., the Allied Central Interpretation Unit) during the Second World War enhanced the technique and established it after the war as a primary research tool in archaeology. Although political regimes in some European countries severely restricted overflying, it developed without major interference in the UK (J.K. St Joseph, A. Baker, J. Pickering, D. Riley, D. Wilson), France (J. Baradez, R. Agache), West Germany (I. Scollar, R. Christlein, P. Filtzinger, O. Braasch, K. Leidorf), Belgium (C. Leva, J. Semey), and Denmark (H. Stiesdal). The 1994 Klienmachnow conference (in Germany) was a key moment in raising awareness of AA among archaeologists from Central, Eastern, and Southern Europe.

Stereoscopy was a successful technology especially applied during WWII. Nowadays, it is frequently used in AA when working with vertical photographs to give an illusion of depth. A 3D effect can be achieved using two photographs offset by 60 %. The stereoscope shows the left eye one photograph and the right eye the second, the brain then creates a 3D image of the area.

Since the late 1960s, AA has seen dramatic technical advances. In addition to the traditional platforms (e.g., kites, model planes, balloons, aircraft, helicopters), remote sensing now makes use of multispectral imagery captured by *satellites* to explore past landscapes and features at a wide range of scales. Satellites (since 1960s) orbiting at 600–1,200 km from the Earth's surface have recorded a wealth of information.

The declassification by the USA in 1995 of an archive of images acquired by the first generation of US photo reconnaissance satellites (CORONA – 1960 and 1972) and the KH-7 GAMBIT and KH-9 mapping camera programs in 2002 was a milestone for archaeologists who quickly recognized the potential of these archives for extensive survey coverage of the Earth, including territories currently lying in no-fly zones (e.g., Turkey, Syria, Armenia) (Ur 2003). The ERTS satellite (later renamed LANDSAT) was launched in 1972 to continually photograph the Earth's surface. Many countries and organizations have sent satellites equipped with cameras and sensors into orbit to acquire information on surface events by using electromagnetic radiation across the spectrum (Parcak 2009).

Use of the wider spectrum of different bands of wavelengths of electromagnetic radiation (daylight, infrared, ultraviolet, thermal radiation) means that AA can be classed as a method of *remote sensing*. Radiation of different wavelengths detects different physical features. The majority of satellite survey work in archaeology has focused on the band of *visible light* to detect archaeological features and past landscapes. However, visual data is only a small proportion of what cameras and other sensors can detect. A multispectral scanner registers a small number of bandwidths. By comparison, a hyperspectral scanner registers 100 or more bandwidths – including those which are beyond the visible spectrum, e.g., radar, ultraviolet, thermal radiation, etc.

For assessing what can be detected, two parameters are especially important – spectral resolution and spatial resolution. *Spectral resolution* denotes the detection that is possibly owed to the chosen wavelength. The range of visible light is from 0.380 to 0.780 μm (panchromatic image). If a sensor registers visible light, then it covers four channels (spectrum bands) – blue (0.45–0.52 μm), green (0.52–0.60 μm), red (0.63–0.69 μm), and infrared (0.76–0.90 μm). The spectral response pattern of soil is generally governed by the properties of the soils: color, texture, structure, mineralogy, organic matter, free carbonates, salinity, moisture, and the oxides/hydroxides of iron and manganese. Thus, analysis of results from parts of the spectrum provides information about the physical-chemical characteristics of any detected features. For example, analysis of green and red bands may give information on the contents of iron (Fe) in soil. *Normalized Difference Vegetation Index* (red and infrared bands) is a method for measuring vegetation vigor which may indirectly infer the presence of archaeological features.

Ground (spatial) resolution measures the minimum size of a feature detectable on the ground. A feature larger than the spatial resolution will be visible on the image, while a feature appearing smaller than a pixel on the image will not be seen. High ground resolution therefore is extremely important. Images of 80 m resolution (Landsat series MSS 1, 2 and 3) or 30 m (Landsat TM 4 and 5) are sufficient to determine geological or geographical aspects but not to detect archaeological features. Current resolutions can be achieved down to 1 m, which enables individual features such as storage pits, barrows, or sunken houses to be identified. The IKONOS satellite's panchromatic imaging (the whole visible spectrum, which means more energy reaches the sensor) provides a surface resolution of 1 m, although multispectral imaging resolution falls to 4 m.

Satellite images are currently used in prospection of archaeological features, study of their environmental contexts, spatial analysis, past landscape studies, 3D modeling, preservation assessments, and protection and management of archaeological heritage.

Airborne Laser Scanning (ALS), developed in the 1990s, uses the LiDAR (Light Detection and Ranging) system for rapid, high precision survey of the surface of the ground (including forested areas) (Crutchley and Crow 2009). In this method, laser range-finding beams are fired at the ground from an aircraft with exact position measured by GPS, creating clouds of points (with x, y, z coordinates), which are used to compute a digital terrain model (DTM) and digital elevation model (DEM)

Fig. 3.4 Wrześnica, Pomerania Region, Poland. DTM derived from LiDAR of the forested area presenting detailed topography and showing up the presence of geomorphologic structures as well as clusters of early medieval burial mounds (By Ł. Banaszek and MGGP Areo, 2012)

(Bewley et al. 2005). Digital graphic processing generates views of the surface in micro-relief. The most spectacular discoveries made using this technique include medieval field systems, road courses, barrows, queries, etc., especially those hidden in forests (Devereux et al. 2005; Doneus and Briese 2011) (Fig. 3.4).

LiDAR data also provides additional information on the intensity of the reflected light, as the emitted signal is usually in the near-infrared (NIR) spectrum. It is therefore possible to use it to analyze moisture, chlorophyll content, and other factors that characterize cropmarks.

Theoretical Context

AA has been a key branch of *field archaeology* for more than a century. Its initial success was applied to generating *culture history*, featuring interpretations based on *evolution* and *diffusion*. This took the premise that a photograph is neutral and objective in its representation of the world. As image registration is "mechanical" in nature, photographs were seen as recording real anomalies devoid of a subjective human factor. These anomalies added to the world's stock of sites and monuments, from which the narratives of prehistory and history can be written. By the same token, repeat visits to certain landscapes led to the realization that the sites were disappearing. *A Matter of Time* (published in 1960 by the Royal Commission on Historical Monuments of England) established a role for AA in conservation practice in the UK, leading to *The National Mapping Programme* and the development of set standards.

Processual archaeology was a major factor in the technological "revolution" in AA. It emphasized the objectivity of the research process and the consequent importance of the precise measuring of cultural and natural features. This mission was aided by new analytical technologies, particularly computerized *data bases* (including mapping) and *Geographic Information Systems* (GIS). Gaps in the record raised questions about the visibility of sites, and prompted research into *formation processes* as applied to cropmarks and soilmarks. Results obtained from remote sensing influenced the classification and construction of models describing the relation between cultural systems and the natural environment, and the application of technological innovation.

Postprocessual archaeology questioned the "realism" of aerial photographs, and emphasized the role of perception and interpretation in the creation of the record. Interpretation issues are now the subject of intense discussion on the way the cultural context affects aerial survey, the photoreading process, and their role in forming how we imagine the past (Brophy and Cowley 2005).

Interpretation

Understanding that there is an interpretative process by which the information from aerial photograph becomes an archaeological record is crucial. The interpretation of archaeological features and landscapes is a skill built on experience and knowledge, where intuition and subjective judgment are acknowledged as major factors. The ability of the archaeologist to interpret and depict is as important as the technical processes of rectification and georeferencing.

As archaeological use of digitally recorded data has developed, it has become increasingly clear that it is not an "objective" dataset. Methods of primary data collection and processing parameters have a significant impact on output; the ability to "see" is heavily dependent on software for manipulation and visualization. These factors are a complex mix of objective parameters (e.g., point density) and subjective judgments that are inextricable from the pervasive issue of archaeological interpretation.

Archaeologists decide which platform to use (aerial, satellite, ALS) and which electromagnetic emission to record. Similarly, data-processing, the selection of suitable algorithms, and their mode of visualization are matters decided by researchers. The final image undergoes visual editing and interpretation according to knowledge and interpretation experience and is accepted when a result is deemed to be satisfactory. Thus, like all other forms of archaeological data, the corpus of aerial photographs is the result of reconciling observation and imagination, of matching what we want to know, what has survived, what we currently recognize, and the methods available for their detection and recording. These methods are improving all the time as fresh interpretations raise our expectations and ambitions further.

More information relevant to this section will be found in EGA under Aerial and Satellite Remote Sensing in Archaeology, Archaeological Theory: Paradigm Shift, Cultural Heritage Site Damage Assessment, Cultural Landscapes: Conservation and Preservation, Landscape Archaeology, Post-Processual Archaeology, Processualism in Archaeological Theory, Prospection Methods in Archaeology, Site Formation Processes.

Chapter 4
Surface Survey: Method and Strategies

Simon Holdaway

Introduction

Archaeological excavation takes time, and while it provides a great deal of information about the nature of past activities, it provides only indirect information on how these activities were distributed across space. Surface materials, on the other hand, are quicker to record not because the recording is any less detailed but because the material to be recorded is immediately visible. For a given set of resources, many more surface locations can be recorded and their contents analyzed. As a consequence, archaeologists working in many countries have conducted surface surveys over large areas. In doing so, they have taken advantage of advances in survey technologies like *Global Positioning Systems* (GPS) and total stations together with software like *Geographic Information Systems* (GIS) and relational databases to greatly enhance their ability to record the spatial distribution of artifacts and sites.

Strategies

In both the Americas and Europe, modern survey emerged from the 1970s as a means of investigating settlement patterns, past population densities, and socioeconomic complexity (Whitmore 2007; Kowalewski 2008). Cherry (2003), for instance, combined probabilistic designs with systematic, pedestrian survey on Melos involving people separated by regular intervals, walking across the land surface, recording exposed artifacts. Transect lines, 1,000 m wide and orientated north–south, were staggered across the island. Chronology was obtained from the typology of

S. Holdaway (✉)
The University of Auckland, Auckland, New Zealand
e-mail: sj.holdaway@auckland.ac.nz

M. Carver et al. (eds.), *Field Archaeology from Around the World*,
SpringerBriefs in Archaeology, DOI 10.1007/978-3-319-09819-7_4

artifacts, established through earlier excavations, and the probable function of the artifacts was assessed in the field to provide an indication of the functional status of the sites identified. This basic scheme characterized later projects although the intensity of survey (as measured by the spacing between field walkers) and the tendency to survey continuous blocks rather than transects changed as did the concern for processes that might have altered or obscured the surface archaeological record.

Changes in the intensity of field survey are correlated with the numbers of sites recorded. However, increasing survey intensity comes at a cost, since the more time spent surveying in one area, the smaller the region that can be covered. Critics suggested that some intensive surveys were too small in extent to reveal useful socio-economic interpretations (e.g., Kowalewski 2008). One solution to this problem was to combine the results from a number of independent surveys, thereby permitting the analysis of results from large areas; however, as Alcock and Cherry (2004) indicated, there are difficulties involved in combining the results from multiple survey projects where data recording standards are not equivalent. Making inferences based on the number of sites, for instance, depends on site areas being calculated in the same way between projects, with obvious biases introduced if common standards are not adopted. Similar issues occur within individual survey projects. Different processes effect *survivorship* of the archaeological record and hence its visibility, both at the scale of the archaeological site and at that of the individual artifact (Terrenato 2004). Pottery, for instance, degrades with age, depending to some extent on the way it was made. Therefore, ancient sites may be less visible than more recent sites. The complexity of the natural processes involved in any one region means that their impact needs to be considered on a case-by-case basis. Equally important, some activities in the past led to the deposition of many artifacts, while others produced many fewer objects.

Australian challenges

Survey work in arid regions of Australia shares many of the issues raised in the Mediterranean. Surface scatters of stone artifacts as well as the remains of hearths with stone heat retainers dominate the surface record of western New South Wales (NSW). Sites are difficult to define since the boundaries of individual scatters are diffuse. The surface carpet of artifacts in western NSW might be thought of as a single archaeological site of variable density stretching over nearly a million square kilometers. Making useful distinctions across this artifact carpet requires that not only artifact density but also artifact assemblage composition be assessed at numerous locations within a landscape. To do this, self-tracking (robotic) electronic total stations together with GPS are used to locate artifacts individually using a nail as a marker (Fig. 4.1). They are numbered individually and surveyed with the total station. Artifacts are picked up and attributes recorded before returning them to the ground (a requirement of the Aboriginal Traditional Owners) (Fig. 4.2). The total station is also used to map the extent of artifact exposure and any features that

Fig. 4.1 Self-tracking total stations allow the rapid location of artifacts in three dimensions. *Colored nails* are used to mark stone artifacts

Fig. 4.2 Stone artifacts are marked with nails, numbered with preprinted numbers, and analyzed in the field using portable computers (*inset*)

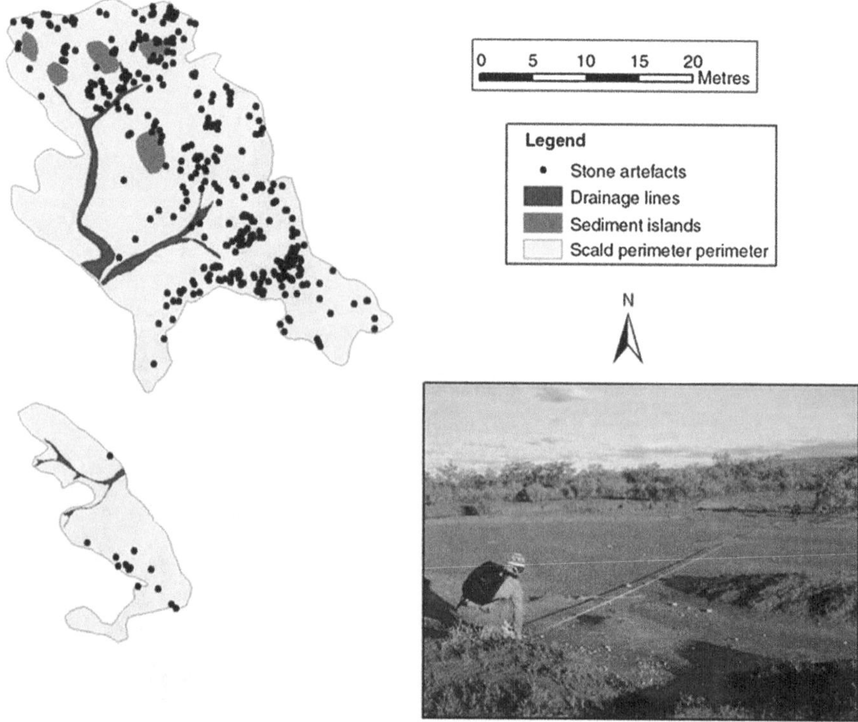

Fig. 4.3 GIS plot of the location of stone artifacts (*black dots*) in eroded areas (termed scalds, *inset*) that are used as spatial sampling units for landscape scale surface survey. The GIS shows the location of artifacts in relation to the size of the eroded area and the presence of sediment islands that obscure visibility

obscure surface exposure (e.g., sediment islands, Fig. 4.3). A distributed system based on a relational database design means that multiple instruments and teams can all work at once, and as a consequence, recording is very quick (overcoming to some degree the intensity versus extent criticisms noted above).

Software allows all sets of information to be integrated together based on a relational database design. The total station writes data files in GIS formats, and the GIS software permits the spatial integration of attribute data. Observations on the geomorphic context of the artifacts are also combined in the GIS. Because each object is recorded with an x, y, and z coordinate, its spatial position can be analyzed in relation to other objects to control for a variety of postdepositional processes (Fanning et al. 2008). Data quality is controlled through "intelligent" data entry software that reduces the chance of human error (McPherron and Holdaway 1996 and through the quantitative analysis of observer bias. An understanding of the relationship between past human activity and the nature of artifact deposition is critical which also involves experimental assessment of the attributes recorded on surface artifacts (Douglass et al. 2008).

Key Issues

Despite the desire to understand "big picture" distributions of archaeological sites by undertaking extensive, low-intensity surveys, understanding why archaeological materials are visible at certain points in the landscape requires that the range of processes that leads to this visibility, both cultural and natural, be understood. The cultural resource of arid regions of Australia, like that in other comparable regions of the world, is dominated by stone artifacts. Because vegetation is sparse, surface visibility is often high and full-coverage regional surveys are possible. Stone artifacts are abundant, as are the remains of heat-retainer hearths with smaller numbers of earth mounds and burials in some regions. Recording artifact scatters by *ground surface survey* is thus a common response.

But the remoteness of parts of Australia, coupled with the abundance of artifacts record in some localities, means that the large-scale regional surveys, like those in the Valley of Mexico (Charlton and Nichols 2005) or in the Mediterranean (Cherry 2003; Bintliff and Snodgrass 1988; Bintliff 2000), have only been undertaken infrequently. Australia lacks pottery that, when seriated, might provide the means to develop a chronology applicable to an extensive surface archaeological record. In addition, stone artifacts, while abundant, have not proved amenable to the detailed time-space descriptions used to date sites in other regions of the world. Alternative approaches to survey are therefore needed.

While arid regions may give the appearance of an unchanging landscape, the opposite is often the case. In much of Australia, geomorphic dynamics are such that a land surface results from a set of individual erosion and deposition events operating at different temporal and spatial scales. Averaged over tens to hundreds (and maybe thousands) of years, different parts of the landscape will exhibit accumulation of sediment (i.e., dominantly depositional), removal of sediment (i.e., dominantly erosional), or no change (i.e., residual). Maximum exposure of the archaeological record is found in those parts of the landscape that are dominantly erosional, while least exposure is found where deposition of sediments is dominant. Too much erosion, however, will remove the deposits on which artifacts rest effectively, removing any trace of the archaeological record.

Sediment chronologies, developed by obtaining age estimates from valley-fill deposits or the ages of remnant flood deposits, indicate periods of erosion interspersed with depositional periods. Regional discontinuity in deposition is the norm, leading to a patchwork distribution of land surfaces differing markedly in age and therefore accumulating archaeological deposits of different ages (Fanning et al. 2009). Truly ancient and more recent artifact deposits may be separated by distances of only a few hundred meters. Following conventional site survey techniques, it is tempting to interpret artifact concentrations directly in behavioral terms, as though their content reflects the operation of a single settlement system even though different locations reflect accumulation over substantially different periods of time. Using a geomorphically based approach to survey overcomes this problem.

An appropriate survey strategy therefore requires intensive chronological, geomorphological, and archaeological studies at predetermined localities (Holdaway and Fanning 2008). The formation of the archaeological record is a sedimentary process (Stein 1987), and a geomorphological approach to understanding the history of landscape use is employed as part of the survey design. Particular attention is paid to recording data sets with reference to the time scales over which the archaeological record has accumulated.

This approach to fieldwork has influenced the interpretation of early Australian communities. Archaeologists in the 1980s saw communities as changing in the mid-Holocene from highly mobile groups existing at relatively low population densities to groups practicing extended occupation with increased social complexity (Lourandos 1985). Data to support this "intensification theory" included documenting increases in the number of archaeological sites dating to the mid- to late Holocene. However, critics noted that site preservation might also account for the perceived increase in site numbers (Dodson et al. 1992). For example, at the Rutherford Creek catchment in western New South Wales, it was shown that the number of dated heat-retainer hearths relates to the ages of the surfaces on which they rest. Summing the radiocarbon determinations from the hearths produces a pattern similar to that used to support an increase in site numbers (and by implication population size); yet this pattern was the result of differential erosion and site preservation rather than human behavior (Holdaway et al. 2008). As this example illustrates, it is essential to understand the geomorphological history of the deposits before a behavioral interpretation can be made directly from survey data.

See also the entries in EGA for Landscape Archaeology; Dry/desert conditions; Floors and Occupation Surface Analysis in Archaeology.

Chapter 5
Nondestructive Subsurface Mapping

Immo Trinks

Archaeological *excavation* provides unparalleled detail of past lives, but it is a costly process and destructive to the site under investigation. Cost and respect for the resource means that excavation can only be applied over limited areas. By contrast, subsurface mapping methods can cover wide areas while leaving the site intact (Scollar et al. 1990). These methods, once regarded only as a means of finding sites (prospection), represent now a complementary tool kit for detailed archaeological investigation of a site and its surrounding landscape. The methods provide overviews of human activity and buried structures of archaeological and historical interest in increasing detail over considerable areas. Subsurface mapping also permits the selection of high-potential areas for targeted scientific excavations and provides a broader settlement context for sites already excavated. Recent developments based on high-resolution multichannel near-surface geophysical technology and advances in state-of-the-art remote sensing now permit the cost- and time-efficient spatiotemporal archaeological investigation and documentation of buried features across entire landscapes. This has applications in both research and rescue projects.

The most commonly used ground-based archaeological subsurface survey methods are magnetic, electromagnetic and geoelectric (Gaffney and Gater 2003). Less frequently employed are geochemical methods, the best known being phosphate mapping. Traditionally *surveys* are conducted manually in rectilinear grids using tape measures and survey lines placed on the ground for orientation and facilitating exact sample positioning and spacing. The advent of automated positioning systems in form of *Global Positioning Systems* (GPS) or *total station survey instruments* (TST)

I. Trinks (✉)
Ludwig Boltzmann Institute for Archaeological Prospection
and Virtual Archaeology, Vienna, Austria
e-mail: immo.trinks@archpro.lbg.ac.at

M. Carver et al. (eds.), *Field Archaeology from Around the World*,
SpringerBriefs in Archaeology, DOI 10.1007/978-3-319-09819-7_5

permits the rapid high-precision location of *anomalies* (high and low readings) recorded by geophysical instruments. The output of these surveys is essentially a map of these subsurface anomalies in two dimensions, although georadar adds the third dimension by presenting the anomalies in "depth slices" (see below).

Magnetic Methods

Magnetic archaeological survey, also known as magnetometry, is based on the passive measurement of the earth's magnetic field using highly sensitive magnetometer instruments (Aspinall et al. 2008; Becker 2009; Fig. 5.1). Magnetic archaeological prospection can be used for the detection of ferromagnetic objects, such as iron objects or slag from metal production sites, causing a relatively strong localized disturbance in the earth magnetic field, as well as for the detection of thermoremanently magnetized, burned archaeological structures, as, for example, hearths, kilns, bricks, or ceramics. The topsoil displays in general a substantially increased magnetization compared to deeper soil horizons and the underlying geological layers, a fact known as the *Le Borgne effect*, which is thought to be based on natural (e.g., forest fires, lightning strikes, oxidation of magnetite to maghemite) and anthropogenic influences (use of fire in prehistoric times). Hence, under favorable geological conditions, it can be possible to successfully locate and map archaeological trenches, pits, and postholes containing prehistoric topsoil in a matrix of relatively lower magnetization (Fig. 5.2). In order to be able to detect the small magnetic field variations caused by archaeological structures in the presence of a strong earth magnetic field, two magnetometer sensors are placed vertically above each other, resulting in an instrument known as a gradiometer: both sensors measure the effect of the earth's magnetic field as well as any of its temporal variations, which can be caused, for example, by solar activity, while the sensor that is closer to the ground measures the stronger effect of any structures buried within the shallow subsurface. State-of-the-art archaeological magnetic survey is conducted using one or more magnetometers (*fluxgate/Foerster* type, *Overhauser*, or *optically pumped cesium magnetometers*) along measurement

Fig. 5.1 Motorized magnetometer prospection at the Iron Age site of Uppåkra in southern Sweden using a multichannel Foerster gradiometer array mounted on a nonmagnetic cart (Image courtesy of Ludwig Boltzmann Institute for Archaeological Prospection and Virtual Archaeology)

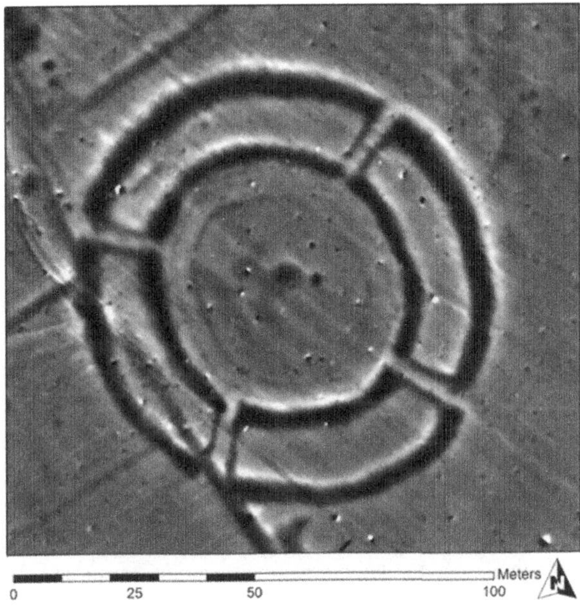

Fig. 5.2 Magnetic prospection result showing the Neolithic ring ditch of Steinabrunn in Austria measured with a multichannel cesium magnetometer system. The amplitude range of the *gray* scale image is −8/+12 nT (*white/black*) (Image courtesy of Wolfgang Neubauer)

transects with no more than 50-cm parallel spacing and 10-cm inline sample spacing. In general, no definite information about the depth of structures causing variations in the magnetic data can be derived from magnetic prospection.

Geoelectric Methods

Geoelectric survey, also termed resistivity or earth resistance survey, is based on the measurement of the resistance of artificially injected electrical currents into the subsurface (Hesse et al. 1986). The electrical soil resistance (or its reciprocal value, the electrical conductivity) is strongly dependent on the presence and amount of soil humidity, pore space, and salt and ion content in the shallow subsurface, as well as archaeological features present, which can cause measureable electrical effects at the surface. Positive features, such as stone walls, contrast with negative features, where the soil filling usually retains a greater amount of moisture. In suitable ground and weather conditions, resistance measurements can be used to locate stone structures, walls, and cavities due to their relatively increased electrical resistance, while filled ditches and pits can show by virtue of their relatively increased electrical conductivity. Geoelectric measurements are generally conducted by injecting an alternating electrical current into the soil using two electrodes. The electrical potential associated with the injected current is affected by an electrically heterogeneous subsurface, which can cause a measureable variation of the electrical potential at the ground surface. Therefore, two additional electrodes are employed in commonly

Fig. 5.3 Automatic Resistivity Profiling with two ARP(c) systems. The electrodes are the toothed wheels (Image courtesy of Geocarta, Paris)

used four-electrode arrays in order to measure the electrical potential over a fixed distance. At the surface, soil resistivity represents an average of the values along the flow path of the electrical current and is hence called *apparent resistivity*. The depth of investigation is a function of the distance between the current electrodes. By varying this distance it is possible to investigate the change of apparent soil resistivity with depth. Using a linear multielectrode array, it is possible to record the soil resistance with increasing electrode spacing at different depth levels, resulting in a so-called *pseudosection*. Most geoelectric archaeological prospection surveys are conducted manually using a fixed electrode frame or fixed multielectrode arrays with 0.5- or 1.0-m probe spacing, resulting in relatively limited spatial measurement progress. In the UK and in France, experiments have been conducted employing towed carts equipped with spiked electrode wheels. In recent years motorized geoelectric cart systems have been developed in France, permitting considerable spatial coverage rates with three simultaneously measured depths of investigation (Fig. 5.3).

Electromagnetic (EM) Methods

Electromagnetic (EM) archaeological survey methods comprise magnetic susceptibility, the Slingram method, induction methods, and metal-detecting and ground-penetrating radar (GPR), also known as soil radar or georadar.

Magnetic susceptibility is a dimensionless measure indicating a material's degree of magnetization in response to an applied magnetic field (*magnetizability*).

On the earth all materials are naturally exposed to the earth's magnetic field. Using dedicated instruments, sometimes called *Kappameter*, the magnetic susceptibility of soil layers, stones, and objects of archaeological interest can be determined in the field, or soil samples can be taken into the laboratory for measurement. An increased magnetic susceptibility of soil samples can indicate cultural layers due to thermo-remanently increased magnetization. Spatial measurements of the distribution of the soil magnetic susceptibility can thus reveal areas of archaeological activity.

The *Slingram* method utilizes a transmitter and a receiver coil with constant spacing between them. A primary low-frequency EM field generated by the transmitter coil is projected into the ground where it induces eddy currents in electrically conducting objects and materials. These induced currents give rise to a secondary EM field that can be detected by the receiver coil, simultaneously measuring the apparent resistivity and magnetic susceptibility of the ground. The method is used widely for the characterization of soils (*pedology*) and in precision farming. Other EM *induction meters* can be used to locate and map changes in clay content and soil humidity, filled-in trenches, walls, as well as areas of increased magnetic susceptibility, indicating cultural layers, fire places. A typical EM induction meter consists of a rod with transmitting and receiver coils mounted at its opposite ends. The system is carried or towed on a sledge horizontally over the ground along measurement transects. Measurements are usually recorded with an inline spacing of several decimeters, while transect spacing in case of instruments with 1-m coil separation should be around 50 cm. The depth of investigation corresponds to approximately half the transmitter-receiver spacing. Data positioning can be implemented using a global positioning system antenna or reflectors and a robotic TST. State-of-the-art EM induction meters using several receiver coils permit the simultaneous recording of electrical conductivity and magnetic susceptibility of the soil at four depth levels. Using motorized vehicles these systems can cover several hectares per day with 80-cm transect spacing (Fig. 5.4). A great advantage of the EM method over geoelectric survey (or georadar) is the fact that it does not require a contact to the ground and that it can be used efficiently in environments with high soil conductivity (e.g., wet soils, clay, saltwater beaches, arid regions with high electrical topsoil conductivity).

Metal detectors are manually operated EM induction devices designed for the detection of metal objects in the topsoil and shallow subsurface. In the case of the popular very-low-frequency (VLF) or induction balance detectors, the effect of the oscillating primary EM field generated by the transmitter coil onto the receiver coil is electrically balanced in the absence of a nearby metal object. In the presence of a metal object, this balance is disturbed and the machine emits a visual and audio signal. Modern computerized metal detectors permit the discrimination of metals and the cancelation of effects caused by soil mineralization. The depth of investigation of a metal detector for metal objects the size of a coin corresponds approximately to the diameter of the search coil used. In many countries the use of metal detectors is regulated by law.

Ground-penetrating radar is an active survey method based on the reflection of a short electromagnetic impulse off subsurface layer interfaces and structures with differing dielectric properties, such as buried foundations, cavities, and stones in

Fig. 5.4 The DUALEM-21S sensor for simultaneous measurement of apparent resistivity and magnetic susceptibility mounted in a sled, pulled by an all terrain vehicle with DGPS and Lightbar Guidance System (Image courtesy of Wim De Clercq, Gent University)

the shallow subsurface (Conyers 2004). A short electromagnetic impulse with a frequency band between 100 megaHertz (MHz) and 1 GHz is emitted into the ground from a transmitter antenna located on the ground surface, and the reflected radar signal is recorded by a receiver antenna as function of the time that has passed since pulse emission. Transmitter and receiver antennae are placed next to each other in commonly used soil radar systems. Depending on the pulse frequency, the power of the antenna output and the electrical conductivity of the soil, signal penetration depths between 0.5 and 5 m depth can be achieved. Georadar measurements are conducted along straight transects and measurements are made with close inline spacing of, for example, 2 or 5 cm. State-of-the-art in professional archaeological survey is a transect spacing of not more than 25 cm when measuring with a 500-MHz GPR antenna. Exact data positioning is achieved with help of a distance wheel mounted on the GPR cart or sledge and guidance lines placed on the ground with constant intervals, or through the use of a differential GPS with centimeter accuracy. Modern multichannel georadar array systems (Fig. 5.5) offer dense high-resolution measurements with as little as 8-cm transect spacing (Fig. 5.6). Densely measured 2D georadar sections, which can be thought as vertical scans through the subsurface, can be merged into virtual 3D data volumes. Subsequently these data volumes can be cut into horizontal slices, showing structures at approximately the same depth (*GPR depth slices*). Archaeological structures contained in georadar data are

Fig. 5.5 Motorized GPR survey with the 16-channel MALÅ Imaging Radar Array at the UNESCO World Cultural Heritage site Birka-Hovgården. Data positioning is conducted with the GPS antenna mounted on top of the GPR system (Image courtesy of Ludwig Boltzmann Institute for Archaeological Prospection and Virtual Archaeology)

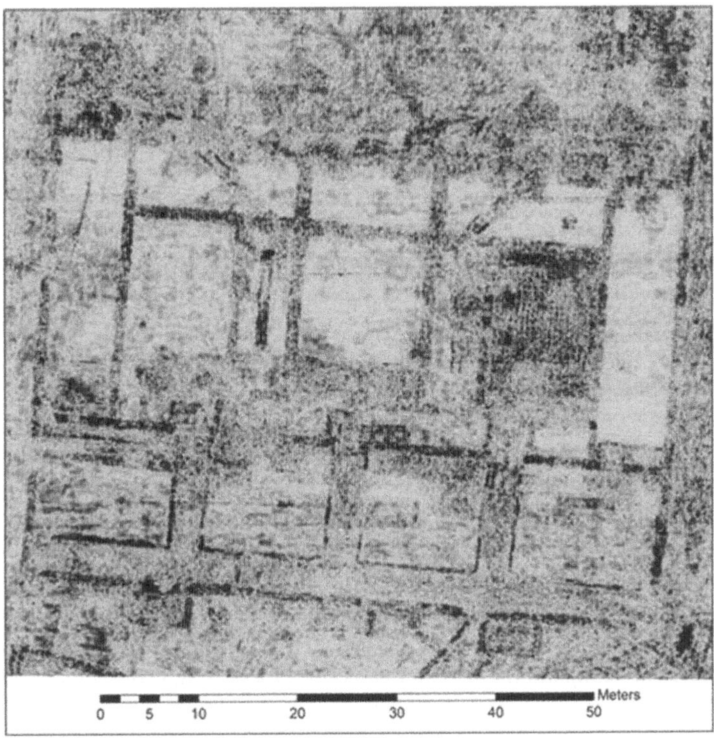

Fig. 5.6 Georadar depth slice measured with the 16-channel 400-MHz MALÅ Imaging Radar Array (MIRA) with 8-cm transect spacing showing the southern part of the main building at the Forum of the Roman town of Carnuntum. In the high-definition data for the first time the individual brick columns of the hypocaust system under the floor of the easternmost room became visible (Image courtesy of Archeo Prospections®)

often more recognizable when presented in plan view as horizontal depth-slice images. Of all archaeological subsurface methods, GPR generates the largest amount of data and offers highest spatial measurement resolution, horizontally and vertically, and the best chance of assessing the depth of features.

Seismic Methods

Geophysical seismic reflection and refraction methods are only rarely used for archaeological onshore prospection due to the rather time-consuming data acquisition and data processing involved, as well as due to the relatively low imaging resolution. Special application cases are, for instance, the seismic investigation of the depth to bedrock at an archaeological site, or the nondestructive testing (NDT) of architecture using ultrasound. In marine and underwater archaeology seismic geophysical prospection methods, such as *sonar* (e.g., chirp sonar, side-scan sonar), boomer, pinger, sparker, and *sub-bottom profiler*, are successfully used for the detection and mapping of archaeological and historical structures (e.g., wrecks, harbor constructions) on and below the seafloor.

Geochemical Methods

Geochemical archaeological survey methods are based on the mapping of distribution and amount of specific chemical elements and compounds within the soil for localization and delimitation of archaeological sites, as well as for a more detailed analysis of known sites and the function of subareas (Oonk et al. 2009). Compared to the number of geophysical surveys, the number of reported geochemical surveys is small, due to the relatively slow data acquisition involved. Most commonly employed have been soil phosphate measurements using sample intervals between 1 and 50 m with the goal of locating and delimiting prehistoric settlement sites. Increased phosphate values can indicate the presence of cultural layers of archaeological interest due to the release of phosphate ions during the decay of deposited organic material (occupational waste and manure) and their subsequent binding to soil particles. Other geochemical prospection methods involve the analysis of heavy metals in archaeological soils to identify metalworking sites. Aside from increased phosphate, archaeological soils commonly show anomalous levels of calcium, copper, magnesium, potassium, sodium, and zinc. One concern regarding geochemical mapping for archaeological prospection is the comparability of data values obtained from different soil phases. Geochemical methods are also erosive since samples have to be taken.

Future Directions

Archaeological subsurface surveys all map variations in the physical or chemical properties of the topsoil and the near subsurface. Digital systems generate the maps as gray scale (Figs. 5.2 and 5.6) or color-coded raster images located on the local or national grid. The use of Geographical Information Systems (GIS) aids interpretation by presenting these geophysical maps within the context of previous discoveries or modern land use (Neubauer 2004). Improved digital imaging is an important part of current R&D.

The most important parameters affecting the efficiency of subsurface archaeological prospection methods are sensitivity, speed, and sample spacing (Becker 2009). Considerable advances have been made using motorized multichannel systems with GPS positioning and navigation. Understanding of the nature of structures observed in geophysical data is being improved empirically by comparison with the results of subsequent excavations. Research into the visibility of buried archaeological structures using different survey methods continues. Of particular interest in this regard are "ghost" structures visible in the geophysical record that fail to show during subsequent excavation.

See also the entries in EGA for Archaeometry, Landscape Archaeology; Prospection Methods in Archaeology; Archaeological Prospection Laboratory; Magnetic Susceptibility of Soils and Sediments.

Chapter 6
Excavation Methods

Martin Carver

Introduction and Definition

Archaeological excavation is the procedure by which archaeologists define, retrieve, and record cultural and biological remains found in the ground. Past activities leave traces in the form of house foundations, graves, artifacts, bones, seeds, and numerous other traces indicative of human experience. These *strata* survive very variously, depending on the type of location and geology (hilly, lowland, wet, dry, acid, etc., known as the *terrain*). Survival and visibility also depend on how far the remains of the past have already decayed or been disturbed by later activities, such as cultivation or building. These *site formation processes* give a site its modern character, and this has a strong influence on the excavation method that is used.

Excavation usually (but not always, see below) requires the removal and permanent dispersal of strata so they can never be reexamined. So the method is also influenced by the need to conserve cultural strata as far as possible – never dig more than you need to understand the site. Many sites are situated in socially sensitive areas, where excavation (particularly the removal of skeletal remains) is to be avoided or kept to a minimum.

Successful excavation depends on our ability to see or detect these traces, so that they can be measured and sampled, and this in turn depends on the *techniques* and the skilled workforce available. Like other sciences, excavation requires us to devise new techniques that enable us to see more, so that excavation method is in a state of continual development.

The way an excavation is done is therefore determined by what you want to know, the state of preservation of the site, the techniques and skills available, and the social context of the country in which the excavation takes place. In best practice,

M. Carver (✉)
Department of Archaeology, University of York, York, UK
e-mail: martin.carver@york.ac.uk

M. Carver et al. (eds.), *Field Archaeology from Around the World*,
SpringerBriefs in Archaeology, DOI 10.1007/978-3-319-09819-7_6

these are brought together and balanced in a program specially designed for each project. Contrary to popular belief, success is much less dependent on the application of a standard method (or *default system*) to every situation (Carver 2011).

Excavation Areas

The type of area opened in an excavation is determined by its purpose. Small-scale excavations, such as *shovel tests* and *test pits* and *trenches*, are used in the reconnaissance stage to locate sites or in the evaluation stage to help assign their current value. Shovel tests are the size of a shovel blade say 15×15 cm, test pits are 1×1 to 4×4 m, and test trenches are 1–3 m wide and can be very long (100 m or more). They are especially valuable for testing deep strata, since the sides can be held up by shoring, so protecting the excavators from the danger of collapse (Fig. 6.1).

Sets of test pits and trenches also have a wide application in addressing particular research questions over a wide area. In this case the pits and trenches are distributed over the landscape with a view to obtaining examples (*samples*) of assemblages and local sequences from which an occupation or behavior can be generalized

Fig. 6.1 Excavation through part of the tell settlement at Çatalhöyük, Turkey, showing edges protected from collapse by sandbags and a deeper trench supported by timber shoring (M. Carver)

Fig. 6.2 Area excavation at Portmahomack, Scotland. The horizon is being exposed by a troweling line and will be recorded with the assistance of observation from a tower (M. Carver)

(see Hester et al. 1997, pp. 58–74; see America, p. 193). *Box excavation* consists of a number of test pits (up to 5×5 m in area) set adjacent to each other in a grid, each separated from the other by a *balk* (about half a meter wide) along which excavators can walk and earth be removed. The balk also serves to retain a *section*, a vertical slice of strata, drawn by excavators to record the sequence of layers at that point. Box excavation was pioneered in Russia and adopted in China, and a version was also enthusiastically promoted in England by Mortimer Wheeler (see Britain, p. 203).

Area excavation refers to an excavation where the area opened is continuous (Fig. 6.2). In research excavations, the size of the area is closely connected to the questions addressed: early pioneers in Denmark used areas of up to 3 ha to reveal the shallow but extensive traces of Iron Age villages consisting only of pits and postholes. In CRM excavations the size is related to the area to be affected by development; these are often very extensive, such as the Framework Excavations in advance of London's Fifth terminal at Heathrow, or the excavations by the National Road Authority in Ireland (p. 107).

Excavation Techniques

Archaeological strata are defined in the horizontal plane by scraping the surface until boundaries (anomalies) are seen in the soil. These denote the edges of *contexts*, deposits that are made at different times (Fig. 6.3). The object of excavation is to define contexts and put them in order to produce the story of the site.

Fig. 6.3 The dark curved patterns of post pits and ditches revealed by troweling. On this sandy terrain, the edges are rendered more visible for visible with the aid of a light spray (M. Carver)

Initial definition of a deposit is often achieved with a mechanical excavator with a front bucket or backhoe, used for example to remove topsoil or a concrete platform. The surface may then be cleaned with a shovel and further defined with a trowel, a tool which archaeologists have adopted from the building trade (a pointing trowel) and made especially their own (Fig. 6.4). The ability to define strata and to see objects depends on the technique and the intensity of effort applied. For example, clearance of the topsoil with a back-actor is fast but visibility is sacrificed – smaller objects and more subtle edges in the soil will not be noticed. By contrast, to ensure that everything is noticed in a feature of special importance, such as furnished grave, the excavator will proceed with the greatest caution, not only taking care to define every tiny anomaly in the ground, but *screening* (sieving) all the waste soil (*spoil*) to make sure nothing escapes.

These different levels of digging at which excavation may operate also imply the application of different levels of *recording*. For example, the character and location of a wall exposed by a bulldozer will not be as accurately known as one carefully revealed by the trowel and brush. Accordingly, the more detailed the excavation, the more detailed should be the records. It can be seen too, that the more detailed the digging, the longer it will take and the more it will cost. The question of how much trouble to take is therefore a vital one to consider at the design stage. One useful way of controlling the application of appropriate level of digging and recording is to use *Recovery Levels*, lettered A–F (Fig. 6.5), a handy template which lays down

Fig. 6.4 Hand tools in use. (**a**) The pointing trowel favored in Europe. (**b**) The handpick favored in East Asia (M. Carver)

LEVEL	COMPONENT	FIND	CONTEXT	FEATURE	STRUCTURE	LANDSCAPE	e.g.
A	(not recovered)	Surface finds PLOT 2-D	Inferred by sensor OUTLINE PLAN	Inferred by sensor OUTLINE PLAN	Inferred by sensor OUTLINE PLAN	Inferred by sensor	Field walking
B	(not recovered)	Large finds RECORD EXAMPLES KEEP EXAMPLES	Defined by shovel DESCRIBE	Defined by shovel SHORT DESCRIPTION. OUTLINE PLAN	as features	PLOT STRUCTURES on OS	19th C House
C	(not recovered)	All visible finds. RECORD ALL. KEEP EXAMPLES. MAY PLOT BY m^2	Defined by coarse trowel DESCRIPTION (Munsell for mortars and natural)	Defined by coarse trowel FULL DESCRIPTION. DETAILED PLAN HEIGHT	Defined by coarse trowel EXCAVATE AS ONE. PHOTOGRAPH	1:100 PLAN PROFILE	16th C Pits
D	SAMPLE SIEVING of spoil on site for presence of specified material (spoil not kept)	All visible finds PLOT 3-D and KEEP ALL	Defined by fine trowel DESCRIPTION (Incl. Munsell) PLAN 1:20	Defined by fine trowel FULL DESCRIPTION. DETAILED PLAN 1:20 (colour coded) CONTOURS PHOTOGRAPH (B/W)	Defined by fine trowel EXCAVATE AS ONE. PHOTOGRAPH by PHASE	1:100 PLAN CONTOUR SURVEY	Timber trace building
E	TOTAL SIEVING of spoil on site for presence of specified material and KEEP SPOIL	All visible finds PLOT 3-D and KEEP ALL	Defined minutely DESCRIPTION (Incl. Munsell). PLAN (natural colour) 1:10 or 1:5 contour	Defined minutely FULL DESCRIPTION. PLAN (colour) 1:10 or 1:5 CONTOUR. PHOTOGRAPH	Defined minutely EXCAVATE AS ONE. PHOTOGRAPH by PHASE	(as LEVEL D) CONTOUR SURVEY	Skeleton
F	MICRO SIEVING soil block in laboratory	(as component)	(as LEVEL E) and LIFT AS BLOCK	(as LEVEL E)	(as LEVEL E)	(as LEVEL D)	Storage pit fill

Fig. 6.5 Recovery levels used to control the levels of precision applied to digging and recording in excavation (M. Carver)

in advance the minimum recording required for each type of digging. This ensures not only that the full record is made but that features excavated at the same level can be compared: the assemblages of two garbage pits excavated at the same recovery level are comparable, since they were retrieved at the same level of intensity and subjected to the same screening regime.

Recovery levels are decided in the design stage. In general, Level A is used for the clearance of the top of a site by machine: Level B usually refers to tidying with a shovel and Level C to preliminary definition with a trowel. The vast majority of features are excavated at Level D or its equivalent. Here definition is as good as can be achieved by the naked eye, each context is recorded individually, 25 % of the spoil is screened, and there are detailed written and photographic records of all features. Level E tends to be applied to features of special importance like an undisturbed floor or a furnished grave. Here the tools used are the dental pick or the scapula, rather than the trowel, and the excavator works very slowly and close to the ground. There will be occasions when a feature is so unusual, and in such good condition, that the excavators cannot do justice to it on site. In this case (Level F) it is boxed and lifted and taken to the laboratory, where it can be slowly dissected in controlled conditions. A pioneering example was the lifting of an entire burial chamber at Högom in Sweden. At Monruz in Switzerland, an Upper Paleolithic floor was defined on site and then lifted and put on permanent display – a combination of Levels E and F excavation.

Nano-excavation

Recent technical advances have further enlarged the ambitions of excavators to detect, and record in ever more detail, the phenomena encountered on archaeological sites. Archaeologists started screening and taking bags of soil (*context samples*) back to the laboratory some decades ago, in order to extract material that was suspected of being there, but not visible to the naked eye. Examples are grains of pollen or the husks (carcasses) of insects, which give information about the vegetational resources and the local environment, respectively.

Further developments, which might be termed Level G, use chemical and geophysical readings taken on site, to infer the former presence of certain activities. ICP analysis was used at Sutton Hoo to detect traces of iron and copper from a vanished cauldron and the residue of bones from a burial chamber that had been scoured by tomb robbers (Carver 2005, pp. 49–53). Minute traces of bone can now be identified to species by *proteomics*, using the weight of specific proteins. In Greenland, an archaeological team described 500-year sequence of animal farming, using DNA drawn from a sequence of samples taken from a vertical core driven down into an open field (Hebsgaard et al. 2009). Magnetic instruments have proved revealing on site, for example, at Pinnacle Point where Paleolithic hearths have been detected using magnetic susceptibility measurements. Perhaps the most interesting advances, from the excavators' point of view, are the results of using

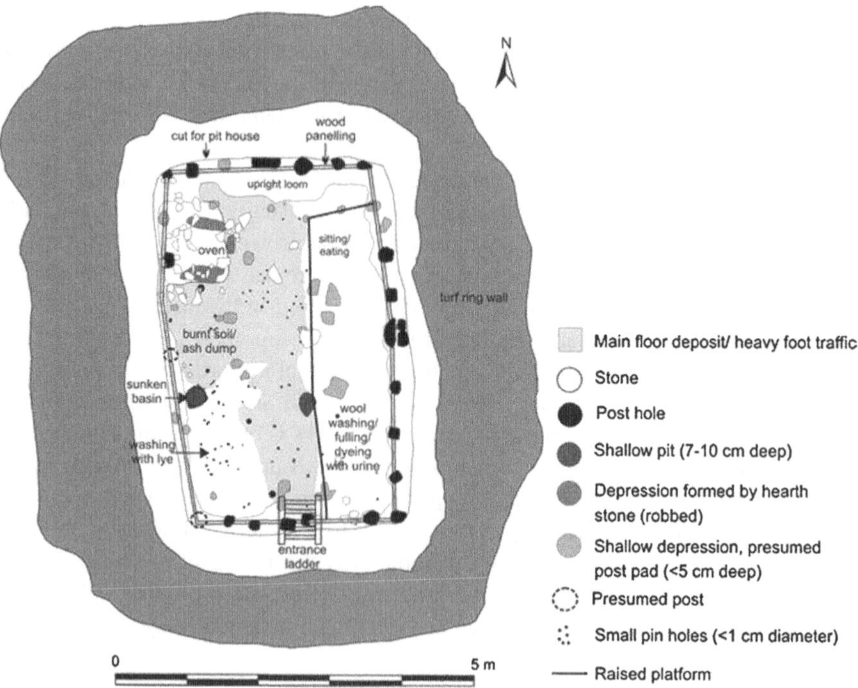

Fig. 6.6 An interpretation of Hofstathir pit house G, owed to microchemical and geophysical mapping (Courtesy of Karen Milek)

geophysical and geochemical techniques in combination. An example is Karen Milek's analysis of the floor of Viking houses in Iceland where magnetometer readings and chemical readings allowed her to infer the presence of wool washing, latrines, and beds and map their location (Milek 2006, 2012a, b; Fig. 6.6).

Arbitrary and Stratigraphic Excavation

Since the basic sequence of an archaeological site is given by the contexts (layers), the ideal is to record each of these in the order in which it was deposited. This is *stratigraphic excavation*, which, in its simplest form, maps each layer separately (Roskams 2001) and in more sophisticated schemes records all the layers but also higher-order concepts like features and structures (Carver 2009; and see Recording Fieldwork, p. 63). The order of deposition may be partially captured in *section* and is worked out for the site as a whole with the aid of *stratification diagrams*.

Arbitrary excavation divides the deposit into horizontal slices 5–10 cm thick, known as *arbitrary levels* (or spits). This is naturally a much faster method of digging than defining each original cultural layer in three dimensions. It is often justifiable in the case of deposits where stratification is extremely difficult to see, for example, in *cave sites* or *LBK settlements*. Even when layer interfaces are visible, it is sometimes championed as more scientific than the definition of individual contexts, which is subject to the variable skills of excavators. If a deposit is precisely sliced, horizontally and vertically, the records of these surfaces provide an unequivocal, and checkable, account of where interfaces were located and what layers looked like.

Analysis and Publication of Excavations

The minimum duty of every excavator is to conserve the records made in a publically accessible archive and provide an account of the sequence of activities encountered on the site. Many thousands of CRM excavations are conducted each year that meet these minimum requirements on behalf of clients. The full yield of research requires a comprehensive program of analysis, in which all the artifacts and biota (the *assemblages*) are studied and the *use of space* is analyzed and the *sequence* and date determined. In general the assemblages indicate the activities on site; the spatial analysis discovers the shape of buildings and how floors, yards, and routes were used. The sequential analysis puts the structures and activities in order and gives them a date. These results are synthesized to give a documented account of the events that occurred in order of date, often divided for convenience into phases or periods. What every excavation should offer is a strong, evidence-based local story, which can then be deployed to understand bigger questions couched in more generalized theoretical frameworks.

Relevant entries in EGA include Floors and Occupation Surface Analysis in Archaeology; Stratigraphy in Archaeology: A Brief History.

Chapter 7
The Archaeological Study of Buildings

Jason Wood

Introduction

The study of buildings has always formed a significant part of archaeological endeavor (Wood, 1994, 2006; Malm 2001; Morriss 2000; Parron-Kontis and Reveyron 2005; Schuller 2002). In Britain, research, illustration, and publication began to mount through the first half of the nineteenth century, not least through the national work of John Britton and Robert Willis and their regional contemporaries. These early students of historic buildings applied archaeological standards of draftsmanship and subsequent dissection, phasing, and analyses that permitted logical insights about dating, periodization, and typology. Indeed, Willis used the term "archaeology" to describe his recording techniques and their application at several English cathedrals. He knew the value of demonstrating structural and dating arguments through making proper records, and his work remains as valid today as it ever was. Of course, succeeding generations would set new standards and devise new procedural models, but Willis stands close to the start of the archaeological tradition that requires accurate measurement and drawing before an analysis is undertaken.

Research and Understanding

For Willis, and the subsequent researchers that he inspired, it was enough to demonstrate the academic benefits that accrued from the study of buildings. The notion of "pure" research for its own sake, simply to find out, may be unfashionable these days, but it is still alive. In this age of public accountability, however, academic

J. Wood (✉)
Heritage Consultancy Services, Lancaster, UK
e-mail: jwhcs@yahoo.co.uk

M. Carver et al. (eds.), *Field Archaeology from Around the World*,
SpringerBriefs in Archaeology, DOI 10.1007/978-3-319-09819-7_7

curiosity and challenge may not be enough to secure the necessary financial or legislative support. Other benefits, such as opportunities for innovation and community engagement, must be demonstrated. Today, the study of buildings needs to be set within a wider intellectual context, and the archaeologist must ensure that research programs are carefully considered and coordinated with others in similar fields before work begins.

In recent years, the role of the archaeologist and the application of modern archaeological practice have been extended to inform the conservation and management of historic buildings. This is based on the firm belief that it is not possible to conserve or manage a building without first understanding its history. There is a need to know how and why a building was constructed, how the spaces within a building and between buildings were altered and used through time, what survives of the building and what has been lost, as well as any association with individuals and events. In this way, the study of buildings is inevitably drawn down the path of research – albeit research directed toward a practical outcome. This understanding is documented through the process of making analytical records.

The ultimate aim of understanding buildings is to define their *significance*, so that the historical asset may be retained and enhanced. In particular, it is essential to recognize those aspects that make buildings important enough to justify the necessary conservation time and effort. It is impossible to say, for example, whether or not a particular roof structure should undergo extensive repair or be renewed until it is known what date that roof structure is and how important it is relative to comparable roof structures elsewhere. To put it in a single word, the importance of a building or group of buildings will need to be "*characterized*" and to gain credibility that characterization must be well documented.

Having characterized a building, the knowledge gained can then be used to address any sensitive management problems. This may lead to more intensive study to inform particular conservation or development proposals. Clearly not all buildings need to be studied in the same detail: different circumstances will demand different responses. The scope and level of documentation need to be economically tailored to particular conditions and will be dependent on a number of factors, such as the type and complexity of the building and the nature and scale of proposed works. Consideration should carefully be given to the appropriate kinds of analytical recording in each case. For instance, further research will be especially important for elaborate works programs on multiphase buildings where a greater understanding of the structural and material performance of the fabric is required to avoid damage and allow for appropriate preservation. Where, for example, it is necessary to deconstruct the timber frame of a building to repair decay, or where partial demolition of its masonry to remove rusting metal cramps cannot be avoided, it will be important to prepare precise records. For the dismantling of buildings for re-erection elsewhere, for example, in a museum, very detailed three-dimensional recording and numbering of all components will be required, in order to recreate the disposition and assembly of as much of the original fabric as practicable.

In such situations, the role of the archaeologist, often working in close partnerships with other disciplines, needs to be properly integrated with the project direction

Fig. 7.1 The major repair project at Ightham Mote, Kent (UK), undertaken on behalf of the National Trust, had the benefit throughout of an archaeologist working alongside the architect and contractor to inform the process and record what was discovered (Photo: Jason Wood)

and monitoring team, usually under the leadership of the project architect. The most satisfactory projects will be those which, from the earliest possible stage, work with and take into account the skills and experience of a wide variety of specialists. As well as archaeologists, these may include architectural historians, structural engineers, materials specialists, and others (Fig. 7.1).

It should be noted that as a part of an historic building conservation or development project, the work of an archaeologist differs significantly from that associated with conventional archaeological fieldwork, in that the data can form a vital part of the subsequent works specification. Scaled drawings and photographs often provide the essential basis for detailed works proposals and consent applications. Such records may also be used for issuing instructions to building contractors. The need for accuracy and legibility are therefore paramount.

Techniques for Studying Buildings

Documentary research is important to establish the architectural and historical interest of a building and to elucidate the evidence for its history and development. This can be achieved in a number of ways. Most research should start with the obvious sources – the relevant statutory designation, a survey of standard reference works and existing secondary sources on both the individual building and of that class of building in general. Local authority record systems and record offices are often a good source of information, as well as national records and specialist archives. It is advisable not to restrict research to locally available material, as in many cases, crucial information will lie in national collections and may have been overlooked in the past.

In general, work should concentrate initially on the sources most likely to reveal evidence for the history of the fabric of the building, such as maps, plans, photographs, and other historic images. Most studies will benefit from a map regression exercise. This involves gathering copies of all relevant maps, starting with the most recent and working back through the whole sequence of every period. Topographical or other drawings, published views, and photographs are especially useful. Their collation can be time consuming, but the effort is not often wasted as these images frequently shed light on the original context and tell much about a building's function and pattern of alterations. Beyond these sources is a whole range of information including title deeds, taxation lists, and rate books, which can all be helpful to construct a simple chronology of ownership and tenancy.

Oral history has an important role to play in the study of buildings. People who have direct experience of a building's use and adaptation in the recent past may present opportunities to gather supporting evidence for changes in form or function. For example, the redevelopment of industrial buildings can benefit from contact with former employees resulting in a greater understanding of any surviving plant and its significance, informing decisions on retention or disposal. Defining significance is now a process that increasingly goes beyond expert values to encompass the wider community and to embrace public history. Capturing peoples' views and attitudes about buildings that are significant to them can be illuminating. A crucial aim must be to encourage people to tell their own stories, to share their personal and often "unofficial" history, and to explore further the forces that link these memories to specific buildings.

Fabric Survey and Analysis

Historical research alone is not sufficient: there must always be some degree of engagement with the fabric of the building. Drawings are an indispensable part of studying buildings. These can be produced using a variety of different survey methodologies, equipment, and related software packages (Dallas 2003):

Hand-measured survey involves the use of tape measures, plumb bobs, frames, and surveyor's levels.

Instrument-based survey involves the use of total station theodolite control, consisting of a closed-traverse run around and through a building, followed by trigonometric intersection of suitably observed points on a façade, or electronic distance meter tacheometry utilizing microprisms for cross sections through complex enclosed structures.

Fig. 7.2 Laser scanning carried out by the University of Birmingham at Chedworth Roman Villa, Gloucestershire (UK), on behalf of the National Trust (Photo: Jason Wood)

Photographic-based survey (often used in conjunction with hand-measured and instrument-based control) includes

Rectified photography, consisting of single photographs or a mosaic of overlapping photographs taken using large- or medium-format cameras aligned square to the object

Photogrammetry, based on stereophotography taken using metric cameras

Laser-based survey using terrestrial laser scanners. These record three-dimensional positions at a predetermined resolution over a chosen area, generating thousands of high-accuracy coordinates. The coordinates are stored as a series of XYZ measurements which visually constitute a point cloud that represents the geometric form of the building being scanned in three dimensions. Laser scanners also operate in complete darkness and are therefore unaffected by varying light levels, unlike more traditional recording methods (Fig. 7.2).

The resulting drawings are usually provided as a set of scaled plans, sections, elevations, and details (Fig. 7.3):

Plans: The requirement may include basement, ground and upper level floor plans, including plans of ceilings, vaults, and roof structures, showing relevant external and internal detail and features. The location of all sections and elevations should be identified. Plans are the fundamental product to which all other material can be related.

Sections: The requirement may include sections corresponding to the bay divisions or axes through the relevant parts of a building. These should normally define the principal wall plane and also include detail through adjacent openings and voids such as windows, doors, passageways, and smaller features such as putlog holes and beam sockets, as well as roof and floor detail. The height locations of all plans should be identified.

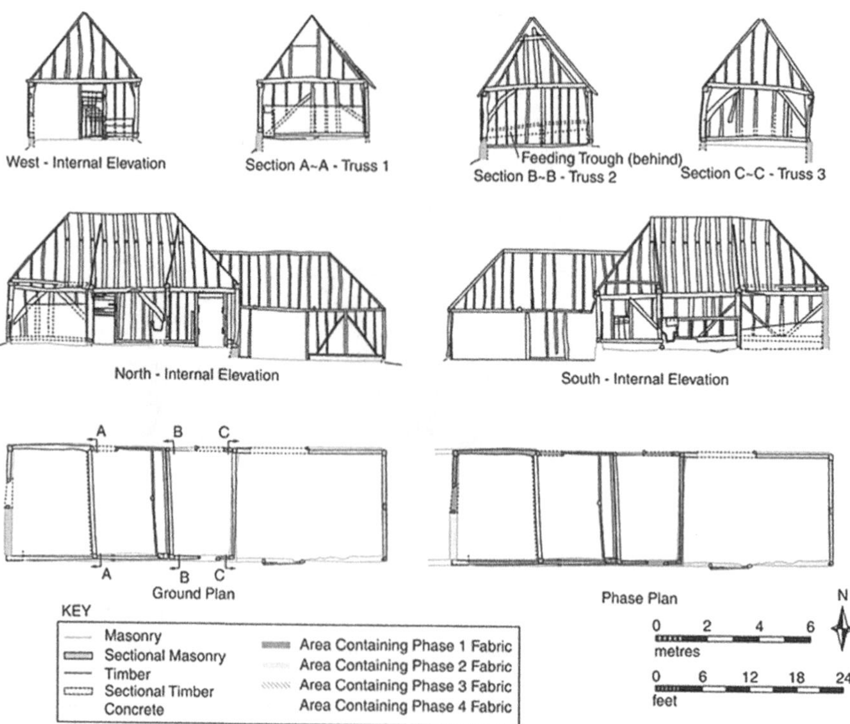

Fig. 7.3 Plans, elevations, and sections of the timber-framed stable block at Abbey Farmstead, Faversham, Kent (UK), recorded in advance of repair and refurbishment works (Drawing: Lancaster University Archaeological Unit; courtesy of Oxford Archaeology and Swale Borough Council)

Elevations: The requirement may include external and internal elevations of the relevant parts of a building, depicting architectural features with associated detail (Fig. 7.4). Walls adjoining elevations should be depicted in section. The height locations of all plans should be identified.

Details: The requirement may include separate plans, sections, and elevations of representative openings and architectural features, with exploded views to supplement the two-dimensional record where appropriate (for example, carpentry joints), and representative architectural, decorative, and ornamental details, both loose and in situ (molding profiles, inscriptions, setting-out lines, tooling, nail positions, masons' and carpenters' marks, graffiti, etc.).

It is not possible, however, to understand an historic building on the basis of record drawings alone. Close analysis of the fabric will be required to establish the relative chronology of the building and its structural phases:

Fig. 7.4 An elevation drawing of the church tower of St. George of England, Toddington, Bedfordshire (UK). Recording and analysis provided accurate base level information about the nature and historical development of the fabric to inform the repair program (Drawing: Network Archaeology Ltd; courtesy of Toddington PCC)

Analytical records: The requirement may include annotating the plans, sections, and elevations to depict boundaries between different types of building material (stone, brick, tile, wood, metal, glass, etc.); surface finishes (mortar, render, plaster, daub, paint, industrial lining, etc.); building periods, phases of construction and repair; constructional detail (wall alignments and thicknesses, bonding patterns, blockings, putlog holes, beam sockets, chase scars, butt joints, building lifts, work-gang breaks, fittings, etc.); occupational detail (wear marks, blackened timbers, industrial residues, etc.); and evidence for abandonment or demolition (robbing, salvaging, fire damage, etc.).

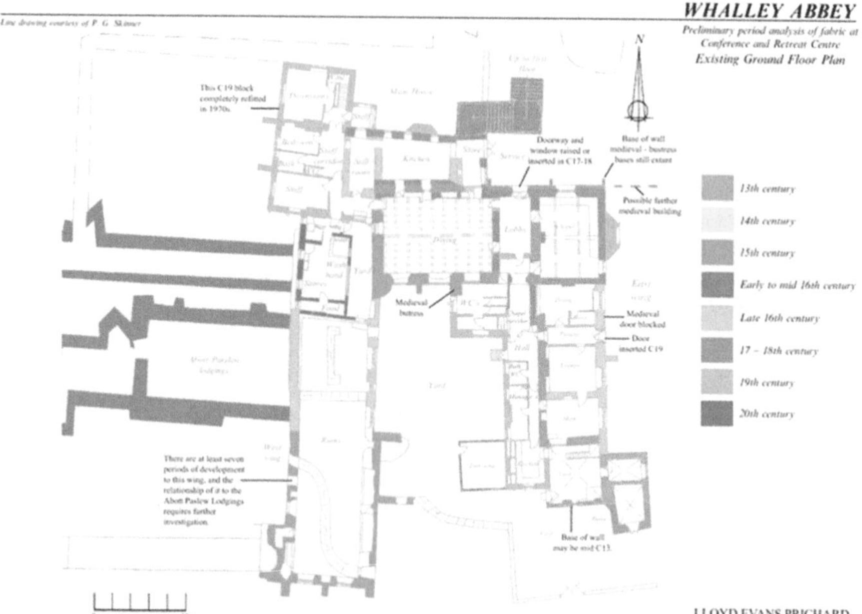

Fig. 7.5 An annotated ground plan showing suggested periods and phases of part of Whalley Abbey, Lancashire (UK) (Drawing: Lloyd Evans Prichard)

Interpretation records: The requirement may include plans, sections, and elevations depicting outline reconstruction of the principal elements and features, for each of the periods identified. Output may be presented as an annotated plane (Fig. 7.5) or three-dimensional or cutaway projection (Fig. 7.6).

Intervention records: "As-built" records, showing the extent of conservation or development works, should depict areas of rebuilding, rebedding, repointing, grouting, new fabric insertions, etc. "As-built" records are particularly important where a component or structure is dismantled, repaired, and then reassembled.

General photographic recording of the external and internal appearance of the significant parts of the building should be undertaken. Close-up photography will also often be required for architectural details.

Finally, detailed physical or chemical analysis of certain building materials, surface finishes, or residues can often provide essential corroborative information including technological and supplementary dating evidence.

Entries in EGA relevant to this section include Buildings Archaeology; Historic Site and Historic Building Preservation: Overview; Historic Building Conservation: Current Approaches.

Fig. 7.6 A cutaway reconstruction drawing of the church at Furness Abbey, Cumbria (UK) (Drawing: David P Cooper)

Chapter 8
Recording Fieldwork

Madeleine Hummler

Theories of Recording

Archaeological field work is a scientific process that relies on recorded observations and measurement. It is accepted that the archaeological record is of course not an exhaustive rendering of the site, even though it may represent much of what is left of it. However, every anomaly recognised in the field must be give a location and a description, since without these no analyses or interpretations are possible. Comprehensive recording has become the guiding principle of archaeological survey and excavation, especially where a site is to be destroyed, since the record has to stand as a proxy for the site itself (Fig. 8.1).

A multitude of factors, including the circumstances of deposition (intentional and unintentional in the past), site formation processes and post-depositional activity, terrain and types of remains and the techniques available, determine what is or could be recorded. We can only record what we know how to detect, something that is in constant evolution, with new research alerting us to fruitful avenues of enquiry. A relatively recent example is the recording of significant chemical traces in floor areas, even though we cannot 'see' them (see Carver 2011, pp. 49–56 for an introduction to some of these techniques).

Recorders strive to strike a balance between measured and intuitive observation, as may be seen in the growing literature on archaeological practice, for example the essays on practices from the seventeenth to the twentieth century in north-western

M. Hummler (✉)
Department of Archaeology, University of York, York, UK
e-mail: madeleine.hummler@york.ac.uk

M. Carver et al. (eds.), *Field Archaeology from Around the World*,
SpringerBriefs in Archaeology, DOI 10.1007/978-3-319-09819-7_8

Fig. 8.1 Recorder at work, showing context records sheets (*right*), feature record sheet (*under* the tape), drawing (on the knee) and Munsell Color chart (*centre*) (M Carver)

Europe (Wolfhechel Jensen 2012), or the discussion by Lucas (2012, pp. 18–73) of philosophies of recording, including different stances on 'total' or 'selective' recording exemplified by Pitt-Rivers and Petrie in later nineteenth and early twentieth century Britain and Egypt (ibid. pp. 45–51). General Pitt Rivers insisted that "every detail should […] be recorded in the manner most conducive to facility of reference" (Pitt Rivers 1887 cited in Lucas 2012, p. 45; see also Darvill, this volume), but was by no means the only one or the first to adopt this stance. Modern archaeological historiography is writing a more varied and less linear account of field experience and precept, for example, the very detailed instructions in 1836–37 for excavations of barrows in Mecklenburg (Germany) by Friedrich Lisch (Eberhardt in Wolfhechel Jensen 2012, pp. 154–56). Similarly, the emergence of open area excavation has been claimed by many different traditions: Germany and Britain in the 1930s (Darvill, this volume), Denmark in the 1930s (Larsson, this volume), Soviet settlement archaeology in the 1920s–1940s influencing Chinese procedures in the 1930s (Zhang, this volume), Leroi Gourhan's *grands décapages* of the 1960s (Courbin 1987; Schlanger, this volume); see also Galanidou and Leesch, this volume.

Recent decades have seen the growth of the critique of the position that recording can be wholly objective. Reynolds and Barber (1984) noted that "the emphasis on recording technique has been […] an attempt to convert the whole site, lock, stock and barrel, into a physical record. In effect, this too often means that observation (an essentially active process) gives place to passive mechanical recording." For Hodder "The key point is that excavation method, data collection and data recording all depend on interpretation. Interpretation occurs at the trowel's edge" (1997, p. 693). Lucas's concept that the archaeological record is an *act of translation* (2012, pp. 237–8) is helpful: translating the physical reality of what is in the ground, transferring it into another medium, giving it meaning, and accepting that interpretation is part of the equation. If recording is translation, then the tension between subjectivity and objectivity becomes a positive force.

Recording in Four Acts

So, records must be made; but which records? Introductions to archaeology and textbooks on archaeological practice give primacy to written, drawn and photographic records (physical or digital), and the definition and recording of sampled materials, and there is much agreement on procedures. A useful way of thinking about the archaeological record – rather than structure it into written, drawn and photographic records – is to divide it into four *purposes* of the record: recording *location* (position, geometry, distribution), recording the properties of *elements that are observed but not kept* (strata, stratigraphy), recording *elements that are kept* ('finds' including biota, samples) and *monitoring* (recording what has been recorded, how and why). The summary that follows will be limited to reflections drawn from experience and the from literature dealing with archaeological practice, especially on excavation (for example Roskams 2001; Carver 2009; Tassie and Owens 2010). Surface and sub-surface surveys make use of some of these procedures (e.g. to record location), although they have their own strategies (e.g. for levels of coverage), and dedicated protocols and software (e.g. for geophysical surveys; see entries by Holdaway, Křivánek, Oestmo and Trinks, in this volume).

Location

The principle of locating a point on the ground is to position it on a horizontal *grid* using an easting and northing (x and y co-ordinates) and to measure its height above a datum point, e.g. sea level (z co-ordinate). The three-dimensional Cartesian co-ordinates (x, y, z) give a unique *map reference* relative to the rest of the known world. This can be measure with tapes and compass, with a square and level, with a Total Station Theodolite (TST) or with a Global Positioning System (GPS), depending on the resources available and the accuracy required (TST being the most expensive and the most accurate) (Tassie and Owens 2010, Chaps. 2 and 6). Paradoxically, the speed and accuracy of electronic measurement can lead to a more mechanistic and interpretative way of recording site geometry, such as deciding where the outline of a layer lies and just plotting points along it rather than drawing detailed surface plans with planning frames (of course combinations of methods can be used or supplemented, for example by photography). Location records produce *maps* (showing everything), *plans* (showing individual contexts, features and structures) and *plots* (showing the distribution of objects). Maps, plans and plots may be generated digitally on site using basic computer-graphics programs.

Recording What Is Not Kept

Let us take a flint tool (an *object*) found in a layer (a *context* or stratigraphic unit). The object will be kept (see below), but lies in soil (the context) that will be discarded or sampled, and has a physical, spatial and stratigraphic relationship that can only be recorded on a unique occasion (when it is lifted) in written, drawn and photographic form. Not surprisingly the burden of recording what cannot be kept lies heaviest on the recorder and has generated the most print on how to do it, such as Harris's principles of archaeological stratigraphy (whose application is explained in Roskams 2001, Chaps. 9 and 11–13), how to record individual stratigraphic units (for example in the Museum of London Archaeology Service [MoLAS] 1994 manual and in countless textbooks) or how to capture graphic and photographic data in many ingenious ways (for example *Antiquity*'s online Project Gallery, http://php.york.ac.uk/org/antiquity/projgall.php, has published in 2011–2012 papers on real-time 3D field recording in southern Jordan, or photogrammetry for recording archaeological structures on the Upper Tigris).

The development of the definition of basic stratigraphic units (contexts) has been widespread and parallel; it is attributed, for example, to Britain in the 1970s, Sweden in the 1960s (Ambrosiani in Wolfhechel Jensen 2012, p. 312) or Poland in the 1940s (Urbańczyk, this volume). In excavation, the *context* is the deposit of material that we define as being different from another, in terms of composition, shape and stratigraphic position. A context does not have to be a layer of soil only, it can be the stones making up a wall (its mortar would be another context). Contexts are not givens (*data*), they are entities that we define (*capta* as they have been called), and therefore we can also assign a context number to an *arbitrary layer* (or spit). Since contexts are defined, it follows that a cut into the soil (for a feature like a pit) can also be a context (it differs in shape and stratigraphic position from other contexts). *Single context recording* (see Roskams 2001) focuses exclusively on these entities, omitting features and structures (see below).

As well as its location and shape, a context record includes a description of its material: something that has become standardised in the interests of analytical potential. Lucas (2012, p. 87) gives a typical example: "compact mid greyish brown sandy silt with occasional inclusions of fine charcoal (2%, <5mm) and subangular gravel (1%, <10mm) [etc]" and laments the fact that the interpretation of this piece of soil is a laconic "pit fill". Indeed too much attention appears to be paid to the composition of strata and the geometry of the feature, and too little to the human agency behind it (the 'pitness' of a pit). It also seems that much of this descriptive detail has little analytical purpose, except perhaps analyses of the presence/absence of charcoal or of Munsell soil colours. This is not to say that we should stop recording context composition, but should look for more analytical outcomes, to match the discoveries of microstratigraphy and micromorphology (Carver 2011, Chap. 2; and see Matthews this volume).

The need for higher level interpretations made on site, such as the recognition and study of a pit, a hearth or a wall, has been met by the formal definition of groups of associated contexts, known in Britain and the USA as *features*. The nature of the feature (also confusingly called master context, locus, structure, group, set, complex, *Befundkomplex* or *fait*) is now well established and a helpful definition is given by Py (1997, p. 30): "if the context is the atom, the feature is the molecule." Examples of forms devised to record features are given in Carver (2009) and Pavel (2010), the latter a valuable collection and commentary of 60 different systems (all illustrated) used for recording on excavations in Europe, America and the Near East. By the same token, sets of associated features may merit a site record at an even higher level of interpretation in the form of a *structure*, for example a building formed by a regular pattern of post-holes (Carver 2009, pp. 138–46).

Recording What Is Kept

That artefacts and ecofacts are recorded and kept seems self-evident, but when we consider how small and even 'invisible' these data can be, it becomes apparent that choices are being made and what is recovered is only a sample of the whole. At one extreme, on sites with huge amounts of pottery (e.g. at Lattes in southern France) it may be that we record the presence of body-sherds of dolia with reference to a typological scheme, but do not keep them all. At the other end of the scale, minute fungal spores would only be found if we took samples of soils in which they survived. In general the trend has been to increase the amount that is recorded, because our perceptions of what is important have changed: excavators of the La Tène inhumations at Münsingen-Rain in Switzerland in the early 1900s kept only the skulls. By contrast the advent of routine sieving and flotation in the later twentieth century has vastly increased our knowledge of the environment and economy through the recovery of fish and small mammal bones or insect and vegetable matter. It follows that a consistent sampling strategy with an analytical purpose is needed. Indeed it would be futile and unmanageable to take 10 l bulk samples of every context just in case there was something there. We need to set out the degree of sampling, processing, analysis and storage that is intended: for example what percentage of what type of deposit is dry or wet-sieved, put through flotation or taken for specific purposes. Helpful tables of such purposes can be found in Carver (2009, Chaps. 8 and 9) and in Tassie and Owens (2010, Chap. 4, Tables 4 and 9–14). It goes without saying that consistency is important, as it would be pointless to compare in analysis deposits that were similar (e.g. fills of storage pits) but which were treated differently (e.g. some excavated summarily, others with treated with full recording and comprehensibly sampled). Obvious as this is, this need for consistency has implications for the recovery levels (see below) deployed on excavations.

Monitoring

As important as recording the stuff on site is recording the recording: what was done, not done, decided, discussed and interpreted. In short, monitoring, which also includes the metadata (the documentation generated to keep track of what has been recorded, such as numerous indexes). So, in addition to the proformae used on site, a *site notebook* is an essential tool, to record the day-to-day running of the site, evolving ideas, changes in strategy, in short all the things that are not accommodated in standard forms, but which inform the outcome of the excavation. That outcome is dependent on the decisions taken about how to treat different parts of the site; indeed we dig and record at different levels of intensity, for example removing the topsoil by machine, shovelling rubble or carefully excavating a skeleton. Most recording proformae have boxes to record the levels at which individual contexts and features have been excavated and recorded, but this can be done more efficiently by referring to a structured scheme, such *Recovery Levels* (p. 48). There are obvious advantages to adopting a Recovery Level structure – it formalises procedure and promotes consistency, but also allows flexibility. However, that very flexibility has its dangers: having a Recovery Levels scheme should not give licence to implement arbitrary "gear changes" (e.g. "we decided to treat this deposit at level B rather than level D because we were pushed for time"). It is therefore important to stick to the recovery levels, once a project design has been agreed, so that like can be compared with like in analysis.

The records generated inform analysis and publication but they also exist for future generations to interrogate. Therefore they need to be deposited in permanent archives and made easy to consult. Archives typically contain not only the 'raw' data and the metadata in physical and electronic form, but also the documentation pertaining to the conduct of the project and its analysis up to publication. How this is achieved will vary from country to country, as will the form of storage, whether as a physical archive or electronically; examples of pioneering digital systems can be found for Lattes in France (Py 1997) and in Britain an early example of an integrated archive was presented by Powlesland in 1998 (articles in *Internet Archaeology* 5). Good advice on archives in general, derived from the British experience, will be found in Brown (2007).

Prospect

To sum up, archaeological recorders are objective, subjective, consistent, selective, accountable and creative all at once. There is no universal prescription, but there is a consensus that location, stratigraphy, composition, monitoring and archiving underpin recording systems. Whether devised or adopted ready-made (you can for example download the MoLAS manual, or the recording forms from a CD in Tassie and Owens 2010), this is only the beginning: systems should not be set in stone, they can be adapted to suit new analytical purposes. In this way the sophisticated investigations of the future will be integrated with the basics recorded now. Stratigraphic units will become more exciting: the tedious and analytically under-exploited "loosely compacted 7.5YR 6/4 silty sand with occasional subangular gravel" will become the container of much more information: perhaps about tethered cattle which stood there chewing the cud (from chemical residues in a context stratigraphically later than another, which was a secondary deposit derived from a midden containing protein residues from fish processing). To contribute to documenting a (purely hypothetical) change from hunter-fisher-gatherers to an economy based on domesticates is not a bad aim for the hard-pressed recorder struggling in the wind and rain.

Chapter 9
Spatial Analysis

Bisserka Gaydarska

Spatial analysis deals with the use of space in the past. Such analyses are performed at two main scales: (a) *intra-site level* (some archaeologists argue for further differentiation within a site, defining micro and semimicro levels) and (b) *inter-site* or landscape level. Both analyses are concerned with finding patterns of distribution, whether of finds and features (usually at site level) or of sites and monuments. Spatial analysis at both site and inter-site level may also contribute to the elucidation of *sequence*. While the employment of some methods at both levels is broadly similar – e.g., *GIS*-based mapping or various statistical analyses, others are unique for each level. For example, GPR is more suitable for the establishment of intra-site patterns, while digital terrain modeling is more cost-effective on a landscape level. The number of methods and techniques used in spatial analyses is ever-growing and diversifying.

On Site (Intra-site)

On site, the plotting of artifacts and features allow the identification of certain activity areas (marked by objects), sleeping areas (blank spaces in a building), community areas (open spaces in a settlement), and so on. The mapping of finds may also indicate intrusions that are natural (the course of a stream) or anthropogenic (the line of a ditch) that are otherwise hard to see. Most often the analyses are performed after excavation and fieldwork is finished, which is why proper recording of locations during the investigations is crucial (see Recording Fieldwork, this volume). Analysis of the context records and an understanding of taphonomy and deposition (Formation processes, this volume) is key for the correct understanding of, e.g., whether matching fragments of artifacts found in different contexts alludes to

B. Gaydarska (✉)
Department of Archaeology, Durham University, Durham, UK
e-mail: bisserka.gaydarska@durham.ac.uk

M. Carver et al. (eds.), *Field Archaeology from Around the World*,
SpringerBriefs in Archaeology, DOI 10.1007/978-3-319-09819-7_9

contemporaneity of the features (Kobyliński and Moszczyński 1992) or to the social practice of curation (Garrow et al. 2005). The relative size and disposition of structures and the routes between them are used to infer the relative importance (hierarchy) of buildings and the social routines practiced within a settlement.

At a smaller scale, *access analysis* explores the use of space by mapping the relative ease with which rooms may be approached within a house, allowing archaeologists to propose the location of high-ranking or special users. An eloquent example of access analysis was used to study social inequality on Bulgarian tells (Chapman 1990). Four more or less fully excavated tells (Ovcharovo, Targovishte, Radingrad, Poljanica) served as the basis for an analysis of the development of social space throughout their use (Fig. 9.1). The settlement maps showed the houses, the number of rooms within them, and access to each room from the main entrance. At Targovishte and Radingrad (Fig. 9.1a), one or two rooms were accessible from the entrance and two or three further rooms reached in succession with minimal choice. By contrast at Ovcharovo and Poljanica (Fig. 9.1b), houses eventually contained up to 11 rooms with multiple choice of access, a pattern that was held to reveal to the successful reproduction of social inequality. The simpler access pattern at Targovishte and Radingrad was interpreted as being owed to a relatively unstratified community, and it was suggested that failure to find an adequate material way to contain social rivalry led to the relatively short lifetime of these two tells.

In the Landscape (Inter-site)

In one of the most commonly practiced types of landscape investigation, the documentation of surface finds can provide information about the intensity of discard and, thereby, infer occupation (see Chap. 4, "*Surface Survey: Method and Strategies*", this volume). The mapping of features registered by noninvasive techniques (such as Chap. 3, "*Aerial Archaeology*" and *subsurface investigations*, this volume), supplemented by detailed archival research (including historical records), is also used to create a narrative picture of landscape habitation. In most modern studies, a combination of survey methods is applied. The spatial particularities of the mapped distribution of features and artifacts in a landscape usually provide the basis for studies of settlement patterns; subsistence strategies; political, military, and ideological utilization; and reorganization of the landscape. The recognition of time depth is important in a landscape, as it is in an excavated site. The idea of a *palimpsest* (Aston and Rowley 1974) acknowledges that landscapes are "layered" as century follows century, giving so-called diachronic patterns. Thus, the establishment of changes over time by interrogating the evidence for erased episodes of human occupation, or identification of multiple phases of occupation, is a major task assisted by spatial analysis.

Early examples of spatial analysis at the landscape level generated maps with dots, representing sites and/or finds to which various analyses would be applied to improve the pattern using statistical packages such as *cluster analysis*. Such analyses set out to define not only the location of sites, but their relative importance

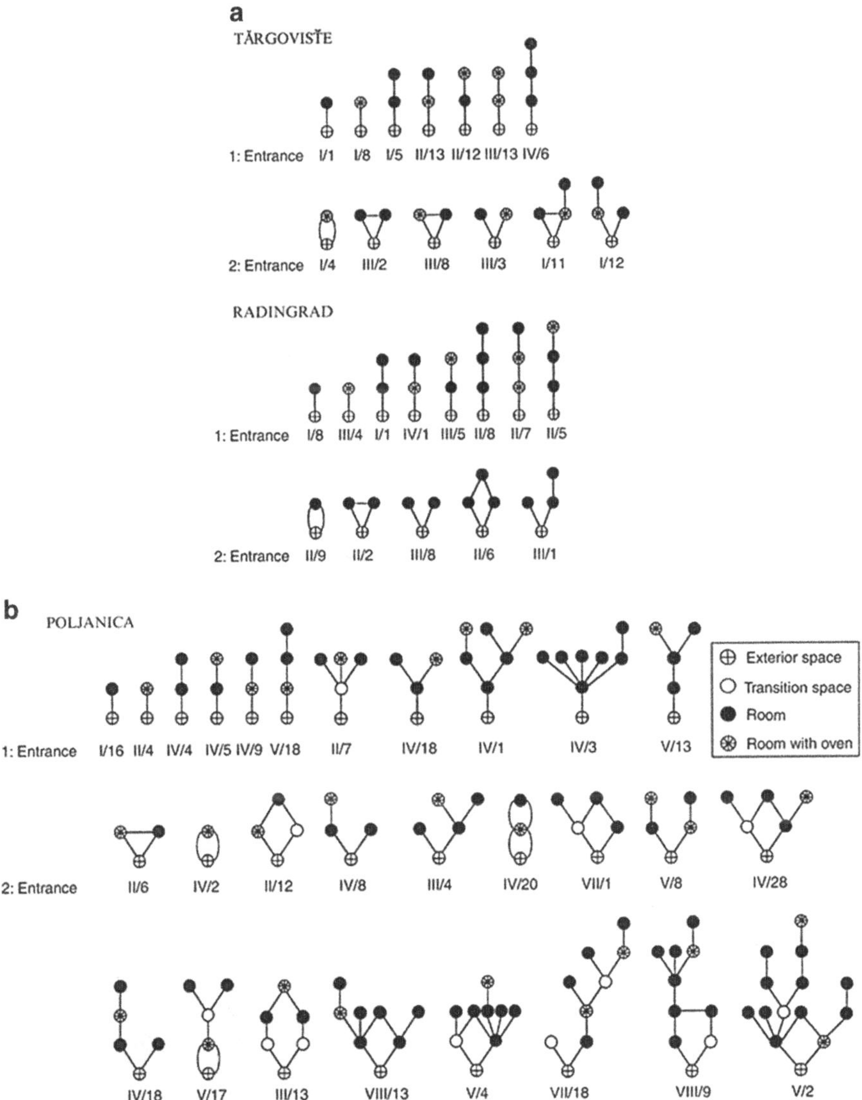

Fig. 9.1 Access levels of Bulgarian tells showing number of rooms and complexity of house organization (**a**) Targovishte and Radingrad; (**b**) Poljanitsa

(from their size or the quality of finds). The sites discovered are most often seen as settlements, but the same principles have been applied to cemeteries, burial mounds, and hill forts. *Central place theory* uses the size of settlements to construct dependent territories around them. The land was also routinely modeled by surveying the surface in three-dimensions and representing it in the form of *contours* or *hachures*.

More recent landscape studies have added to the power of spatial analysis by collecting different variables (for example, placenames, surface finds, settlement locations) and entering their coordinates into a computerized data base to make a series of digital maps. The stack of digital maps forms a *geographic information system* (GIS), which can be interrogated in a large number of ways in order to bring out spatial relationships between variables that are often unsuspected. The surface of the landscape itself can also be digitized using *LiDAR* imaging. The data collected from the air is used to generate a three-dimensional surface on the computer – a *digital terrain model* (DTM). Using graphics programs, the DTM can be viewed from different angles to offer a realistic vision of the landscape from different locations, in different periods (*hillshade models*). The same database can be used to generate models showing which parts of the land could be seen at other parts (*viewshed*). These new tools enable the ancient landscape, its settlement patterns, and the routes through it to be envisioned in considerable detail.

A recent project in the area of Homs in Northern Syria examining the distribution of settlement types was able to group them in revealing new combinations (Philip et al. 2011). Traditionally, the area of southwest Asia is perceived as a tell-dominated landscape and the southern marl-based part of the study area confirmed this observation. The northern study area, however, with its basalt environment seemed to have facilitated a different type of occupation. Single and clustered irregular and rectilinear units of different sizes, a stone enclosure, and many cairns mostly on slopes and ridges were mapped, revealing settlement clusters (Fig. 9.2).

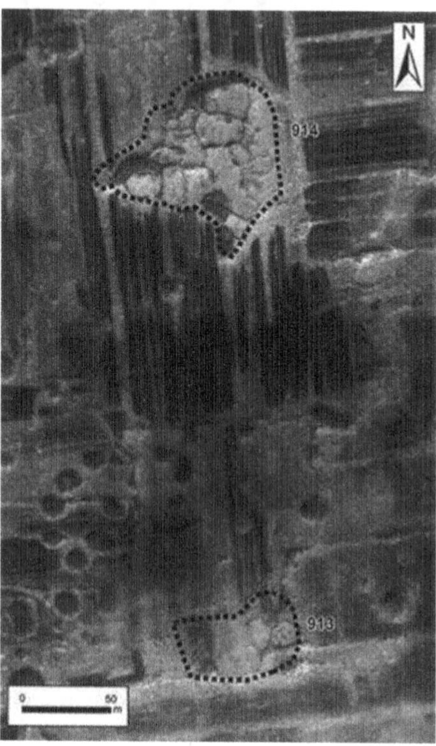

Fig. 9.2 Structures in the North basalt study area of Homs, Syria, showing settlement clusters (After Philip et al. 2011)

Functional and chronological differentiation was established between the grouped irregular and the grouped rectilinear structures, thus suggesting changing strategies of engagement with the landscape. Several "waves" of occupation/settling have been proposed, starting with the well-documented settlement expansion in southern Syria during the Chalcolithic/Early Bronze Age and reoccurring in Roman and Byzantine periods, mostly associated with field systems – a pattern of land use that remained in place till modern times. The presence and mapping of thousands of hitherto overlooked cairns poses questions about the long-term landscape management of a stony environment that is intimately related to perpetuated social practices. The main result of this project is the demonstration of the diversification of the settlement patterns in Northern Syria in both space and time.

See also the entries in EGA for Landscape Archaeology; Floors and Occupation Surface Analysis in Archaeology.

Chapter 10
Sequence and Date

Martin Carver

Introduction

For the field researcher, a primary task is assigning a date and a sequence (order of occurrence) to the features and structures they record. Occasionally an archaeological site has already been recorded in history, for example, the celebrated urban excavation at Five Points (Chap. 31), New York City, exposed a plan of buildings and streets that had appeared on a map in 1855. Even sites mentioned in documentary references seldom offer a date as precise as this, and dated events which might *seem* to refer to an excavated site have to be used with great caution.

In general, very few objects, activities, or structures discovered by fieldwork can be given a precise calendar date, and archaeologists are obliged to build a *chronological model*, which balances all the available information (Fig. 10.1).

Dating Objects

As applied to objects, the methods at our disposal are *typology*, which offers a *relative dating* for artifacts (e.g., pottery) and structures (e.g., architecture). Typology uses the likely order of manufacture, based on form and style, combined with the dates given elsewhere. For example, pottery, one of the most useful of artifacts since it occurs widely and endures well in the ground, has an enormous range of types. Some periods of manufacture are known from kiln sites, but most are deduced from which types occur together; in this way archaeologists have built up extensive typologies that help to date every kind of site built by pottery users.

M. Carver (✉)
Department of Archaeology, University of York, York, UK
e-mail: martin.carver@york.ac.uk

M. Carver et al. (eds.), *Field Archaeology from Around the World*,
SpringerBriefs in Archaeology, DOI 10.1007/978-3-319-09819-7_10

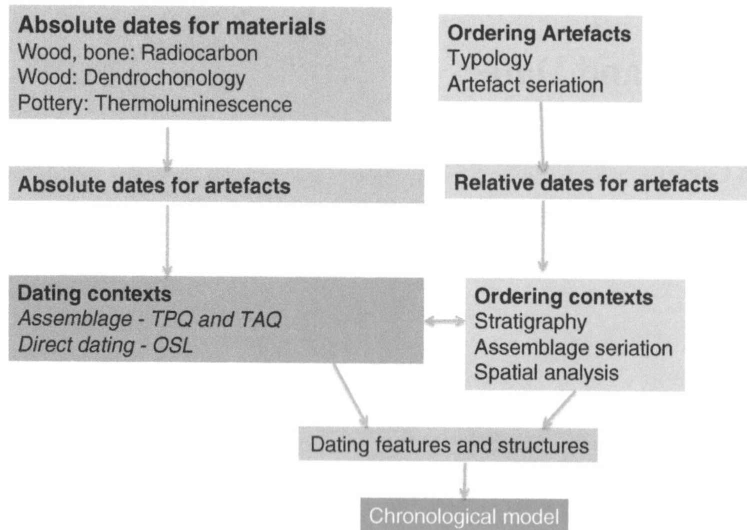

Fig. 10.1 Chronology in field work (Carver 2009, p. 267)

Artifacts may also be given an *absolute dating*, by scientifically measuring the *age of materials* they are made from. Well-known examples here include *radiocarbon dating*, which measures the age since the death of a living plant (i.e., wood) or creature (e.g., bone); *dendrochronology*, which measure the age of timber since it was felled, from the numbers and spacing of annual growth rings; *archaeomagnetism*, which measures the age of a hearth since it was heated; and *optically stimulated luminescence* (OSL) which measures the time that has elapsed since a layer of sand was last exposed to sunlight (Hedges 2001). These dates, which have an error range from 1 year (dendro) to 25 % or more, indicate when an organism died or a mineral was buried.

Dating Contexts

Absolute and relative dates for artifacts, or groups of artifacts, can be used to date the archaeological layers they are found in – but the relationship is not a simple one. A layer is always deposited later than the latest object found in it, for example, a floor with a coin of 400 CE beneath it must have been laid in 400 CE or later (since the coin must have existed before the floor was laid). This relationship is called a terminus post quem (TPQ). A wall which has a date written on it (say 1929) must have been constructed before 1929. This relationship is called a terminus ante quem (TAQ). However, these equations are by no means always valid or helpful. A coin may be not just earlier, but centuries earlier, than the floor that covers it. A coin within a floor may be *intrusive* and so later than the floor. A coin found on top of a floor may be later than the floor, if dropped on it soon after manufacture and never moved, or much earlier than the floor if carried around for decades in someone's pocket. Similarly a coin or a potsherd found in a foundation trench is usually earlier than the wall in the same trench, but it may also be much earlier since it has been displaced – is residual – from an earlier phase or site. Since we rarely know the circumstances in which a coin was discarded, it is risky to use coins to date structures. They are at least very rarely contemporary. In spite of this, equating the date of a building with the date of the coins found in it remains a widespread practice.

Structures, features, and contexts may also be dated directly – by typology and by scientific dating. Typology may be applied to the shape of hearths or kilns, or the ground plans of houses, comparing them to others found elsewhere and so presuming that they can be assigned to the same culture and date. Absolute dating can sometimes be applied, for example, *dendrochronology* will date the timbers of a timber-framed house (Kuniholm 2001). However, it is frequently found that such a house, in the form it survives, is composed of structural timbers of different dates. Even the earliest of these may have been recycled from another usage – for example, in a ship. *Radiocarbon* dating is applied to carboniferous materials, such as charcoal or bone, but here the association with the deposit is of crucial importance (Taylor 2001). The charcoal in a hearth may represent the date of last burning but only if it derives from twigs or animals. Otherwise the wood may have already have been cut down long before it was burnt (the 'old wood' effect). Similarly the bones in a grave should date the digging of the grave very well, but animal bone may have been disturbed and redeposited and so give a date before, perhaps long before the deposition of the layer in which it was found.

An important method applied by excavators to contexts, features, and structures is stratigraphic ordering. This does not date them but provides a *relative order* for each deposit in the overall sequence. The traditional method of presenting the order of occurrence is the section, which shows the deposition of layers from the side, and is recorded by drawing (Fig. 10.2), and these may still be valuable even if they only

Fig. 10.2 A vertical section through consecutive layers at the early monastic site at Portmahomack, Scotland (M. Carver)

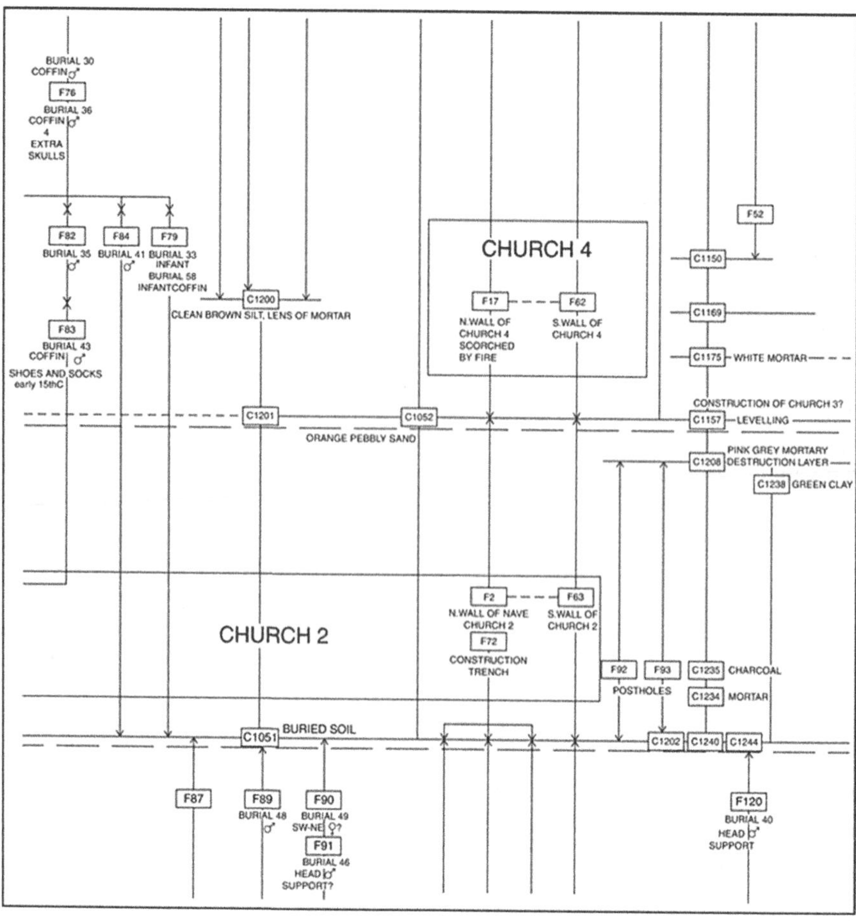

Fig. 10.3 Extract from a stratification diagram, showing part of the sequence encountered in the excavation of a church at Portmahomack, Scotland. Contexts are designated with the prefix ‘C’. Contexts belonging to features are contained within the feature box (prefix ‘F’). Some features are grouped with the structures they have been assigned to (‘Church 2’, ‘Church 4’). The features are shown as *vertical arrows*, locating their limits in time. The stratigraphy is modelled to show where chronological (vertical) variation is possible (Courtesy of FAS-Heritage Ltd)

report the sequence in a specific slice through the strata. A more comprehensive method of stratigraphic ordering that applies to the whole site is the stratification diagram – which models the sequence in two dimensions, the earliest contexts at the bottom and the latest at the top (Fig. 10.3). These have developed from pioneer examples in the 1970s (e.g., Harris 1989) to more comprehensive models which include features and structures and represent uncertainties in the sequence (Carver 2009, p. 296). These uncertainties form an important aspect of the modelling process and show where other interpretations are possible.

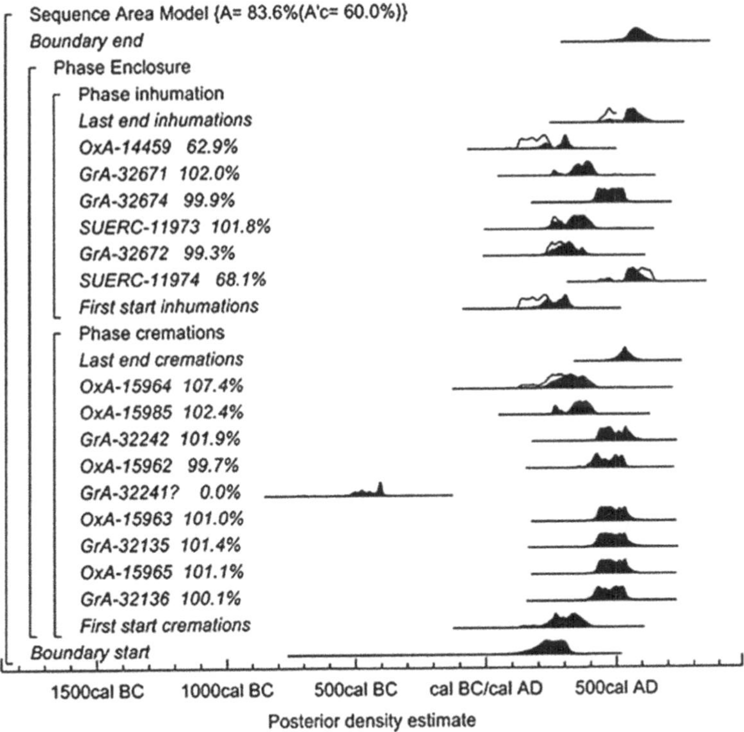

Fig. 10.4 A sequence of graves from the Anglo-Saxon cemetery at Wasperton, England, placed in their best order by Bayesian analysis. The outline shows the error range of the calibrated date; the solid black profile is the more precise "posterior density estimates" derived from Bayesian modelling (Carver et al. 2009: Fig. 4.1)

The stratigraphic ordering of graves containing bone or hearths containing charcoal can be dated with much greater precision by using radiocarbon dating combined with *Bayesian analysis*. The radiocarbon dates give a range of error, but this range is reduced by knowing the order in which deposition occurred. The Bayesian analysis produces shorter ranges of probability for each date (posterior density estimates, Fig. 10.4). This is giving archaeological sequences of high precision dating back to 20,000 years ago (Buck 2001).

Relative Ordering by Space

The business of establishing a sequence makes also use of *spatial analyses*. For example, a settlement that is spatially coherent (like the grid of a *planned* town) suggests that all the streets and houses were laid out at the same time. Features that are *aligned* are also thought to reflect contemporary use. For example, inhumation graves in a cemetery may have different orientations, but those that are most closely aligned are said to be close to each other in date. Similarly, graves that mimic the orientation of a building are later in date than the building. On the scale of a landscape, alignments are important indicators of sequence. Roads and field boundaries seen from above may indicate a sequence where they "respect" one other. For example, the field boundaries may join up to a preexisting road, or the road may cut straight across the line of the fields, showing it was imposed on a preexisting agricultural landscape.

Modelling

At the scale of a landscape, archaeologists use such spatial mapping as an indication of sequence. It is often possible to apply typology, for example, to infer the likely culture and date of cropmark forms encountered in *aerial investigation*. Similarly, forms recorded in *subsurface survey* are sometimes recognized by virtue of their shape alone: a straight road or a circular ditch or a settlement grid. When using *surface survey* to find sites, archaeologists rely on typologies to provide a broad date for the pottery or stone implements or metal artifacts they are mapping. The distribution of this material provides the location of sites belonging to a particular culture and period.

On excavated sites, stratigraphic ordering provides the surest indication of relative sequence. The alignment of features and structures often give an inference of where these might be contemporary. The broad dates of objects and structures (and the very occasional documentary reference) allow a sequence to be anchored more closely in time. In well-stratified sites, such as towns, the stratigraphic sequence is treated as primary. Poorly stratified sites (the majority) rely more on relative and scientific dating of objects and samples. The method is to examine and record the detailed possible relationships of objects and strata in every case and then to use typology, stratification, spatial analysis, and absolute dating to build up a robust chronological model.

Entries in EGA relevant to this section include Dating Techniques in Archaeological Science; Dating Methods in Historical Archaeology; Radiocarbon Dating in Archaeology Stratigraphy in Archaeology: A Brief History.

Chapter 11
Ethnoarchaeology: Approaches to Fieldwork

Gustavo G. Politis

Introduction

Field methods of ethnoarchaeology are based on those of ethnography, but because of the type of information that is sought, there are some record types that are more specific to archaeology. In other words, fieldwork in ethnoarchaeology is also based on participant observation in living societies, with an attitude of minimal interference in the community under study and a clear research design. However, little has been written and reflected on ethnoarchaeological fieldwork (for exceptions see David and Kramer 2001, pp. 63–90), and in general it is not clearly specified in the reports. There are three defining elements of ethnoarchaeology that have implications in their field methods: *the study of a living culture*, with reference to the *material derivatives of human behavior*, and (when it is in traditional society) the *postcolonial context.*

Approaches

Ethnoarchaeological fieldwork has some peculiarities. First, the overall goals are more limited than those of classical ethnography, since they are usually related to material culture, with the settlement and with the exploitation of the environment and landscape changes. This makes ethnoarchaeological work generally more specific and shorter than those of classical ethnography (although there are exceptions like the works of John Yellen (1977) among the Kung or those of Russell Greaves (2006) among the Pumé). Although post-processual ethnoarchaeology – more

G.G. Politis (✉)
Facultad de Ciencias Sociales, CONICET-INCUAPA UNICEN, Buenos Aires, Argentina
e-mail: gpolitis@fcnym.unlp.edu.ar

M. Carver et al. (eds.), *Field Archaeology from Around the World*,
SpringerBriefs in Archaeology, DOI 10.1007/978-3-319-09819-7_11

Fig. 11.1 J. Peter White at the Legaiyu village, Asaro Valley Eastern Highlands, New Guinea, in 1964, among an ethnic people identified as Gahuku-Gama. White had asked the indigenous people to flake stone cores (Photo courtesy of J. Peter White)

hermeneutic – has looked for understanding the cultural context of production of material culture and has paid more attention to emic category, this has not resulted in a substantial increase in the duration of fieldwork campaigns.

Since ethnoarchaeologists study living cultures with archaeological eyes, they record data such as places for garbage disposal, marks and breaks on a bone and its dispersion in domestic spaces and in the landscape, operational chains and sequence of artifact production, plant, and location of households and villages (Fig. 11.1). Thus, ethnoarchaeologists draw plans, analyze bones, record artifacts, and make maps with the skills that are specific to archaeology. Ethnoarchaeological work often includes the collection of objects and debris, such as faunal remains, the debris of a sequence of stone flaking, or broken pottery sherds, for further study in the laboratory, following analytical techniques from archaeology or taphonomy (see, e.g., O'Connell 1987; Lupo and O'Connell 2002). Likewise, information is often quantified, especially in terms of size, distance, weight, and time (see, e.g., the study of Bird et al. 2009, on daily foraging trips and hunting strategies of the Martu). With the advent of post-processual ethnoarchaeology, there has been a greater emphasis on understanding the context of material cultural. The article on pottery decoration by David et al. (1988) is a good example of this trend. Moreover, from post-processualism onwards, a more emic perspective has been developed, and efforts have been put into trying to understand how the same people conceptualized and thought about their objects and their behavior and to understand its causes and motivations.

To simplify something much more complex, it is important to differentiate ethnoarchaeological observations from ethnoarchaeological projects. The former generally occur during a campaign of archaeological fieldwork. Observations made on these occasions are very useful in interpreting a specific context, but cannot always elucidate more complex systems or generate more general models. These observations are also frequent producers of "cautionary tales," which help mitigate the ethnocentrism of archaeologists and overthrow assumptions based solely on common sense. Furthermore, ethnoarchaeological projects have an agenda and specific designs and seek to transcend the regional application; generally they seek to create general models which allow for the connection between human behavior and material culture (the classic studies of Binford 1978, on Nunamiut are a good example of this; see also discussion in Roux 2007) or for understanding the meaning of material production within its social and cultural context (see, e.g., Gosselain 2000).

There are two main types of ethnoarchaeological projects. Those incorporated within archaeological projects, and those undertaken on their own account, without direct links to local archaeological research (although these may have originally served as inspiration). Carol Kramer's study (1982) on a vernacular architecture of Iran and Warren DeBoer work (1974) on the pottery from Peru Conibo are classic examples of the former. Ethnoarchaeological studies on Pumé conducted by Greaves (2006) or Kelly et al. (2006) and collaborators of Mikea of Madagascar exemplify the second type. Although less frequent, ethnoarchaeological research can also be conducted within the framework of ethnographic/social anthropology projects. The famous work of John Yellen among the Kung is one of the exceptions, as it was done as part of the Harvard University Bushman Studies project, led by Richard Lee and Irven DeVore.

Methods

In general the methods and techniques of data record in ethnoarchaeology have three variants. The first is the record of the activities as they happen, with special attention to the materials derived from them and the social and ideational framework within which they occur (see, e.g., Politis 2007). This is the ideal case and should be the most successful for generating analog models. The second variant is when the ethnoarchaeologist requests the execution of specific activities in order to obtain certain types of information. This variant may allow for a better control of observation, as in experimental archaeology, with the difference that the one holding the experiment is the cultural "other." This situation is common, for example, when the researcher wants to record the making of some artifacts that are no longer made or that were not made during the period of fieldwork. The weakness of this second strategy is that it is more difficult to frame the phenomenon in its original cultural context (and so understand its causes and motivations), since induction is applied by the researcher. In both variants, ethnoarchaeologists are making

Fig. 11.2 J. Peter White in 1973 in Horaile parish, near Lake Kopiago, where the local people are Duna speakers. Picture taken while they were making the film (Photo courtesy of J. Peter White)

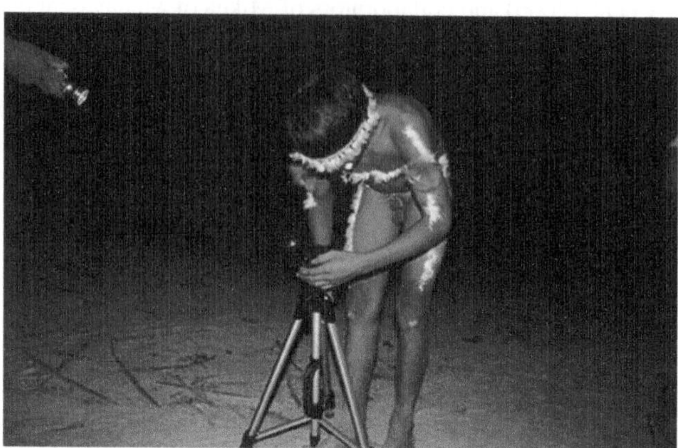

Fig. 11.3 A young Awa inspecting the digital camera during night filming of in a Juriti village ritual (Brazil), 2008 (Photo courtesy of Almudena Hernando and Alfredo Gonzalez Ruibal)

increasingly frequent use of film in addition to graphic and sound recording (Fig. 11.2), especially taking advantage of digital cameras (Fig. 11.3).

The third variant uses previous knowledge about the societies to make broader ethnoarchaeological models, spatially and temporally. In this case the ethnoarchaeologist does not "observe" anything but receives oral information about some aspects of the behavior of people in the past and their material implications. Models of residential mobility among Nunamiut made by Binford (1978) are good examples of this third strategy as it incorporates the memory of traditional territories of

Fig. 11.4 Lewis Binford visiting Anaktuvuk Pass in 1999. He is talking to Johnny Rulland who was his "brother" and one of his primary informants (Photo taken by Grant Spearman. Courtesy of Amber Johnson)

this people. In practice, two or three of these variants are combined in the field. In all three variants, key informants are also used (Fig. 11.4).

Despite the relatively widespread belief that ethnoarchaeologists also dig sites, this happens rarely now. In general, ethnoarchaeologists generate the models that serve as analogies for human behavior, but are not primarily interested in recovering what is left after a place was abandoned. The generation of "archaeological record" is usually observed in real time during the fieldwork and is the interface between the living culture dynamic and static registration, which focuses the ethnoarchaeologists. Thus, the excavation of a site where observations of the living culture have been made does not have much relevance for ethnoarchaeology; the study of differential preservation of the remains belongs to the field of taphonomy and the study of the natural processes of site formation.

Ethics

The ethical aspect of fieldwork is crucial (Hodder 1982, p. 39; Fewster 2001; David and Kramer 2001, pp. 84–90). The governing ethical standards and good practice applied to general anthropological research have first priority: this includes full respect for the community and its customs, minimal interference, and informed consent. This last is sometimes difficult to obtain in its entirety, due to both linguistic and cultural differences. It is often difficult to explain the ethnoarchaeologists' passion for systematically recording (sometimes obsessively) everyday behaviors and conserving what the people studied consider junk. This is of course related to the degree of

"Westernization" of the ethnic group in question, but for many traditional societies, the activities carried out by ethnoarchaeologists remain incomprehensible: why pick up and put in bags a lot of dirty bones which do not have any meat? Why draw and map the sherds of broken pottery? Full and real informed consent can be obtained quite easily in some cases, but it is unrealistic, for example, in the case of more recently contacted communities such as the Colombian Amazon Nukak or the Upper Orinoco Hotï. What it is obtained is the agreement for the ethnoarchaeologist to accompany, join, and "observe" in a particular way some people in their everyday activities, but this by no means implies that the observed are fully aware of what the ethnoarchaeological research in question means. This is an ethical dilemma that is hard to solve.

Finally, the continual disruption of traditional or preindustrial lifestyles, the growing processes of ethnogenesis, and the steady advance of globalization are leading to the demise of practices which help observers interpret the past. Within this orbit, ethnoarchaeology is reorienting its strategies and objects of study, and some variants of this new trend are turning to what has been called the archaeology of the present (Gonzalez Ruibal 2009). This has led to a redesign of the field methods that are closer to those of ethnography, sociology, or what is known as studies of material culture.

Entries relevant to this section in EGA include Binford, Lewis R. (Theory); Ethnoarchaeology; Ethnoarchaeology: Building Frameworks for Research.

Chapter 12
Publication in Field Archaeology

Martin Carver

Every publication in any field is designed for the people who are intended to read it. Archaeological fieldwork is carried out for different sectors and sponsors and it therefore generates a variety of output. A recent overview proposed eight different modes of publication designed to serve eight different types of "consumer" (Fig. 12.1).

The preparation of a *field record* (no. 1) is a primary duty of the fieldworker, whether engaged in CRM or research. These records are generally stored in an archive within the museum that retains the assemblages of artifacts and biota. In principle, records and assemblages are public property and remain accessible in perpetuity. In practice museums often find this difficult to achieve but hope to make the material available to researchers and special interest groups. The increasing range of records and material retained by excavators combined with the enormous quantity of material generated by CRM is creating a major problem of long-term storage for industrialized countries. This is one reason for the development of the online *lab report* (or Field Report) (no. 2), which sets out to present a complete account of the main discoveries from fieldwork in a digital form. This will include summaries of the primary records, an album of selected photographs, an atlas of the main spatial form and relationships, site journals and interpretations made on site, and analyses made in the laboratory after fieldwork was completed. These analyses may include studies of stratigraphy, artifacts, animal bones, plant remains, and scientific dating. In many cases the specialist reports in their original form may appear only in this medium, their essence being summarized for printed forms. The *Archaeological Data Service* (http://ads.ahds.ac.uk) is a major service provider in this field, hosting online archives for research projects as well as many thousands of client reports from CRM operations which are otherwise inaccessible.

M. Carver (✉)
Department of Archaeology, University of York, York, UK
e-mail: martin.carver@york.ac.uk

M. Carver et al. (eds.), *Field Archaeology from Around the World*,
SpringerBriefs in Archaeology, DOI 10.1007/978-3-319-09819-7_12

MODE	CONTENTS	MEDIUM	CLIENTS
1. Field Records	Site records, primary data	Hard copies	Sponsor, Other researchers
2. Lab Report	Commissioned studies and analyses	e-repository	Sponsor, other researchers
3. Client Report	Description of the investigation and results	Hard copy with limited distribution ["grey literature"]	Sponsors
4. Research Report	Description of the investigation, findings, their interpretation and context	Article (hard copy or on-line), monograph with multiple distribution	Researchers
5. Popular book	Abbreviated research report	book	The public
6. Popular output	Selected significant aspects	Magazine articles, site guide, TV programmes	The public
7. Display	Selected significant aspects	Exhibitions in museums,	The public
8. Presentation/ Interpretation	The site and its surviving parts; local trails	Conserved monuments; display panels;AV	The public

Fig. 12.1 Modes of publication (After Carver 2009, p. 316)

The production of a *Client Report* (no. 3) is normally a condition of contract for the CRM firm that undertakes fieldwork in advance of development. The "client" is the organization that paid for the archaeological work. In regulated countries this is often local or national government. In deregulated countries it is more usually the organization that is undertaking the development; archaeology is included in its costs. In both cases, the clients or their consultants provide strict instructions about the content of the report and the timetable for its delivery. These contents include details of the location, the work done there, the methods used, and the discoveries made. In the current profession, many of the methods are standardized and repeated in successive client reports. The value of the archaeological discoveries themselves is expressed in terms of their *significance*, a measure of how far they have added to knowledge. However, CRM projects rarely include research time, and so client reports can rarely expect to explore this significance in the wider context of modern research. For this reason, the majority of client reports remain as "grey literature" delivered to the client or at best placed in an online archive where it is generally accessible (see above).

Research Reports (no. 4) are intended to report the most significant new discoveries of the day. They are, accordingly, selective in two senses: first, only fieldwork productive of important research is eligible for consideration, and of that, only carefully selected data and succinct argument are appropriate for publication. Research publication is subject to peer review, undertaken on behalf of publishers to ensure the highest standards of integrity and reasoning. The criteria for acceptance usually run along the lines: "Was there a research question?" "Did it need to be addressed?" "Are the results clearly presented, validated, and discussed?" and "Is the conclusion credible?" There have always been numerous other forms of open-ended, unspecific, imaginative, and non-scientific writing about the past, but few have been successfully applied to the publication of results of fieldwork.

The current research community in archaeology overwhelmingly prefers paper-copy publication in journals or monographs over data-rich digital repositories. Research publication is therefore expensive, another reason that it remains competitive and selective. It should also be noted that the main beneficiary of such selectivity is the reader. By filtering the mass of information and opinion that is generated by the archaeological community, the publishing industry hopes to select the fieldwork of most significance and most lasting value at the least cost to researchers and other readers.

The content of a research report will include the basic information about the purpose of the project, the research questions that were addressed, where it took place, the theoretical basis for the design, the methods used, and the results obtained. A site model is argued on the basis of selected analyses of assemblage, space and sequence, and a free-ranging account of its context and wider significance presented in a discussion section. The conclusion assesses the success in answering the questions expressed in the original Project Design, presents new ones, places the fieldwork results in history or prehistory, and announces the planned future of the archive, the site, and its environs.

Members of the public, and indeed students when they are starting out, may not have the background to appreciate or assess research reports. If a field project has become well known, it may become the subject of a range of more general outputs. "Popular" books (no. 5) attempt to place the archaeological discoveries in the mainstream. Commercial publishers do a wonderful job here, usually ensuring good quality and taking the financial risk on themselves. Mainstream publishers may produce a range of summaries and pictures in magazines, newspapers, and on TV (no. 6) over which the field archaeologist generally has less control but may still welcome them on the basis that "there is no such thing as bad publicity."

Direct communication with the public is available in two other media. In exhibitions (no. 7), the findings of fieldwork may find vivid expression in a museum, where artifacts and structures and their sequence are brought together. Some sites, particularly those which have been the subject of research projects (less so those excavated in advance of development), are still conserved and may be visited by members of the public. The art of presenting sites (sometimes known as "interpretation") is to explain to visitors what they can still see and relate what was found and what it might mean (no. 8). This is undoubtedly a form of publication and a special one since it takes place in the landscape, that historic environment which field method sets out to enhance.

Part II
Exemplary Projects

Chapter 13
Landscape Mapping at West Heslerton

Dominic Powlesland

Archaeological research at West Heslerton, Yorkshire, England, began in 1978, following the chance discovery of Early Anglo-Saxon burials during sand quarrying (Powlesland et al. 1986). Subsequent excavations in advance of quarrying and plowing covered some 35 ha of the Vale of Pickering, exposing prehistoric, Roman and Anglo-Saxon settlements and cemeteries (Figs. 13.1 and 13.2). Revealing a portion of ancient landscape at such a large scale emphasized that the narrative of human occupation was expressed by a continuum of activity rather than by a number of dispersed sites of different ages. It also raised the question of the wider context of the excavated area and the nature of the landscape of which it formed a part. The Landscape Research Centre (LRC) was created to map the total archaeology of the Vale of Pickering, testing and developing methods of remote mapping and analysis. Now in action for more than the 30 years, the LRC has recorded over 1,000 ha of contiguous settlement in unprecedented detail.

The 1980 research design argued that a proactive campaign of archaeological survey was necessary both to provide a context for the excavations and to identify the scale, complexity, variability, and levels of preservation of the archaeological resource. The preliminary area to be examined was a transect 1-km wide and 10-km long laid at right angles across the varied terrain of the valley. Two packages of remote mapping methods were applied, the first from the air, the second on the ground.

Crop-marks are sensitive to conditions that vary with the seasons and from year to year, so that most discoveries in England are made by chance. To improve the viability of total coverage, LRC initiated a program of intensive and repeated aerial survey flying over the same fields again and again, and documenting crop-marks that were only visible from the air for a few days at a time. New technology in the form of airborne multispectral imaging offered the potential to record crop-marks in

D. Powlesland (✉)
The Landscape Research Centre & The McDonald Institute, University of Cambridge, Cambridge, UK
e-mail: d.powlesland@btinternet.com

M. Carver et al. (eds.), *Field Archaeology from Around the World*, SpringerBriefs in Archaeology, DOI 10.1007/978-3-319-09819-7_13

Fig. 13.1 The Vale of Pickering viewed in Google Earth with overlays showing the distribution of sands and gravels in *orange*, areas with crop-marks in *yellow* and areas covered by geophysical survey in *red*

wavelengths beyond the visible parts of spectrum, particularly from infrared and thermal wavelengths. A research experiment funded by the Natural Environment Research Council (NERC) in 1994 provided an opportunity to test the viability of multispectral imaging for landscape scale crop-mark mapping, to test the potential for identifying crop-marks in nonvisible wavelengths in fields under permanent pasture and in fields that had no prior crop-mark record. The 1994 NERC flight combined conventional large format vertical color photography with digital imaging using the Deadelus 12 band multispectral scanner; by chance, the flight was undertaken at a perfect time when a very large number of crop-marks were visible (Fig. 13.3). The vertical photographs from this single survey included a large percentage of the features identified over many years of ad-hoc air photography. The scientific test to identify features using wavelengths beyond the visible part of the spectrum was confirmed, but the limited resolution of the Deadelus scanner generating images with a ground resolution of 2.0 m rather than the .08 m per pixel resolution of the photographs meant that the returns from the multispectral imaging were diminished (Powlesland et al. 1997).

Another NERC supported flight undertaken in 2005 collected LiDAR data. The LiDAR survey, despite its relatively low ground resolution of 2.0 m per pixel, provided an accurate surface model covering c. 80 km^2 around West Heslerton Village. It was quickly realized that the LiDAR surface model was imperfect in that it represented the current rather than ancient topography. The current landform has been radically altered by desiccation of the extensive peat deposits in the center of the Vale as a consequence of climate change, man-made drainage, and agricultural effects.

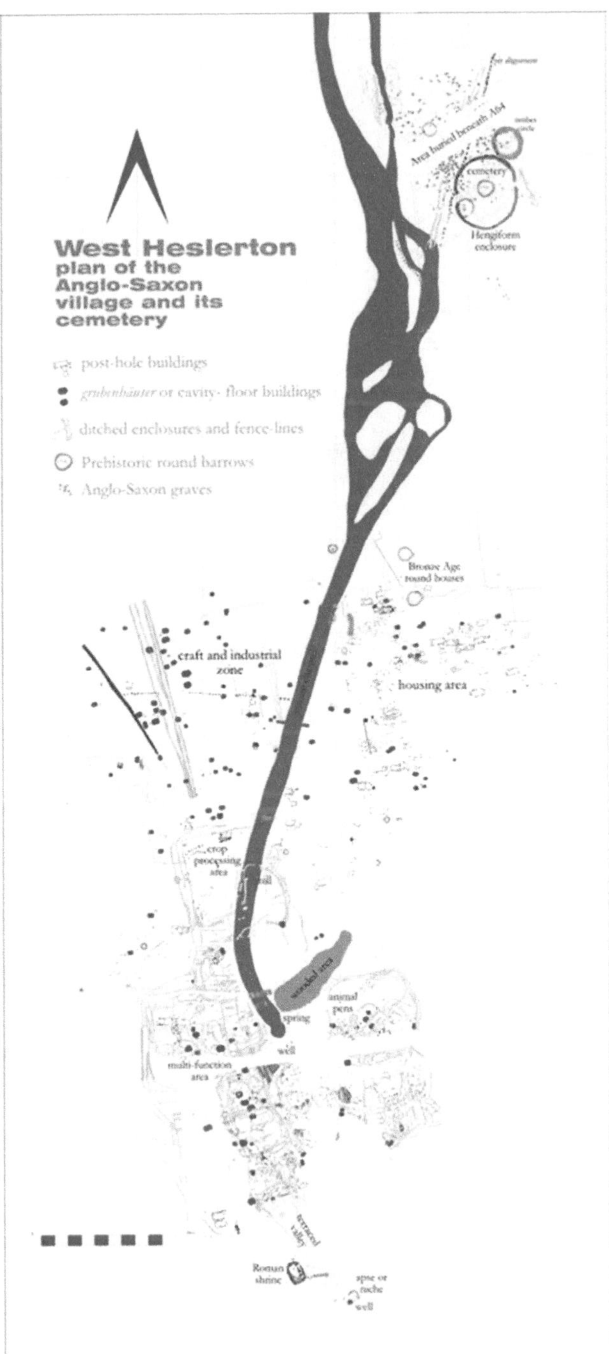

Fig. 13.2 Plan showing the excavated Anglian Settlement and associated cemetery at West Heslerton

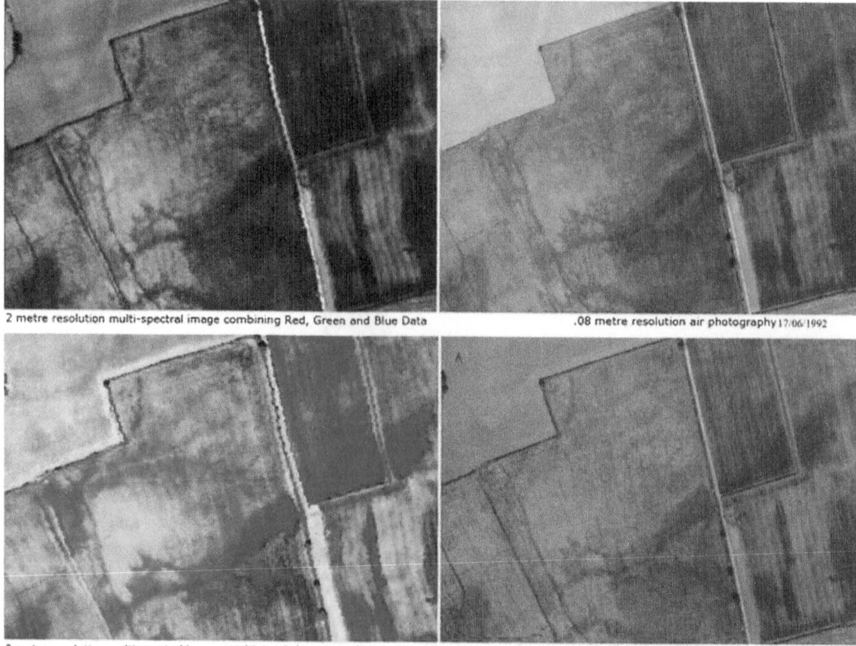

Fig. 13.3 *Four views* covering an area of crop-marks derived from multispectral and high resolution airborne imaging. Showing the limitations imposed by resolution and the difference in crop-marks only a few days apart

Attempts to identify buried archaeology using ground-based remote sensing in the early 1980s initially produced poor results, a consequence both of the available hardware and local conditions. With the support of English Heritage, a program of large scale and contiguous geophysical surveys designed to cover multiple adjacent fields was begun in 2001 and continued for nearly a decade; these completely transformed the picture of past activity in the area (Fig. 13.4). Survey was first targeted on an area of c. 350 ha between the villages of Sherburn and East Heslerton; work began using a single Geoscan FM16 fluxgate gradiometer, collecting data over 30 m^2 walked at 1-m intervals, recording points at .25-m intervals on a north-south axis with a field team of two. The sandy soils of the southern side of the Vale of Pickering both to the east and west of West Heslerton proved to be exceptionally responsive to geomagnetic prospection in particular. The initial 350 ha target area was sufficient to expose an extraordinary number of archaeological features but was insufficiently large to give an understanding of the underlying structure of the prehistoric and later landscape or develop a long-term management strategy.

In order to increase the rate of area coverage, a Bartington 601 dual gradiometer, with two probes set 1 m apart, was purchased; this significantly reduced the amount of walking required to cover each area. The limitations in single or dual probe survey employing manually established 30 m grids were recognized at an early stage of the large area surveys; it was difficult to secure high quality and uniform results

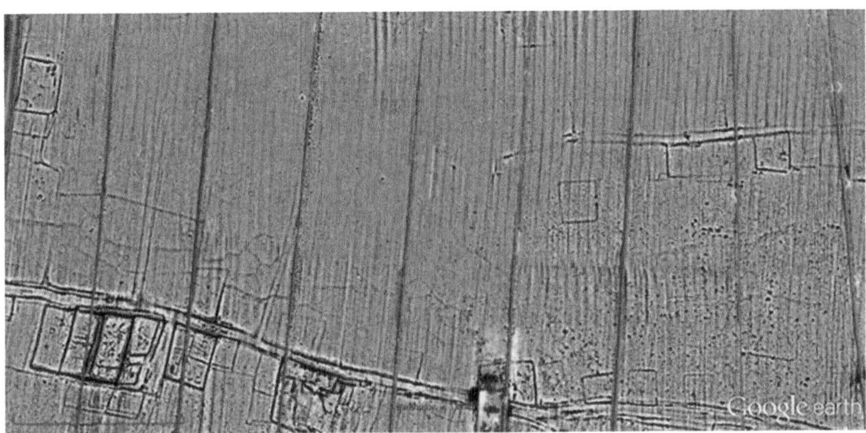

Fig. 13.4 A section of the LRC landscape scale geophysical survey covering a 1-km strip on the southern side of the Vale of Pickering revealing evidence of prehistoric, Roman and Anglo-Saxon domestic activity in addition to major trackways and probable cemeteries

at a rate of more than 2 ha per day. By the mid-2000s, new instruments employing multiple probes mounted on carts were developed by English Heritage in the UK and a number of geophysicists in Europe. In 2007, we began to use a Foerster Kartograph which carried four probes with a .5 m separation between them and collected magnetic values at .1 m intervals in the direction of travel; a Real Time Kinematic GPS mounted on the cart meant that each point collected was precisely positioned with an accuracy of less than 5 cm. The increased density of the collected data greatly improved the resolution of the mapped magnetic anomalies, revealing features that would not have been observed in lower resolution data, and made interpretation of the results more reliable. The use of the onboard GPS meant that there was no need to manually lay out a traditional survey grid and, by using a 2 m wide cart, larger areas could be covered in a day.

The integration of the geophysical and airborne remote sensing results within the LRC's geographic data management system employed the same approach as was applied in the excavations. Each identified feature is individually identified, documented in a database, and digitized as a filled polygon to produce an interactive map which can be viewed and interrogated at any scale. Conventional GIS software, while well suited to multiscalar data, rarely supports the sort of 3D imaging needed to appreciate the landscape setting of the evidence and, more significantly, the fourth dimension, time. This challenge was addressed using Google Earth as the platform for a digital atlas incorporating the results; this resolved the three primary issues – the delivery of the integrated results of the research using the Internet to nonspecialist and specialist audiences, the delivery of the interpreted data within an interactive 3D landscape, and the facility to scroll and animate the results through time. This represented a significant breakthrough in terms of the publication of a landscape dataset; the time depth of the data was addressed through the design of the underlying database, which indicates the active period for each identified feature (Powlesland 2012).

The detailed feature dataset now comprises over 30,000 features ranging from individual small pits to trackways running for many kilometers. This densely utilized landscape has challenged established models of population density and land use from the Neolithic to Medieval periods in England. It has also brought home the character of the archaeological resource as a continuous historic environment.

See also the entries in EGA for Landscape Archaeology and British Isles: Medieval Archaeology.

Chapter 14
Seascape Survey on the Inner Ionian Sea Archipelago

Nena Galanidou

Meganisi and its satellite islands lie in the Inner Ionian Sea Archipelago, a relatively short distance from Aetoloakarnania and Lefkas (Fig. 14.1). The abundance of top-quality flint and the presence of small wetlands and karstic cavities were the first points that attracted our attention to this corner of western Greece. But there was something more. In the Pleistocene, the short distance between these islands and the neighboring Lefkas and Aetoloakarnanian coast, combined with the shallow seabed in this area, meant that changes in sea level during glacial and interglacial periods would have caused the islands to become alternately connected to and isolated from the larger landmasses. Thus, over time, new living conditions and environments were constantly created for the Paleolithic communities of southeast Europe, which responded to these in their turn. The islands of the archipelago form fragments, the higher tips, of the original Pleistocene landscape, a large part of which now lies submerged under the sea. It was only after the first millennia of the Holocene that the coastline assumed its present form and offered to the communities of late prehistoric and historical times a new set of insular attractions (Fig. 14.2). Marine and fresh water resources have been bountiful, and it is no coincidence that the coastline of our research area is today protected by Natura 2000. From a diachronic perspective, then, Meganisi and its neighbors posed a methodological challenge for the realization of a hybrid island archaeology – alternating as it was between mainland and islands, passing points, and landing places – on a small and viable spatial scale.

N. Galanidou (✉)
Department of History and Archaeology, University of Crete, Rethymno 74100, Greece
e-mail: ngalanidou@phl.uoc.gr

M. Carver et al. (eds.), *Field Archaeology from Around the World*,
SpringerBriefs in Archaeology, DOI 10.1007/978-3-319-09819-7_14

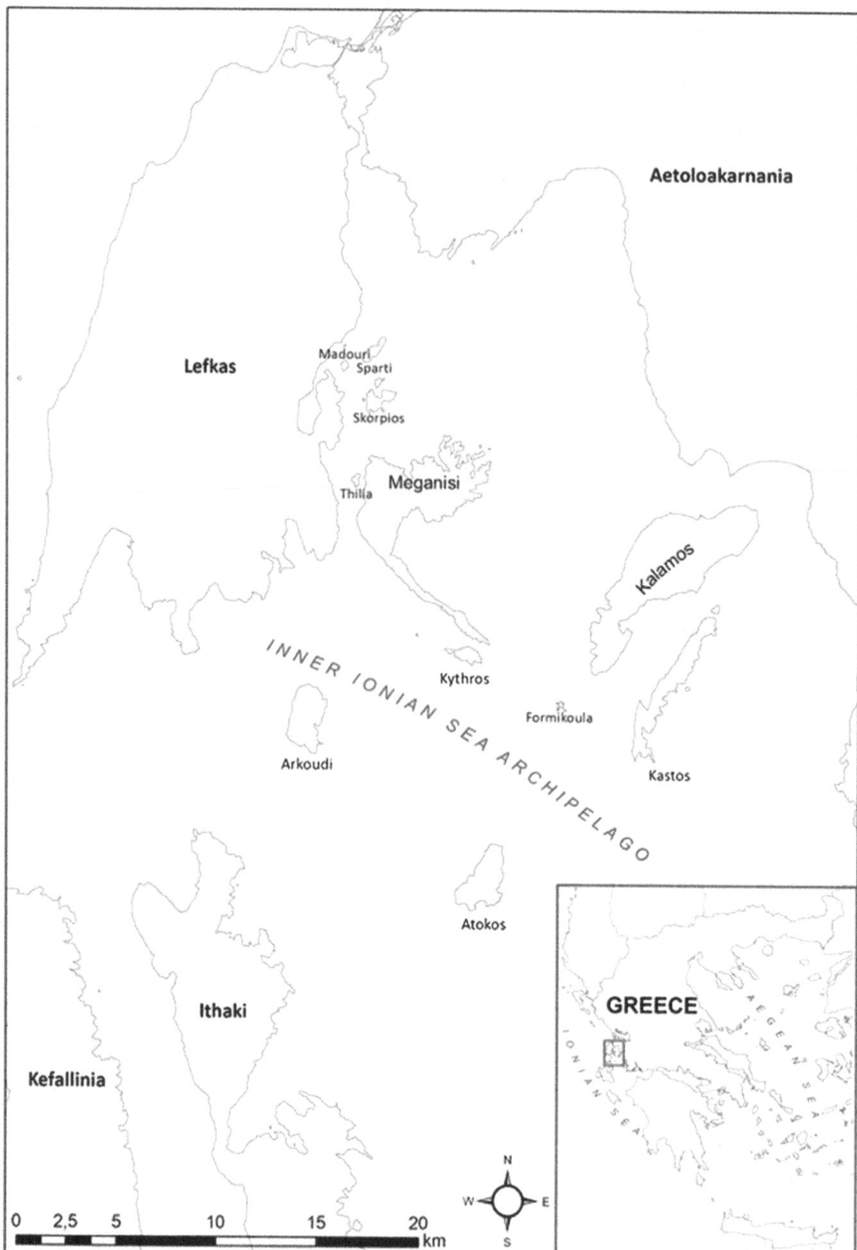

Fig. 14.1 Map showing the area of study, the Inner Ionian Sea Archipelago in west Greece, delimited by the mainland Greece (Aetoloakarnania), Lefkas, and the northern tips of Kefallinia and Ithaki

Fig. 14.2 Panoramic view of the Inner Ionian Sea Archipelago taken from east Lefkas (Photo courtesy of Costas Zissis)

The project was a University of Crete initiative undertaken in collaboration with the Greek Ministry of Culture. It had two main objectives: (1) the study of the archipelago's prehistoric and historical trajectories and links to the trajectories of the larger landmasses to the east and west (*regional* scale) and (2) the identification of prehistoric sites that could be further tested by excavation in the future (*site* scale). The *project design* comprised *archaeological survey* to shed light on human activity through time and space as well as *archival and anthropological research* to reconstruct natural and cultural landscape history. It was guided by interdisciplinary collaboration of archaeologists working with specialists in geology, geography, oceanography, biology, social anthropology, and architecture.

The *archaeological survey* was conducted in Meganisi, Thilia, Kythros, Petalou, Nisopoula, Formikoula, Atokos, and Arkoudi in two field seasons in summers 2010 and 2011. A geographical information system (designed in ArcGIS 9.3) provided the platform for the work in the lab and the field. At the outset, multiple layers of *cartographic information*, in the form of topographic maps (1:5,000), historical maps (Fig. 14.3), geological maps, and satellite images, were compiled, superimposed, and consulted. As surface inspection progressed, data on finds, sites, and monuments was also gradually integrated. The larger islands were divided into 100×60 m transects with a numeric designation (Fig. 14.4a); the smaller islets were explored as individual transects. Information on place names, landscape features (e.g., a doline, a cave), and structures (e.g., a threshing floor), collected by local informants or through surface exploration, was mapped on transects and guided the priorities of research.

Surface exploration proceeded in *transects* by teams of five fieldwalkers spaced at 12-m intervals. Team members walked in parallel lines, each scanning the ground to right and left (Fig. 14.4a). They collected and bagged all artifacts seen on the surface and recorded visible structures or architectural remains. Each team worked with a coordinator, an experienced archaeologist responsible for positioning his/her team in the field with the aid of a portable GPS, compass, satellite, and topographic maps of the day's plan of coverage. Upon completion of a few transects, the teams stopped

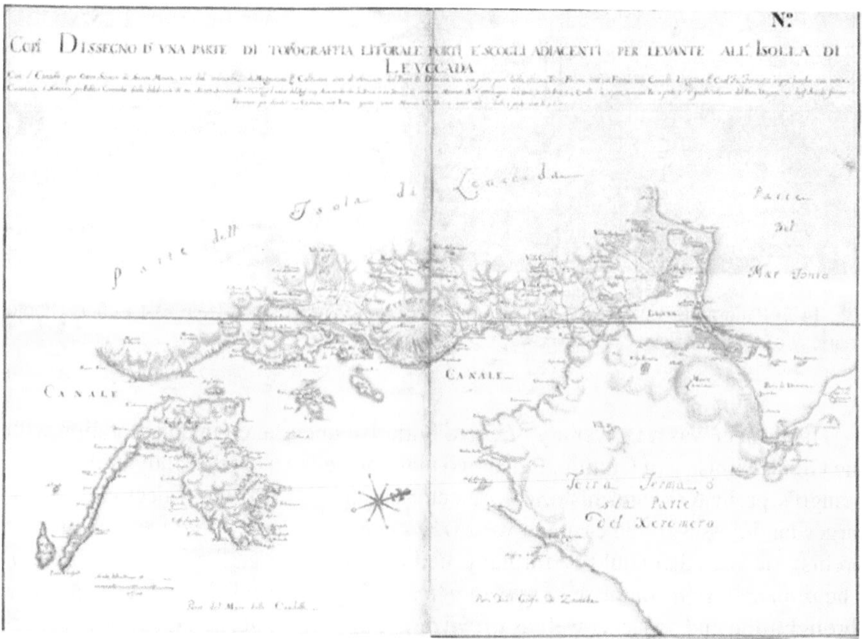

Fig. 14.3 A 1729 map of the survey region by Santo Semitecolo (Map courtesy of the Lefkas Historical Archive)

for evaluation. At this point coordinators wrote in the day book, made plans of any notable structures, and sorted finds. Leaving behind the natural flint debris was necessary since students were often unable to distinguish those from artifacts in the course of ground scanning. Under a tree or in the open air, these stops for inspection, find sorting, and evaluation were opportunities to teach students the archaeology fundamentals and the nature of the materials.

Sites were designated on the basis of three criteria set up by the pioneering work by Cherry et al. (1991) at Keos Island: high artifact *density*, *continuity* in artifact distribution over a contiguous area, and *discreteness*, that is, the area has a distinct edge, beyond which artifact density falls of markedly. Site coordinates were recorded with a portable GPS and transferred to the GIS database.

The original plan was to cover one third of the archipelago's 30 km^2. In practice, a little less than 7 km^2 was examined. Vegetation, steep relief, and seabird habitats proved to be the major obstacles to meeting our original coverage plan (Figs. 14.4b and 14.5). Although team coordinators were prepared for the topographic and accessibility conditions of the next day's assigned units of work, more often than not the satellite images (even those only a few years old) were depicting a landscape that had changed dramatically due to either vegetation overgrowth

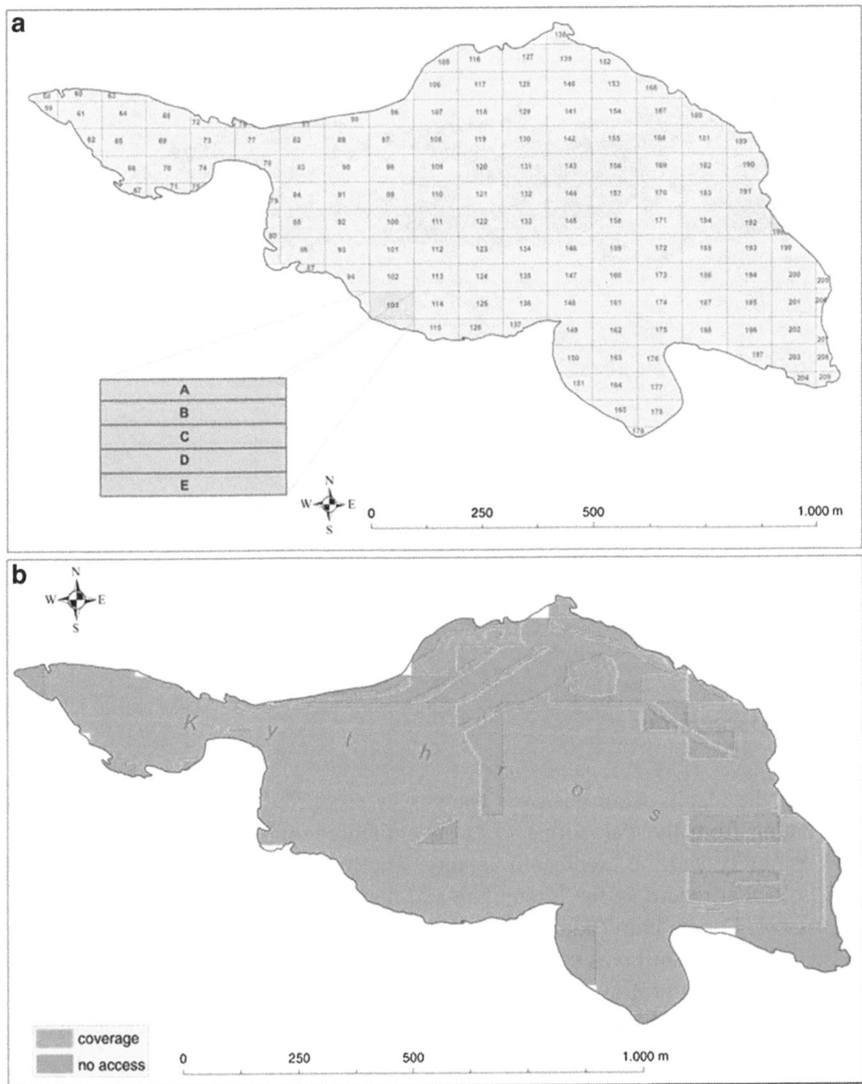

Fig. 14.4 (**a**) *Top*: the Kythros grid. (**b**) *Bottom*: map showing the coverage at Kythros (*green*) and the areas with no access (*pink*)

(western Greece receives more rain than any other part of the country) or intense construction activity and road opening especially along the coastal areas of Meganisi. In the smaller islands covered by thick and thorny vegetation, fieldwalking could only take place along paths created by grazing animals or water erosion.

Fig. 14.5 The steep coast at southwest Meganisi. Arrows show the locations of a cave with submerged floor (*lower*) and a multiperiod site on top of a limestone cliff near the recently opened road (*upper*)

Future Directions

However the results were positive. The survey recovered 20,000 artifacts and 30 sites dating from the Paleolithic to the twentieth century, with a hiatus between Late Antiquity and the eighteenth century. The finds bridge the gap between the archaeological record of the Ionian Sea and that of mainland Greece (e.g., Bailey et al. 1997; Forsén and Tikkala 2011; Wiseman and Zachos 2003). More importantly they lend themselves to discussing and interpreting the island record in terms of cultural and natural events that are distinctive to the coastal areas of Western Greece. Working on very small islands in a geologically active part of the world, we have been aware that archaeological site preservation and visibility is largely dependent upon eustatism, tectonic movements (including coastal uplift or subsidence and local sea-level rates of change) and high-energy events (including wave action and tsunamis). Thus although the Inner Ionian Sea Archipelago survey begun on land, we have developed a special interest in the sea and in the information still locked up on the drowned prehistoric landscapes of the Ionian shelf.

Relevant entries in EGA include Environmental Reconstruction in Archaeological Science; Glacial Landscapes: Environmental Archaeology; Greek Islands (Excluding Crete), Archaeology of ; Island Nation Sites and Rising Sea Levels; Submerged Prehistoric Landscapes; Survey Archaeology in the Greek Aegean World.

Chapter 15
Archaeology in Advance of Motorway Construction in Ireland

Rónán Swan

In the late 1990s, the Republic of Ireland decided to upgrade, develop, and expand its motorway network. Unlike other countries in Western Europe, Ireland's motorway network had been largely undeveloped, with limited works in the 1980s and 1990s. Under Irish legislation and associated government policy, archaeological sites are afforded protection and there is a duty on developers to minimize their impact on archaeological sites through either avoidance, preservation in situ, or, as a last resort, preservation by record (i.e., by scientific archaeological excavation).

The original strategy for dealing with archaeological sites on the early motorway projects was that known sites identified during the environmental impact assessment (EIA) would be excavated prior to construction while the discovery of previously undocumented sites would be left to monitoring during the main construction works, the subsequent excavations thus impeded the progress of the road-building program. Such an approach was unsatisfactory for several reasons. Archaeologically, it meant significant sites might not be discovered until construction had commenced, with archaeological layers being truncated and damaged by the heavy plant and machinery, and perhaps leading to a loss of archaeological sites. It also resulted in claims from the construction companies arising from delays and additional costs relating to their work program.

R. Swan (✉)
Archaeology, National Roads Authority, Dublin, Ireland
e-mail: rswan@nra.ie

M. Carver et al. (eds.), *Field Archaeology from Around the World*,
SpringerBriefs in Archaeology, DOI 10.1007/978-3-319-09819-7_15

Cognizant of these challenges and the need to address archaeology in a responsible manner, the National Roads Authority and the Minister for Arts, Heritage, Gaeltacht and the Islands developed a code of practice in 2000 which created a framework for the treatment of archaeology on national road schemes. As a consequence, Project Archaeologists were appointed as members of road design teams to advise on the archaeological implications of decisions as they happened throughout the lifetime of the project. The code of practice also set out the duties and responsibilities of both parties as well as the Project Archaeologists themselves (http://www.nra.ie/Publications/DownloadableDocumentation/Archaeology/file,3476,en.PDF).

One of the first initiatives of the Project Archaeologists was to commission archaeological works to begin as soon as practicable ahead of the main construction works. For instance, during the design of the M3 and the M7/M8 motorways in the early 2000s, extensive archaeo-geophysical surveying was undertaken of the entire route, and the line of the route was altered to minimize its impact on potential archaeological sites (Fig. 15.1). Another initiative was for a detailed program of advance archaeological works to be undertaken to ensure early identification and full excavation of previously unknown sites. Consequently, the entire road corridor would be investigated by tracked machines excavating centerline trenches with off-sets under close archaeological supervision; typically more than 10 % of the route would be sampled in this fashion. Commencing these works early on also afforded opportunities to redesign routes (e.g., at Woodstown, Co. Waterford, thus avoiding a newly discovered Hiberno-Norse enclosed settlement).

In the intervening period since the adoption of the code of practice, there has been considerable archaeological work undertaken on national road schemes. Over 1,000 km along the routes of planned roads have been investigated providing a significant sample (skewed, for the most part, to avoid known archaeological sites) for the study of the archaeology of Ireland. In the course of these archaeological works, it has become apparent that the previously unknown archaeology is every bit as rich as the monumental archaeology that so often characterizes Ireland, with over 2,000 sites being discovered, excavated, reported on, and published from absolutely every period from the very earliest settlement of the island up to the modern period (Fig. 15.2).

This work has fundamentally changed our view of Ireland's past. Taking just one example, previous studies depicted the Iron Age in Ireland as a blank period about which very little was known other than limited high-prestige artifacts and high-profile royal sites; however, recent research from the University of Bradford using the results from the archaeological works on national road schemes paints a picture of widespread and ubiquitous activity throughout this period (Becker et al. 2010).

Another key aspect of motorway excavations in Ireland has been the emphasis on communicating the results of these works not only to fellow archaeologists but especially to the Irish taxpayers who ultimately pay for this work to be conducted. As a consequence a comprehensive strategy has been developed for communicating the results through site tours, exhibitions, conferences, websites, on-line databases, magazines, periodicals, and books (e.g., O'Sullivan and Stanley 2008; Deevy and Murphy 2009).

Fig. 15.1 M7/M8 Portlaoise-Cullahill which was moved to avoid impacting on archaeological sites discovered during archaeo-geophysical surveying (Illustration: Margaret Gowen & Co. Ltd)

The approach adopted by the NRA to archaeology on national road schemes provides a model which has ensured that archaeological goals and objectives can be achieved while still providing the essential national transport infrastructure.

Fig. 15.2 Neolithic Trackway which dates from 3640 to 3370 BCE (Wk-20960) discovered Edercloon, co. Longford during the advance archaeological excavations on the N4Dromod-Roosky scheme (Photograph: CRDS Ltd)

Further information relevant to this section will be found in EGA under Cultural Heritage Management Quality Control and Assurance; Environmental Assessment in Cultural Heritage Management; Legislation in Archaeology: Overview and Introduction; Trackways in Archaeological Conservation and Preservation; Landscape Archaeology.

Chapter 16
Digging Through Permafrost in Siberia

Vladimir Pitulko

Permafrost is defined as ground that remains below 0 °C for at least 2 years. As a natural conservation agent, it provides an archive of environmental proxy records including biological materials of vegetable, animal and human origin, and artifacts, particularly those made of organic materials such as wood, bone (antler, ivory), or fibers deriving from plants or animals. Permafrost may contain up to 60 % of ice or virtually none at all. Atmospheric heat and water alter deposits quickly, and dramatically affect the preservation of archaeological sites. Finding sites in this terrain still depends on artifacts or cultural layers exposed by chance. Test pits, aerial and geophysical methods have not been successful except for the most recent sites of approximately past 2,000 years or so. Early Holocene and Pleistocene sites, particularly in Siberia, still remain fully frozen. Not many of them are known up to now, but in all cases, they are encased in ice-rich deposits. Experience of excavating such sites is so far limited to three cases – Zhokhov, Yana RHS, and Berelekh (Pitulko 2008). Excavation strategies are determined mostly by the depth of the site and the degree of icing. Where cover is thin, *area excavation* can be applied, but under a thick cover of frozen ground, it is necessary to approach from the side *in profile*. Examples of both these strategies are given here.

On shallow sites, after the frozen deposit is exposed in area, there are three steps in the investigation: (1) thawing, (2) drying (by evaporation and drainage), and (3) regular excavation of the now relatively dry cultural deposits. Steps (1) and (2) require permanent control. Fast thawing creates too much water and saturates the sediment. Forced thawing can be done if the host sediment is not deep frozen and has a low ice content. The best system is to rely on natural melting and evaporation under a summer breeze. Ideally, the area is large enough to be divided into three: one third thawing, another drying, and the last being excavated. Depending on

V. Pitulko (✉)
Paleolithic Department, Institute for the History of Material Culture, Russian Academy of Sciences, 18 Dvortsovaya nab. St., St. Petersburg 191186, Russia
e-mail: pitulkov@rambler.ru

M. Carver et al. (eds.), *Field Archaeology from Around the World*, SpringerBriefs in Archaeology, DOI 10.1007/978-3-319-09819-7_16

Fig. 16.1 Excavations of the Zhokhov site, 2004, by V. V. Pitulko (8,000 BP, New Siberian Islands, Russian Arctic)

weather conditions, this allows the excavation of strata 5–10-cm thick each day. This method was successfully used at Zhokhov (Fig. 16.1), and resulted in the excavation of cultural deposits extending over about 500 m^2, to a depth of 3 m (Pitulko 2008). A sump is required to pump out the meltwater. Screening is achieved using water with a low pressure pump. In other respects, routine archaeological procedures are followed.

Deep sites, with a thick cover of overlain deposits, can only be accessed from a lateral exposure, for example, in a river bank as at Yana RHS (Pitulko 2008; Pitulko and Pavlova 2010). Here the overburden was 7–8-m thick, with an ice content of 40–50 %, and included a polygonal grid of syngenetic ice wedges. It is always possible to clean up and record cultural layers seen in the profile, and even to record some finds in situ. However, real excavations are possible only if the ice wedges are first extracted from the archaeological deposit. This can be achieved by thawing if they are well exposed to the air and the bottom of the wedge is below the cultural layer.

As soon as the top of the wedge becomes thawed, it is shoveled out and the adjacent deposit can be excavated in a strip 1–2-m wide. Then the operation is repeated, gradually reducing the deposit in series of steps (Fig. 16.2). This prevents the remaining thawed deposits from collapse. Material that has been shoveled out is removed by pumping water through the natural erosional channels created by the ice wedges. This kind of excavation requires a large investment of labor. More than 2,000 m^2 has now been excavated at Yana RHS.

Fig. 16.2 Excavations on the river bank at Yana RHS, Northern Area, 2011 (28,000 BP, low Yana River, north of Yana-Indighirka Lowland: excavations by V. V. Pitulko)

The radiocarbon dating of frozen sites in permafrost areas is tricky. Wood, particularly in small pieces, is a floatable material and can be easily transported from elsewhere or deliberately recycled. Although the date of bone will relate directly to the death of the animal, some bone (e.g., mammoth) may be curated over long periods. Sediments themselves may transported through ice action. Dating of the host sediment may give dates approximately 2,000 radiocarbon years older than the date of plant remains they contain (Pitulko and Pavlova 2010). Errors can be avoided by taking many samples from above and below the cultural layers, as well as within them.

Further information will be found in EGA under Frozen conditions: Preservation and excavation; Polar Exploration Archaeology (North).

Chapter 17
A Tropical Rain Forest Site in Belize

Cynthia Robin

Nestled in Belize's lush tropical rain forest, the Chan site was long known to local farmers who still farm the area around the archaeological site. The area was noted by archaeologists in 1994 who were working on a regional settlement survey. The Chan project, a collaborative, international, multidisciplinary research project, began in 2002, bringing together a team of over 120 foreign and local archaeologists, botanists, geologists, geographers, chemists, computer scientists, artists, students, workers, volunteers, and local community residents from Belize, the USA, England, Canada, and China (Robin 2012).

Chan was occupied by a farming community with a 2,000-year history (c. 800 BCE–CE 1200) spanning the major chronological periods of ancient Maya society: the Preclassic, Classic, and Postclassic periods. Unremarkable in terms of community size or architectural elaboration, Chan nonetheless flourished while the fortunes of nearby major Maya civic centers waxed and waned. Research at Chan was aimed at investigating the everyday lives of Maya farmers and the impact farmers had on Maya society. Given that 2,000 years is a long period of time, what did Chan's residents do to facilitate the longevity of their community?

To address these questions, a three-staged research design was developed for the Chan project. Stage 1 involved a full coverage rain forest survey that utilized *Total Station* mapping and a *Geographical Information System* to digitally map the 3.2 km^2 area of the community and record the 274 households and 1,223 agricultural terraces that surround Chan's community center (Fig. 17.1). In Stage 2, extensive *coring* (using a post-hole digger) and full scale *area excavations* were conducted at all buildings in Chan's community center, along with a 10 % sample of households (26 households) and associated outdoor activity and work spaces that represent

C. Robin (✉)
Department of Anthropology, Northwestern University, 1810 Hinman Ave,
Evanston, IL 60208-1310, USA
e-mail: c-robin@northwestern.edu

M. Carver et al. (eds.), *Field Archaeology from Around the World*,
SpringerBriefs in Archaeology, DOI 10.1007/978-3-319-09819-7_17

Fig. 17.1 Undergraduate students Alex Miller, Shelley Khan, and Yasmine Baktash (*left* to *right*) set up a Topcon GTS 605 laser theodolite to digitally map Chan's settlement (Photograph by James Meierhoff)

the temporal, socioeconomic, and vocational variability within the community (Fig. 17.2). Excavation in this terrain involves careful clearance of vegetation and roots to reveal the archaeological features without damaging the stone structures or the trees. Stage 3 research, which was conducted in the field in conjunction with stage 1 and 2 research to facilitate research collaboration, involved the analysis of roughly half a million objects of everyday life, one of the largest archaeological samples from a Maya farming community, and additionally incorporated scientific techniques of soil chemistry, paleoethnobotany, human bone, animal bone, obsidian sourcing, radiocarbon dating, and micro-artifact studies.

The structures and assemblages were classified and analyzed to produce a dated sequence of material practice at Chan over the two millennia. The terraced agricultural landscape was constructed by cooperating farming families, and the agricultural system developed and expanded through time. It avoided soil erosion and maximized water retention, incorporating complex small-scale irrigation and water storage systems. A forest management strategy maintained a diverse mature, closed-canopy, tropical forest even as the population expanded during the Classic period (BCE 250–900), and farmers had a growing need for fuel, construction material, and agricultural land. Extremes of wealth and power were avoided within the community, as all residents from the humblest farmer to the community leaders had access to a similar range of exotic items and lived in perishable houses with similar outward appearances. Ritual and political practices within the community incorporated all residents and focused on the community as a whole rather than individual community leaders.

Fig. 17.2 Archaeological illustrators Merle Alfaro (*seated*) and Nasario Puc (*standing*) illustrate a terminal deposit of broken ceramic on Chan's central ritual structure. Excavators Lazaro Martinez, Everaldo Chi, and Ismael Chan (*left* to *right*) are in the background (Photograph by James Meierhoff)

This long-term stability contrasts with that of the opulent Maya civic centers with their towering temple pyramids that form the usual focus of Maya archaeological research. Avoidance of extremes of wealth and power, more equitable distribution of goods, consistency in health, and communal focus of ritual and politics are some of the socially effective strategies established by Chan residents. The sustainable forest management practiced at Chan is distinct from the more extractive practices seen at the larger Maya civic centers where royals culled the mature forest across the Classic period. The consistent presence of a low degree of biological stress in the Chan skeletal population indicates persistent good health at Chan. This contrasts with that seen at larger Maya civic centers where residents' health declined by the end of the Classic period as indicated by increasing degrees of biological stress.

These studies, drawn from systematic fieldwork at a seemingly unremarkable place such as Chan, thus offer important lessons about human societies, particularly in the matter of social and economic sustainability.

More information relevant to this section will be found in EGA under Agrarian Landscapes: Environmental Archaeological Studies; Maya Geography and Culture: Ancient and Contemporary; Mesoamerica: Subsistence Strategies by Region; Sustainability and Cultural Heritage.

Chapter 18
Excavating a Rockshelter in Northwest Greece

Nena Galanidou

Klithi is a limestone rockshelter on the right bank of the River Voïdomatis in Northwest Greece (Fig. 18.1). Between 1983 and 1989, archaeological excavations here directed by Geoff Bailey brought to light a sequence of Upper Paleolithic deposits exhibiting remarkable uniformity in their artifact and faunal assemblages (Bailey 1997). Hunter/gatherer groups of the late glacial period had used ibex and chamois for food, leather, and bone artifacts. They had collected flint pebbles from the nearby river banks to manufacture an Epigravettian industry dominated by backed bladelets which were employed in hunting. Small endscrapers and other tools were employed in the working of hides and bone. Klithi is a low-diversity site and now features among other specialized ibex-sites that are typically found at high altitudes in or near the sort of rugged terrain that was the habitat of ibex herds.

The *project design* combined on-site excavation aimed at producing data with high precision chronological and spatial resolution, with off-site work intended to place Klithi within its local (NW Greece) and regional (SE Europe) geographical and cultural context. To this end, detailed archaeological survey and paleoenvironmental and paleogeographic research were conducted in parallel with excavation.

The excavation program sought detailed insights into patterns of change and variability in the excavated record, vertically across stratigraphic layers and horizontally in space. Prior to excavation, the shelter floor was cleared of the materials accumulated due to recent herding activity. It was then mapped on a 1×1 m grid with an alphanumeric designation and the major topographic features were projected on it (Fig. 18.2). Each grid was further subdivided into four quadrants, 50×50 cm each, and for the most part, these quadrants were excavated in 5 cm spits as the minimum provenance units to which all finds are referenced. Beyond this arbitrary three-dimensional coordinate system, all excavated finds were also

N. Galanidou (✉)
Department of History and Archaeology, University of Crete, Rethymno 74100, Greece
e-mail: ngalanidou@phl.uoc.gr

M. Carver et al. (eds.), *Field Archaeology from Around the World*,
SpringerBriefs in Archaeology, DOI 10.1007/978-3-319-09819-7_18

Fig. 18.1 Klithi rockshelter on the right bank of the River Voidomatis in Vikos Gorge (Photo courtesy of Costas Zissis)

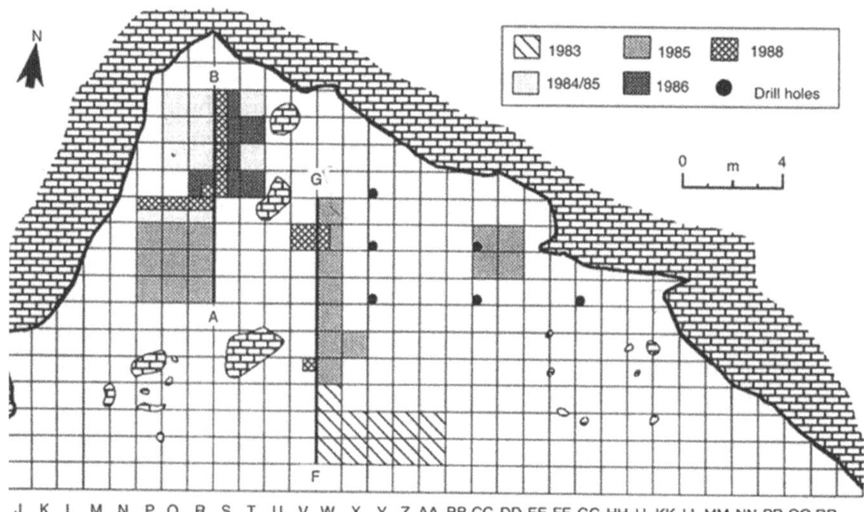

Fig. 18.2 Klithi site plan, showing coverage by excavation year (Reproduced by permission of the MacDonald Institute for Archaeological Research)

Fig. 18.3 Excavating at Klithi with a small brush and a shovel. The excavator kneels on wooden plank and a foam cushion. The high density of artifacts is visible in the exposed surface (Photo courtesy of Geoff Bailey)

stratigraphically referenced in terms of the geological and archaeological features into a two-tier system: *contexts* defined as the smallest units of stratigraphic provenance identified during excavation on the basis of lithology, texture, and color and *strata*, used (at Klithi) to denote groups of layers combined at post-excavation stage to represent a site-wide time unit. Small brushes and shovels were the main excavation tools (Fig. 18.3). Horizontal plans of the deposit featuring specimens larger than 5 cm were systematically drawn throughout. Excavated sediments were routinely dry-sieved and water-sieved (screened) in the river. Sorting, cataloguing, and study of artifacts and bones took place in the open air in the Vikos Gorge, on a river terrace under the plane trees, a magical spot indeed for archaeologists to set up their laboratory.

The *excavation strategy* evolved in the course of the project. First and foremost, a deep sounding was opened at the front of the shelter, reaching a depth of 2.8 m, to preview the stratigraphy and establish the total time span of occupation (1983). Excavation later continued across a horizontal area in order to examine the spatial distribution of finds and features (1984, 1985), following the principles of French "grands décapages" with detailed three-dimensional piece plotting of each specimen to its nearest centimeter. This procedure was eventually abandoned in view of the extremely high densities of archaeological material encountered – on average 26,424 lithic artifacts and 4,472 identified bones per cubic meter. Subsequent experiments with quadrants or miniquads (25×25 cm) (1986) were applied but were still slow, and it was evident that better scientific design could only come from knowing the character of the total deposit in advance. Hollow steel tubes 1 m long and 60 mm diameter were used to sample the deposit in six boreholes drilled in various parts of the shelter floor, including both excavated and unexcavated areas (1986, 1988).

Fig. 18.4 The hearth area at Klithi with tags marking the superimposed layers corresponding to open hearths. The strings mark the site grid used for planning (Photo courtesy of Geoff Bailey)

The deposits were relatively loose and unconsolidated scree sediments, with relatively small clasts and high proportions of finer sediment. The maximum depth of scree deposits reached some 7 m in places, but the dense cultural material was confined to the upper 2 m. These 2 m of anthropogenic sediment corresponded to a mode of animal and lithic resource exploitation that remained stable for 3,500 years.

Refitting of lithic artifacts and quantitative analyses of spatial patterns were recruited to establish the spatial integrity of the deposits. Klithi, like other caves, contained a palimpsest of cultural material from overlapping occupations, a so-called time-averaged deposit, in which some redundant patterns of stable site structure were observed. A single major hearth area at the back of the shelter represented a complex stratigraphy of superimposed open hearths that was in use throughout the span of human presence on the site (Fig. 18.4). The repetitive use of the hearth area suggests a long-term familiarity of the Klithi inhabitants with the site and its physical features. One possible interpretation of this is that the rockshelter was in a remote part of the territory of a single group, which returned to the site periodically, relatively briefly, probably during late spring or early summer, and re-used the existing facilities.

The expedition was completed in 1997 with the publication of an integrated two-volume report, which described the research questions, the methods adopted, the findings, and their interpretations step by step. Over the course of five field seasons, excavation at Klithi exposed 51.5 m^2, representing approx. 1/5 of the total floor area available to the Upper Paleolithic occupants. The remaining 4/5 now lie intact, awaiting the archaeologists of the future to return to Klithi with refined recovery methods and a new set of questions (Bailey and Galanidou 2009).

Entries relevant to this section may be found in EGA under; Floors and Occupation Surface Analysis in Archaeology; Karstic Landscapes: Geoarchaeology.

Chapter 19
Excavation and Survey at Pinnacle Point

Simen Oestmo and Curtis W. Marean

The transdisciplinary project centered on Pinnacle Point (the South African Coast Paleoclimate, Paleoenvironment, Paleoecology, and Paleoanthropology Project-SACP4) has as its primary goal to develop an integrated paleoclimate, paleoenvironmental, and paleoanthropological record for the south coast of South Africa spanning 400 to 30 ka, a time that spans the origins of modern humans. The African Middle Stone Age (MSA), a Middle and Late Pleistocene stone tool phase, dominates the majority of this time span. The MSA in South Africa has gained increasing attention in debates about the antiquity of modern human behavior; some researchers arguing that the South African evidence suggests an early origin of modern behavior, while others suggesting a late origin. Resolution of these debates relies on two advances: improvements in our theoretical approach and an improvement of the empirical record in Africa. Fieldwork was initiated at Pinnacle Point (Mossel Bay, South Africa) to improve the empirical record (Marean et al. 2004).

The field strategy uses state-of-the-art excavation and survey methods and techniques to obtain precise and accurate data, relying as much as possible on digital data acquisition integrated into 3D models of the "paleoscape." The paleoscape is a seamless model of land and sea that projects hunter-gatherer food resources at different climate states. We model that paleoscape with integrations of sea level and coastline change joined to species distribution modeling. A specific part of the transdisciplinary strategy is to use speleothem records to generate long, continuous, and tightly dated paleoclimatic and paleoenvironmental sequences for the MSA combined with other techniques (e.g., faunal change, phytoliths, magnetics) that enrich the environmental reconstructions.

S. Oestmo (✉) • C.W. Marean
Institute of Human Origins, School of Human Evolution and Social Change, Arizona State University, Tempe, AZ, USA
e-mail: Soestmo@asu.edu; curtis.marean@asu.edu

M. Carver et al. (eds.), *Field Archaeology from Around the World*, SpringerBriefs in Archaeology, DOI 10.1007/978-3-319-09819-7_19

Fig. 19.1 Pinnacle Point landscape. The wooden walkway leads to the entrance of cave PP13B

Pedestrian and mountain-climbing reconnaissance techniques revealed sites along the cliffs at Pinnacle Point. Today, wooden staircases and walkways provide access to most of the sites (Fig. 19.1). We use total stations to map all sites and landscape features, coding all visible features directly to handheld computers using drop-down menus programmed into survey software. Using both RTK GPS and direct total station measurements, all coordinates are translated directly into the South African National Coordinate (SANC) reference system (Marean et al. 2004, 2010). The data is integrated into a GIS using ArcGIS, and a 3D paleoscape model is created.

Our excavation recording system is designed so that every measurement made on-site of artifacts, features, sections, surfaces, and everything else is recorded by total station directly to handheld computer (Fig. 19.2). Total stations give all finds a 3D provenience, and finds are given a unique barcode number and assigned to a square, quadrant, and stratigraphic unit. Bar code scanners are connected to handheld computers through USB cables, requiring little to no typing of specimen numbers or other observations. This significantly reduces the transcription errors that plague field recording (Dibble et al. 2007). We record both ends of elongated artifacts by total station to calculate orientation and slope of artifacts within stratigraphic aggregates. We use artifact orientation to gain knowledge about site taphonomy (Bernatchez 2010). All non-plotted materials are gently wet sieved with fresh water through a nested 10^{-3}–1.0 mm sieve (Marean et al. 2010).

We excavate within 50 cm quadrants within squares, naming them by their bearing: NE, NW, SE, and SW. Excavations within these quadrants are conducted following natural stratigraphic units (StratUnits: layers, features, etc.). These StratUnits are grouped into larger stratigraphic aggregates (layers) in the field and then checked

Fig. 19.2 Excavation in progress at cave PP13B (Photographs courtesy of SACP4)

with 3D GIS analysis. All excavator accounts of StratUnits are recorded to forms (supplemented by notebooks) and then typed into a form-based database system. Sediment volume is measured during excavation and sediment samples are taken from every StratUnit. Subsamples of the sediment samples are used to measure magnetic susceptibility (MS) used to identifying evidence for human occupation, mainly due to the use of fire at archaeological sites (Herries and Fisher 2010).

Section drawings are created by combining regular graph paper drawing with dense measurements of all stratigraphy and features using a total station directly to handheld computer, which links the section drawing to true grid space. We then digitally rectify all our section drawing and photographs (Bernatchez and Marean 2011) to true grid space, which allows us to plot on those photographs all artifacts, dating samples, stratigraphic boundaries, and anything else removed from site (Marean et al. 2010). On-site checking of field-acquired data eliminates most potential errors.

Optically stimulated luminescence dating (OSL), TT-OSL, and U-Th dating (also known as uranium series, U-series, 230Th/U) are used to maintain chronological control (Bar-Matthews et al. 2010; Jacobs 2010; Marean et al. 2010). Most OSL ages come from locations where we also conduct micromorphology. Micromorphology significantly enhances our ability to understand sedimentary processes that are potentially problematic for OSL. Pinnacle Point research employs micromorphology regularly, as a foundation to stratigraphic analysis in complex depositional contexts (Marean et al. 2010; Karkanas and Goldberg 2010). We rely heavily on 3D GIS integration of all data and using ages, micromorphology, and stratigraphy to develop "life histories" of the caves (Fig. 19.3).

Fieldwork at Pinnacle Point has yielded the earliest evidence for human exploitation of marine resources, earliest securely dated use and modification of pigment, early use of bladelet stone tool technology at PP13B by ~164 ka, and early evidence

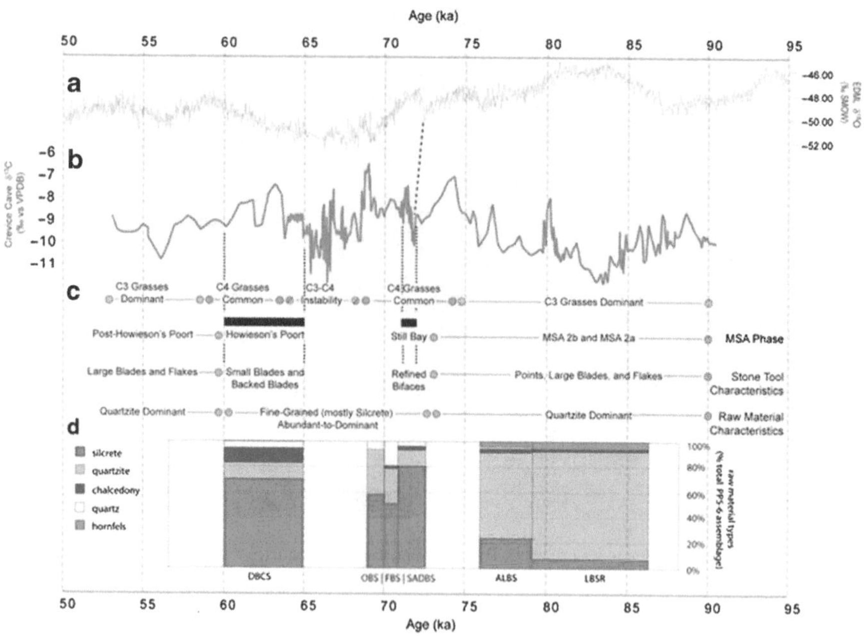

Fig. 19.3 The inferred vegetation sequence from the Crevice Cave speleothem relative to southern hemisphere temperature change and major phases in the production of stone tools and use of raw materials in the southern Cape of South Africa. (**a**) The EPICA EDML d18O record (EPICA Community Members, 2006), (**b**) the Crevice Cave (Pinnacle Point) d13C (*green*) records with inferred grass regimes, (**c**) the major changes in stone tool phase, stone tool type, and raw material abundance in the southern Cape, and (**d**) the raw material abundances at archaeological site PP5-6 (Bar-Matthews et al. 2010: Fig. 11)

for heat treatment of lithics at sites PP13B and PP5–6 (Marean et al. 2007; Brown et al. 2009; Thompson et al. 2010; Watts 2010). We have published, to date, the highest resolution speleothem record for Africa for the MSA for the time span 90–53 ka, which provides us with an unprecedented understanding of changes in rainfall and vegetation (Bar-Matthews et al. 2010). In addition, our tightly collaborative research has allowed us to detect correlations between the coastline distances, strontium isotope ratios in the speleothems, and the abundance of shellfish in coastal sites (Fisher et al. 2010; Jerardino and Marean 2010). We attribute a portion of our success to the reliance on digital acquisition of data, which allows fast- and high-quality analysis of field data, and the synergy created by our transdisciplinary approach, which allows quick insights that cross the traditional boundaries of science.

Entries in EGA amplifying the work at Pinnacle Point may be found in EGA under African Stone Age; Dating Techniques in Archaeological Science; Human Evolution: Theory and Progress; Human Evolution: Use of Fire; Hunter-Gatherers, Archaeology of; Hunter-Gatherer Settlement and Mobility; Hunting and Hunting Landscapes; Out-of-Africa Origins; Lithic Technology, Paleolithic; Island Nation Sites and Rising Sea Levels; Southern and East African Middle Stone Age: Geography and Culture; Stratigraphy in Archaeology: A Brief History.

Chapter 20
An Upper Paleolithic Living Floor at Monruz, Switzerland

Denise Leesch

Upper Paleolithic living floors represent moments in the life of hunter-gatherers in the form of scattered finds and ephemeral features. Such sites are naturally vulnerable to later activities and well-preserved examples are rare.

Investigating how such a site was composed is primarily achieved by fine stratigraphic observation and later by refitting of the recovered flint artifacts, bone fragments, and fire-cracked rocks. The network of lines created by conjoined pieces whose location is recorded three dimensionally allows us to visualize intra-site dynamics and to establish the relative chronology of a site's use. Further crucial information on the time depth of an archaeological horizon is obtained by studying the period(s) of the year during which a site was occupied. Special attention is therefore paid to screening the excavated sediments in order to recover all fragile organic elements that may be used for season determination, notably the teeth from very young animals, less than one year old, and the remains from small hibernating mammals such as ground squirrel and marmot. Another major concern is to differentiate anthropogenic structures (e.g., pits and post holes) from natural features dug by burrowing animals (e.g., collared lemmings or narrow-headed voles). Similarly, it is important to correctly identify naturally accumulated stones or other geological phenomena that may evoke human-made structures. For that reason, the horizontal view of a living floor, however impressive it may be, needs to be completed by detailed stratigraphic documentation of all structures and features observed on the surface.

D. Leesch (✉)
University of Neuchâtel, Neuchâtel, Switzerland
e-mail: denise.leesch@yahoo.fr

M. Carver et al. (eds.), *Field Archaeology from Around the World*,
SpringerBriefs in Archaeology, DOI 10.1007/978-3-319-09819-7_20

Fig. 20.1 The Magdalenian open-air site Monruz (Neuchâtel, Switzerland). The living floor yielded more than 40 well-preserved hearths and remains from at least 56 horses. The layer, though only c. 2–3-cm thick, has proved to be the result of repeated occupation episodes after successful horse hunts (© photo Y. André, Office et Musée d'archéologie Neuchâtel)

Hearths are of special interest because they acted as focal points around which most of the technical, domestic, and social activities took place. In the vast majority of sites, however, charcoal has been destroyed and the soil shows no traces of heat action, thus making it difficult to precisely locate the combustion areas and other hearth-related structures. The approximate position of the hearths is then endorsed by confronting the spatial distribution of all thermally altered objects, notably flints, bones, and stones. In the rare cases of hearths still containing black sediment, the residues are screened separately in the laboratory and sorted under the microscope in order to extract all discrete remains such as charcoal fragments, charred seeds, bones, and fish scales, relevant for reconstructing the use of the hearths.

An exceptionally well-preserved Magdalenian living floor excavated in Monruz, at the edge of Lake Neuchâtel (Switzerland) in advance of motorway construction, offers an example of these techniques in action. The floor belongs to an open-air living and processing site dated to c. 15,500 years ago (Bullinger et al. 2006). Due to high stratigraphic resolution, it was easy in this case to follow the micro-topography of the thin covering layer (c. 2.5-cm thick), so exposing the intact living surface at the very moment of its abandon (Fig. 20.1). Since the detailed distribution of finds and features is of paramount importance, it is necessary to avoid treading on the excavated surface: excavators work from platforms supported by scaffolding (Fig. 20.2). Dense bone and flint scatters, together with extended patches of red

Fig. 20.2 In order to not disturb the original position of the finds, excavation of Paleolithic living floors is operated from a slightly elevated platform made from planks. The sediments are filled into buckets to be wet-sieved per ¼ of square meters, a well-adapted spatial unit for interpreting even discrete find scatters (© photo Y. André, Office et Musée d'archéologie Neuchâtel)

ochre, were associated with more than 40 hearths of various types and dimensions (bowl-shaped and flat structures). By refitting several thousands of fractured stones, it could be demonstrated that all had been originally brought onto the site to cover hearths, so conserving heat – a combustion system characteristic of the Upper Paleolithic period. At that time, fuel was scarce and included only twigs of wood species, such as dwarf willow and dwarf birch, that grow low to the ground. By placing stones on top of the brushwood, the use of the hearths slowly released the heat they had accumulated during the short combustion phase. Stones that fractured in the heat were subsequently dispersed. Through precise mapping of the activity areas, it could also be demonstrated that most of the hearths were of multifunctional character. Maintenance of hunting weapons was systematically performed less than 50 cm from the heat source, and sewing, as shown by the fractured bone needles, less than 1 m away. Hide treatment, probably because it required more space, took place at a slightly greater distance from the hearth. With the focus on the larger hearths, it was possible to propose living units within the overall pattern of debris (Fig. 20.3).

The Magdalenian site of Monruz is interpreted as a site that was occupied repeatedly following successful horse hunts. During each hunting event, only one to a maximum of three horses was killed. After the hunt, the whole group moved from its former camp location to this point where the horses were butchered and consumed. According to the number of killed animals, the occupation lasted for one to a few weeks. While staying at this place, diverse smaller species such as ibex,

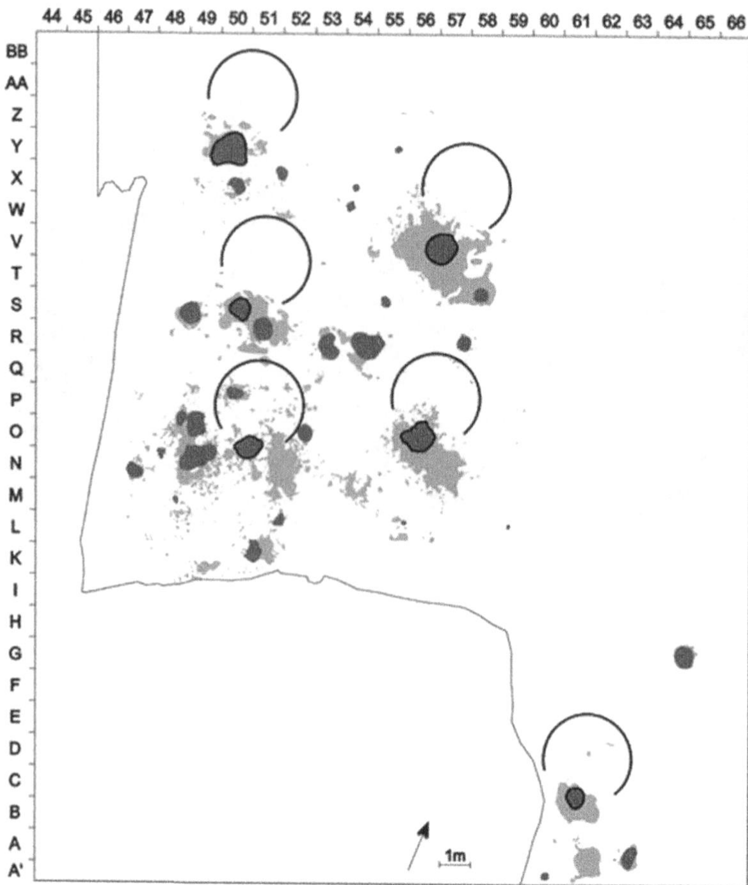

Fig. 20.3 Model of dwelling units based on the location of the large pit-hearths and charcoal scatters (Leesch and Bullinger 2012, Fig. 11)

marmot, alpine hare, and various birds and fishes were hunted in the surrounding area and brought to the camp where they were processed and eaten in the immediate vicinity of the fireplaces. No more than three large hearths functioned simultaneously. Thus, what appeared at first sight to represent a single-occupation level was shown by careful excavation to correspond to a palimpsest created by repeated short habitation episodes during spring and summer.

So perfect an Upper Paleolithic picture did the Monruz deposit provide that part of it was extracted as a single block and removed out of the path of the motorway. It was enclosed in a container made from metal sheet piles and underlain by large pipes filled with concrete (dimensions of the block: 11 × 6 m × 2.5 m; weight: 400 t). The "box" was then loaded onto the platform of a trailer and taken to a new location where it could be studied without time constraint (Fig. 20.4).

Fig. 20.4 Transport of a portion of a Magdalenian open-air site. This unusual operation was entirely financed by the Swiss Federal Roads Office (© photo Y. André, Office et Musée d'archéologie Neuchâtel)

Entries in EGA relevant to this section include Floors and Occupation Surface Analysis in Archaeology; Leroi-Gourhan (André); European Middle Paleolithic: Geography and Culture; European Middle to Upper Paleolithic.

Chapter 21
On the Beach in Remote Oceania

Mike T. Carson and Hsiao-chun Hung

The character and date of the earliest settlement of the remote Pacific Islands remains an important research objective. Tracing human origins in "Remote Oceania" reveals a series of west-to-east migrations, ultimately from southern coastal China before 6,000 years BP (Bellwood et al. 2011). In the far west of Micronesia, the Mariana Islands have become known as the home of the oldest archaeological sites of Remote Oceania, dated 3,500–3,300 years BP (Fig. 21.1).

We are only now achieving some clarity on where to find sites, in a manner that conforms to CRM constraints. The local governments consider excavations to be destructive to cultural heritage resources and harmful to the natural environment. Archaeological excavations are therefore undertaken only in strict compliance with government regulations, which are not always conducive to archaeological visibility. The normal procedures use *shovel tests*, holes 10–20 m apart dug the size of a shovel blade and sieved through a 6 mm mesh, to find sites, and *test pits*, 1 × 1 m in plan taken down by trowel, to investigate them. Monitoring of a machine-dug trench has become standard procedure for archaeological resource management in beach settings.

M.T. Carson (✉)
Micronesian Area Research Center, University of Guam, Mangilao, GU, USA
e-mail: mtcarson@uguam.uog.edu

H.-c. Hung
Department of Archaeology and Natural History, The Australian National University, Acton, ACT, Australia
e-mail: hsiao-chun.hung@anu.edu.au

M. Carver et al. (eds.), *Field Archaeology from Around the World*,
SpringerBriefs in Archaeology, DOI 10.1007/978-3-319-09819-7_21

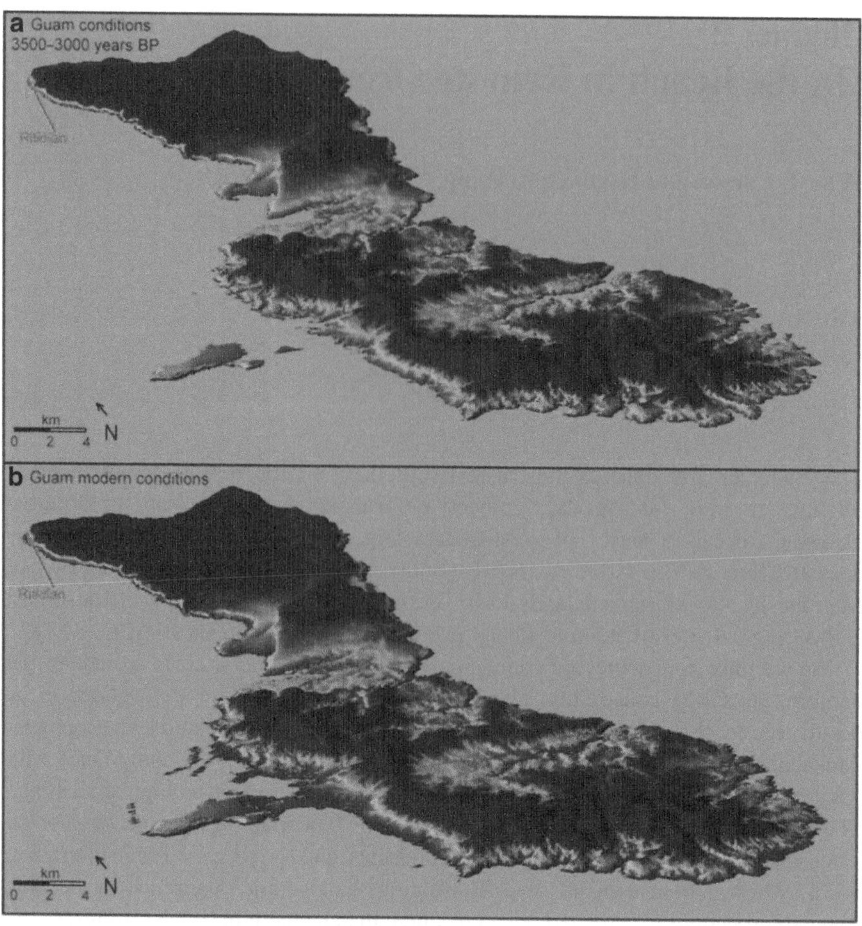

Fig. 21.1 Island-wide terrain model of Guam in the Mariana Islands showing (**a**) conditions 3,500–3,000 years BP and (**b**) modern conditions (Modified from Carson (2011))

Nearly all sites in the Marianas are found through *surface reconnaissance*, walking at close intervals (usually 5 m) through the dense jungle, sometimes augmented by transects of *shovel testing* where the ground visibility is particularly difficult. This approach works well in areas with little or no soil development, where site remnants are easily accessible. In fact, most island terrain fits into this category, bearing perhaps 20–30 cm of rocky silt or clay directly over solid bedrock. Using little or no excavation, this strategy has been successful for mapping and recording sites of the more recent time period, roughly within the last 1,000 years. Megalithic house pillars and capitals (locally called *latte*) mark most residential sites. Broken pottery is littered almost everywhere, along with lesser amounts of stone and shell adzes and other such durable tools.

Fig. 21.2 Setting of 3,500–3,300 years BP beach site at Ritidian, Guam, now more than 100 m from modern shoreline and 2.5 m beneath the surface

For the most ancient sites, dating to 3,500–3,300 years BP, the best chance of finding a preserved archaeological deposit is to search in the beach sand. These locations fortuitously match expectations of where the earliest islanders lived, near productive crop-growing soils and bountiful coral reef ecosystems. The beaches as seen today, however, are recent geological formations. The ancient sea level stood 1.8 m higher than today, plus the earliest sites are at least 1–2 m beneath today's sandy beaches and 100 m or farther inland from modern shorelines. These circumstances teach us two things. First, the coastal terrain has been transformed substantially since the time since the sites were first inhabited. Second, exploratory survey for the most ancient sites cannot rely on surface finds, and researchers must dig deeply in locations that may not appear immediately obvious.

Taking into account these formation processes, a paleo-*terrain model* can be used to depict the approximate coastal topography at the time when the oldest sites were inhabited (Carson 2011). The model has been continually refined by *test pits* and trenches that give precise locations, depths, and dates of ancient sedimentary layers, whether or not they contain archaeological materials. The most thorough work has been in Guam, the largest and southernmost of the Mariana Islands.

At Ritidian on Guam, dozens of small test pits, each 1 × 1 m, were dug at 10-m intervals throughout an area targeted by the paleo-terrain model (Fig. 21.2). The most ancient deposit was found only in one of these test pits, meaning that the origi-

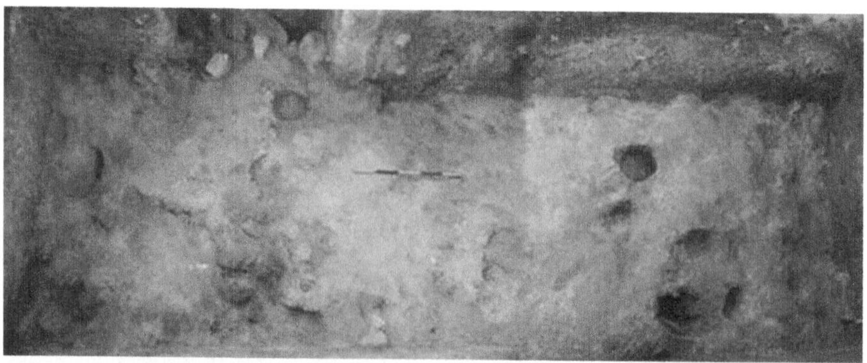

Fig. 21.3 Arrangement of post-moulds, hearths, and other features in ancient living floor 3,500–3,400 years BP, 100 m landward from House of Taga, south coast of Tinian

nal site covered a rather small area less than 20× 20 m in total. The deepest cultural layer was buried more than 2.5 m deep and more than 100 m from the present shoreline. The ancient shoreline context was dated 3,500–3,300 years BP by radiocarbon. Exceptionally thin (1–2 mm) red-slipped pottery fragments were refitted, representing 10–20 % of two different small bowls or jars, plus more than 55 % of another shallow open bowl. The oldest site layer at Ritidian was sealed beneath a zone of 1 m of hardened beach sand (calcrete) that solidified after the site had been buried, creating a barrier that few archaeologists would attempt to breach. The excavation required chiselling of large solid blocks of calcrete, later dissolved in mild (5 %) acid and sieved through half-mm wire mesh for full recovery of the constituent artifacts and midden. Beneath the calcrete, the loose beach sand was removed by trowel and sieved through half-mm mesh for consistent recovery.

The most thoroughly studied early period Marianas site has been on the southern coast of Tinian, 100 m inland from the famous megalithic *latte* ruins of the House of Taga. An excavation slightly larger than 16 m^2 here proceeded by hand troweling of *stratified layers*, each internally divided into *arbitrary levels* 10 cm thick. This strategy uncovered an arrangement of post-moulds, hearths, and other features of an ancient living floor dated about 3,500–3,400 years BP (Fig. 21.3). Among 30,000+ earthenware pottery fragments, more than 150 exhibited finely impressed, stamped, and incised decorations on a red-slipped surface. Chert adzes and flaked tools, shell beads and pendants, fishing hooks, shellfish remains, and bones of fish, turtle, and birds completed the assemblage.

Entries in EGA relevant to this section include Environmental Reconstruction in Archaeological Science; Geoarchaeology; Landscape Archaeology.

Chapter 22
Defining the Neolithic on the German *loess*

Daniela Hofmann

The Linearbandkeramik (Linear Pottery culture, LBK) is the earliest Neolithic culture so far defined in Central Europe. At its maximum extent, it reaches from western Hungary (where it emerges around 5600–5500 cal BCE) to the Paris Basin, into Ukraine, and as far as the Northern European Plain. The LBK is characterized by a distinctive style of pottery (with linear bands) and monumental wooden longhouses flanked by pits. Enclosures and burial grounds also occasionally occur. In the earliest phase (until about 5300 cal BCE), material culture is more uniform, but this gives way to increasing regionalization until the LBK is finally replaced by a series of successor cultures, a regionally varied process completed by about 4900 cal BCE.

Most LBK sites are located on fertile *loess* soils, on the terraces of river valleys. Loess is a wind-borne glacial sediment deposited during the Ice Age which turned to fertile black earth. Subsequent decalcification and brunification have since degraded these soils, a process which began before the Neolithic and continued to at least the Iron Age. It has resulted in the top *A horizon* becoming much more lightly colored, and this has obscured the top sections of any Neolithic features and parts of their stratigraphy. Degraded black earth also began to filter downwards through cracks, so that the cuts of features are now often indistinct and smudged.

After the Neolithic, but particularly after the Roman period, cultivation caused erosion in higher parts of slopes and the consequent deposit of colluvium in the river valleys. Where loess soils are still being plowed today, LBK sites are easy to locate from pottery on the surface, but generally at least half a meter of their deposit has been lost through plowing. Old ground surfaces and floor layers are thus not preserved, leaving only traces of cut features. Conversely, any sites in valley bottoms are now buried under colluvium. Bone is also not well preserved in many areas (Schalich 1988). One difficulty in digging a Bandkeramik site is hence to identify

D. Hofmann (✉)
Department of Archaeology and Conservation, Cardiff University,
John Percival Building, Cardiff, UK
e-mail: hofmannd@cardiff.ac.uk

M. Carver et al. (eds.), *Field Archaeology from Around the World*,
SpringerBriefs in Archaeology, DOI 10.1007/978-3-319-09819-7_22

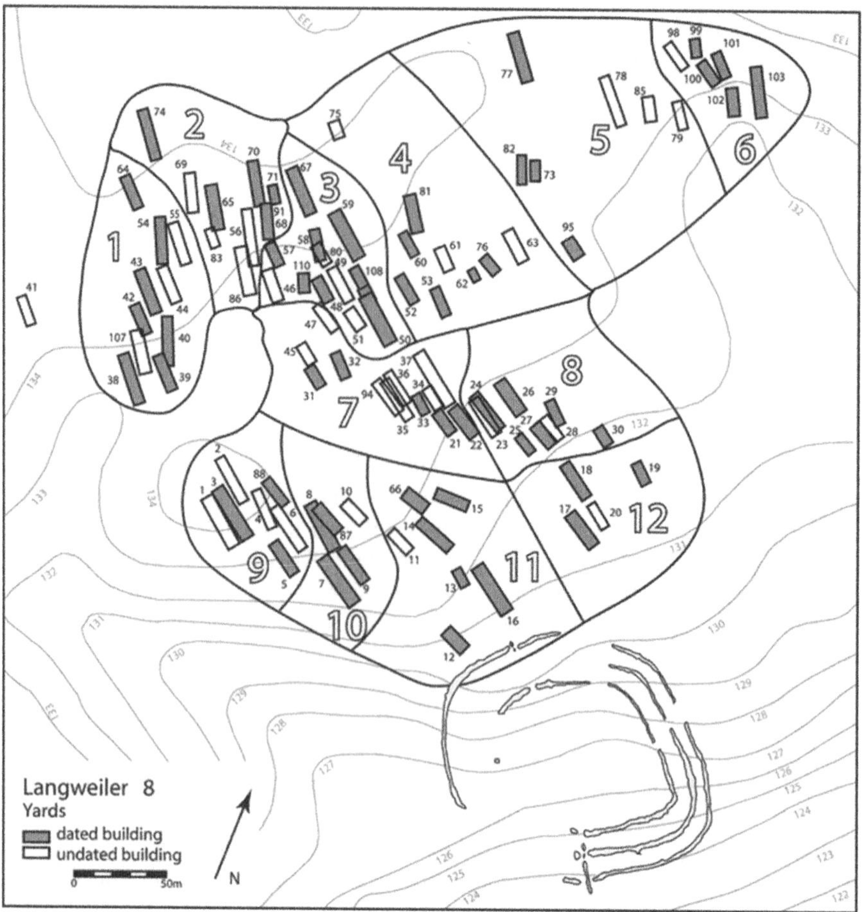

Fig. 22.1 Plan of the settlement of Langweiler 8 (After Stehli 1994, p. 87)

features which have virtually blended into the surrounding loess (and which may only become visible over time, or in specific weather conditions).

The destruction of a large part of the Aldenhoven Plateau in the German Rhineland in the course of opencast lignite mining in the 1970s and 1980s first provided an opportunity to study a whole LBK landscape and has fundamentally framed the way we approach this culture. An entire valley comprising nine LBK settlements and one burial ground was excavated under rescue conditions in a project led by Jens Lüning, revealing hundreds of intercutting houses alongside pits and earthworks (Fig. 22.1).

The main challenge became to understand the chronological development and settlement structure of the sites. Sequencing was mainly achieved by pottery seriation and resulted in the definition of 14 chronological phases. On the basis of dated pits associated with house plans, it was shown that houses shifted within a circumscribed

Fig. 22.2 Part of the Bandkeramik site of Wang (Lower Bavaria) under excavation, showing parts of a house and associated features (Photo: Alasdair Whittle)

area of the settlement, termed a "yard" (Zimmermann et al. 2005). Contemporary houses were hence tens of meters apart from each other, while overlapping house plans were separated by several phases. The duration of each phase was estimated at around 25 years. In addition, on the basis of production waste, it emerged that the largest settlement in the valley, Langweiler 8, imported high-quality flint from the Netherlands, which was then passed on to other sites. Environmental analyses also indicated that the area was rapidly abandoned at the end of the LBK, when there was a distinct reforestation episode (Zimmermann et al. 2005).

Excavation method has usually employed the *spit*, where the deposit is lowered in an artificial horizontal slice c 10 cm thick (American *arbitrary layer*; here often called a *planum*, pl. *plana*). Pits may be *box-sectioned* (where the section is extended into subsoil), and all the material collected together and attributed to the feature. Otherwise a subterranean feature may be divided into *quadrants*, each excavated in artificial spits. Excavating alternate quadrants gives continuous orthogonal profiles through the feature fill (Fig. 22.2). Where layers are hard to distinguish visually or features are complex, the latter is the preferable method as it allows for both horizontal and vertical control. These approaches have their rationale in the difficulty of defining edges, the need to control untrained helpers and time constraints.

Although it is hard to overstress the range and quality of the previous work carried out under difficult conditions, newer projects have challenged many aspects of the original models. For example, at Vaihingen in southwest Germany, two pottery styles existed simultaneously and were associated with different yard clusters, termed "clans" and also defined by other material culture and economic preferences (Bogaard et al. 2011), and this spatial dimension may also be important in the

Rhineland. Rather than self-sufficient households, there could have been factions within each LBK site, an aspect which can only be addressed by excavating large parts of a site and comparing artifact distributions in detail.

Future method should focus on obtaining more stratigraphic information and on the elucidation of formation processes. Layers can be hard to recognize, and how pit fills formed remains elusive. Was chronologically homogenous material deposited quickly, or are we dealing with mixed assemblages, perhaps in a secondary position? To answer these questions, material should at the very least be collected in artificial spits and investigated for refits, with additional methods such as micromorphology employed where possible. However, there is scope for stratigraphic excavation at some LBK sites, and this should be attempted where possible to better understand formation processes and sequence. As always, the methodology adopted must remain flexible and respond to the individual conditions of each project.

There is also much scope for further radiocarbon work. Many existing dates have been taken from the charcoal of long-lived species or from bulk samples. This is of doubtful value. As it is currently debated whether the "earliest" and subsequent phases of the LBK culture overlap, tighter dating frameworks are needed. The problem is even more acute for the beginning and ending of the LBK. Mesolithic groups could have coexisted with the LBK for varying durations, and it is unclear whether the transition to the post-LBK cultures was dramatic and rapid, or a slow mosaic process with several generations of coexistence.

Information relevant to this section may be found in EGA under Europe: Mesolithic-Neolithic Transition; Excavation Methods in Archaeology; Radiocarbon Dating in Archaeology; Neustupný, Evžen; Zvelebil, Marek.

Chapter 23
Crannóg Investigations in Scotland

Anne Crone and Graeme Cavers

Crannogs are types of artificial islands, made or significantly modified by human agency, which, with the exception of one example in Wales, are found only in Scotland or Ireland. The majority of dated examples were built in the first millennium BC but they continued to be built and used episodically until the early modern period. They generally take the form of a foundation of organic materials and stone carrying a platform of timber logs or planks raised above water-level (Fig. 23.1). The island may be connected to the shore by a timber causeway. On top of the timber platform, buildings were erected made of timber, and in later periods, of stone. The great archaeological asset of the crannog is that organic materials such as structural timbers, wooden artifacts, textiles, and food debris discarded in the lake are preserved in cold anaerobic conditions.

Most known crannogs survive as islands surrounded by water, but some are completely submerged and others are now drying out in drained agricultural land. *Site formation* is critical to understanding and interpreting crannogs (see SWAP 2007 for discussion) but is not easy to resolve without large-scale intervention. Although most excavated examples appear to have been constructed by dumping material into the loch to form a mound (known as a *Packwerk* construction), a pile dwelling construction has been proposed for other sites. This clearly has implications for the interpretation of materials found in the core of the mound: do they represent occupation debris which has built up under the pile dwelling or do they represent relict material used in the construction of the mound which predates the occupation of the crannog? Soil micromorphological studies, such as those carried out on some Swiss lake villages (Wallace 2000) and Lithuanian lake dwellings (Menotti et al. 2005), might resolve these issues, but coring through stony mounds has not yet proved possible.

A. Crone (✉) • G. Cavers
AOC Archaeology Group, Edinburgh, Scotland, UK
e-mail: anne.crone@aocarchaeology.com; graeme.cavers@aocarchaeology.com

M. Carver et al. (eds.), *Field Archaeology from Around the World*, SpringerBriefs in Archaeology, DOI 10.1007/978-3-319-09819-7_23

Fig. 23.1 A Crannóg in Loch Nell, Argyll. The majority of crannógs survive as vegetation-covered mounds projecting just above the water

Scottish lochs are particularly cold and murky, and extensive *underwater excavations* have only been carried out in the larger (clearer) Highland lochs, at Oakbank crannog in Loch Tay (e.g., Dixon 2004) and Ederline crannog in Loch Awe (Cavers and Henderson 2005). At both sites, a basket of techniques adapted from shipwreck excavation and the investigation of continental lake villages was employed, with removal of silt carried out using a Venturi system water dredge (see Dean et al. 1992). Although Scottish lochs present a challenging environment in which to excavate, crannogs are generally located in water less than 6-m deep, allowing divers to work for long periods of time using surface-supplied air (Fig. 23.2).

Buiston, in Ayrshire (Crone 2000), is an example of an excavated "dryland site," which had been drained in the nineteenth century and now lay within a boggy but accessible field (Fig. 23.3). Coring demonstrated that, despite the drainage, significant organic deposits survived. The site was initially treated as a *box excavation* with small trenches separated by baulks. Water management soon became a crucial issue and a deep trench was subsequently cut across the site which served as a sump from which the water could be pumped. The trench had another advantage in that the substructure could be fully investigated and it provided greater stratigraphic control; dark organic deposits are much more clearly seen in section than in plan. Water levels were also an issue at Cults Loch and Whitefield Loch, both in SW Scotland, restricting the areas that could be excavated in plan. The Cults Loch crannog is a promontory extending out into the loch, while Dorman's Island, in Whitefield Loch, survives as a tree-covered island which had to be reached by boat. In both cases, narrow, "sacrificial" trenches were dug around the edges of each trench to act as sumps and keep the central area of the trench relatively dry.

Fig. 23.2 Underwater excavations at Ederline crannog, Loch Awe. Divers excavating below water are supported by a safety supervisor based on a scaffolding platform above the site

Fig. 23.3 Excavation underway on the seventh century CE "dryland" crannog at Buiston, Ayrshire. The stone hearth and wooden flooring of a round house lie to the *left* of the photograph while on the *right*, the palisaded walkway, which formed the defensive perimeter of the crannog, curves around

Placing crannogs in their contemporary physical and social landscapes is now recognized as key to their understanding and is central to the research agenda of the Scottish Wetland Archaeology Programme (SWAP 2007). The crannogs in

Whitefield Loch and Cults Loch were selected for investigation following a systematic review of the evidence and subsequent field assessment, which identified the rich later prehistoric landscape within which they both sit (Cavers and Crone 2010; Cavers et al. 2011). Reconstruction of the contemporary landscapes, including excavation of neighboring cropmark sites, formed part of the program.

Information relevant to this section may be found in EGA under Anaerobic Conditions (Bogs, Waterlogged, Subaquatic): Preservation and Conservation; Underwater Sites in Archaeological Conservation and Preservation.

Chapter 24
Investigating Tells in Syria

Wendy Matthews

Archaeological mounds form when activities and settlement were conducted at a site over time and sediment and material accumulation rates exceed those of truncation or erosion. In Southwest Asia an archaeological mound is called a "tell" in Arabic, "tepe" or "chogha" in Farsi, and "höyük" in Turkish. In the ancient Near East, mounds may vary in size from c. 30 m to 1 km in diameter and in height from c. 1 to >43 m (Fig. 24.1). The archaeological investigation of these mounds presents a range of major challenges: (1) low mounds and the bases of mounds may be masked by several meters of sediments from rivers, hill-wash, or erosion; (2) early levels may be buried below many meters of later settlement and difficult to access; (3) materials may be recycled and redeposited throughout a mound by successive construction and digging of pits or graves, for example; (4) with shifting settlement patterns and variations in construction and leveling, mounds are not uniform "layer cakes" and include truncated or eroded areas; and (5) mounds may represent only one aspect of settlement patterns and strategies, but may be overrepresented in field investigations due to their predominance in the landscape. Mound sites nevertheless often provide rich sequences of well-preserved deposits and many aspects of ecological and social strategies. The examples below are largely from interdisciplinary excavations in Syria.

Satellite imagery, aerial photography, surface survey, and *geomorphology* have been applied to study the extensive networks and landscapes of large and small sites in the steppe regions of northern Syria, as in the Tell Hamoukar survey (Ur 2010). Here, satellite pictures showed that many tell sites were connected by radial routeways that formed from at least the fourth millennium BCE. Surveys of artifacts, notably pottery, on large and small tell sites, have identified several major peaks in

W. Matthews (✉)
Department of Archaeology, School of Human and Environmental Sciences,
University of Reading, Reading, UK
e-mail: w.matthews@reading.ac.uk

M. Carver et al. (eds.), *Field Archaeology from Around the World*,
SpringerBriefs in Archaeology, DOI 10.1007/978-3-319-09819-7_24

Fig. 24.1 Aerial view of excavations and large monumental buildings at Tell Brak, Syria (43 m high, >800 m long, and 40 ha in size) (After Gerster 2003: Fig. 32)

settlement in northern Syria, notably in the mid-late fourth and mid-third millennia BCE, as well as decline, as in the late third millennium BCE during a period of climatic stress, when many large sites were partially abandoned and smaller sites along watercourses were frequented (Wilkinson 2003).

At the scale of individual tell sites, specific periods and types of activity areas have been *evaluated* by close integration of studies of *surface materials* and tell *geomorphology* and *topography* to detect in situ materials in actively eroding areas of mounds. By these methods, previously unexplored and otherwise deeply buried levels from the Ninevite five periods of the early third millennium BCE were excavated at several points around the large mound of Tell Brak, including a small temple/shrine (Fig. 24.1; Matthews 2003).

Rapid extensive investigation of subsurface features and buildings at tell sites have been very effectively investigated by *geophysics*, as in the recovery of the whole plan of the lower town of the mid-third millennium BCE at Chuera, by *surface scraping*, as at Tell Brak (Matthews 2003), and by *mechanized sweeping*, as at Sheikh Hamad. Walls, features, and floors were often constructed from compressed mud or mud brick and mud plaster. These may show clearly (Fig. 24.2), but when the fill around them is from similar materials (e.g., from leveling or collapse), they may be more difficult to detect.

Fig. 24.2 Micro-history of a large walled building and surfaces in a street in area HS3, Tell Brak. Location of blocks for microscopic analysis of sequences also shown

The definition of walls and surfaces depends on close observation of the characteristics of deposits and interfaces between layers. The edges of walls can be identified in plan by shaving clean the excavation surface with a hoe or trowel if deposits are moist or by cleaning briskly with a large brush if dry. During excavation, wall and surface faces can be detected by looking and feeling for changes in composition, texture, structure, and fractures along edges or surfaces using a small pick or trowel. Section profiles provide an important *reflexive* record of deposits and features as they are being excavated and should be kept clean (an artist's palette knife is particularly effective) and regularly examined at the edge of trenches or in strategic sections through features and floors. Records are made of structures (buildings), features (walls, hearths), and layers (floor deposits or fills) using digital photography and videos, high-precision architectural survey, plans, section drawings, and written descriptions.

The detailed histories of buildings and settlements have also been studied using techniques for analyzing sequences of floors and activity residues, such as *microstratigraphy* and *micromorphology* (microscopic analysis of layer content and sequences) (Fig. 24.2; Matthews 2003) and *chemical mapping* (as at Çatalhöyük, Turkey). An increasing range of analyses can be conducted in the field. These include portable X-ray fluorescence to characterize architectural and artifactual materials and activity residues (e.g., high phosphorus concentrations), and microscopic analysis of spot samples of sediment to look for plant phytoliths and dung spherulites to identify animal pens, for example, and thereby inform excavation and sampling strategies (as conducted by the Central Zagros Archaeological Project [http://www.czap.org/]). Exemplary interdisciplinary scientific analyses of spectacular burials at the mid-second millennium BCE site of Qatna, in western Syria, include study of the human remains, artifact materials and technology, and organic residues within the vessels.

Large-scale long-term research excavations at major tell sites are providing major insights into the diverse structure and histories of these settlements including changing social and political organization, economies, and ritual practices, which are becoming increasingly well defined. Examples in Syria, from regional and local centers, include Ebla, Tell Brak (Oates et al. 2001), and Tell Beydar in the third millennium; Tell Leilan in the second millennium BCE; and Sheikh Hamad in the first millennium BCE. Rescue excavations are also contributing to research. For example, the integration of the archaeobotanical and archaeozoological data from rescue excavations at several small sites along the Khabur river, sampled prior to their flooding by dam waters, has enabled study of major developments in the intensification of agriculture in the fifth-third millennia BCE in this region (Fortin & Aurenche 1998).

The results from many of these projects have been closely integrated in regional conferences, workshops, and major chronological and environmental research projects and frameworks, such as ARCANE (http://www.arcane.uni-tuebingen.de), and extensively published. Some sites have been conserved and presented for public display and dissemination in situ, within museums and on websites.

Relevant information may be found in EGA under Aerial and Satellite Remote Sensing in Archaeology; Aerial Archaeology; Çatalhöyük Archaeological Site; Surface Survey: Method and Strategies.

Chapter 25
Terp Excavation in the Netherlands

Johan A.W. Nicolay

Before the first sea dykes were constructed in the twelfth or thirteenth century CE, the coastal area of the Northern Netherlands was dominated by extensive salt-marsh. Habitation in this unstable maritime landscape was concentrated on relatively high ridges, often along tidal gullies. Because such ridges were still subject to flooding several times a year, people had constructed artificial dwelling mounds or *terps* (in Dutch: *terpen* or *wierden*) from the first colonization of the salt-marsh area in seventh century BCE. They started with one or more small house platforms, which were gradually raised and extended with layers of sods, dung, and trash. The present-day terps, often still clearly visible in the flat landscape, represent the final phase of their development. Although being constructed for a different reason and in a different landscape, terps can be compared to *tells* in the Eastern Mediterranean, also comprising many overlapping habitation layers that may cover a period of several thousand of years at the same site.

The current method of excavating terps was largely developed during a research project at the site of Wijnaldum-"Tjitsma," in the northwestern part of Friesland (Besteman et al. 1999). Following the discovery of an 17 cm long, gold disc-on-bow brooch (c. CE 600), the universities of Groningen and Amsterdam joined forces to get a better understanding of the archaeological context of this exceptional, probably royal find. Between 1991 and 1993, a total of 8,000 m^2 was excavated, 7 % of the terp's total volume. This project pioneered a new strategy, which involved *stripping* with a mechanical excavator, the systematic use of a *metal detector* (resulting in the unprecedented number of c. 5,000 metal finds), and *wet screening* (e.g., resulting in the discovery of gold drops, sherds of glass vessels, and numerous fish-bones).

J.A.W. Nicolay (✉)
University of Groningen, Groningen, The Netherlands
e-mail: j.a.w.nicolay@rug.nl

M. Carver et al. (eds.), *Field Archaeology from Around the World*,
SpringerBriefs in Archaeology, DOI 10.1007/978-3-319-09819-7_25

Fig. 25.1 Excavating a horizontal level at the terp site of Wijnaldum-"Tjitsma" (Friesland): After the top soil is removed with a mechanical digger, the archaeological level is cleaned using a flat shovel, revealing the outlines of features cut into the clayey soil. Today, precision machining with a grading bucket may leave a surface clean enough to excavate (Photo: University of Groningen, Groningen Institute of Archaeology)

A cross of two areas was opened, measuring 210×76 m. The top soil was removed by a mechanical excavator in layers of 5 cm or less at a time and the surface checked for metal finds with a detector. The first archaeological horizon generally appeared at a depth of 40–60 cm below the present ground surface, whereupon it was cleaned by hand, drawn, and photographed (Fig. 25.1). All *negative features* and *sod-walls* were *sectioned* and documented, and the soil from all features was wet screened with a mesh width of 4 mm. Organic- or find-rich features were also sampled for zoological and botanical remains. This process was repeated at the next level, which was usually 20–25 cm below the previous one. Locations of exceptional finds, like sherds concentrations or human and animal skeletons, were examined in greater detail.

Some reflections on this methodology suggest future developments. The recording of the site using the *planum method* has the disadvantage of disconnecting finds and features belonging to the same cultural layer and disconnecting the horizontal horizons and the vertical sections, since these are recorded separately. The Wijnaldum experience showed that such links can only partly be made afterwards, even by using three-dimensional reconstructions of digitized drawings. Ideally, the original surface of the cultural layers should be excavated, and recorded in three dimensions.

Fig. 25.2 Recording a "free section" at Anjum (Friesland). Interfaces between layers are outlined on the surface of the cleaned section and labeled, before being recorded with written descriptions, measured drawings, and photographs. Objects disturbed or located by metal detector are assigned to their layer of origin. The stratified sequence seen in section provides a basic narrative for the occupation of the terp (Photo: University of Groningen, Groningen Institute of Archaeology)

In practice, large-scale terp excavations have already become too time-consuming and too expensive to encourage the extra burden of stratigraphic excavation.

One new research method that is economic and effective makes use of existing sections already cut through known terp sites. Between 1840 and 1945, about two-thirds of all terp sites in the Northern Netherlands were completely or partly dug away, to be sold as humus to enrich the sand and peat soils in the hinterland. These sites can be investigated by cleaning the escarpment of the surviving intact mound (Fig. 25.2). In this way sections of 100–200 m long and 3–4 m high can be studied in only 4–5 weeks without eroding the remaining terp. Added to the results of "traditional" excavations, these *free sections* give valuable insights into the structure, chronology, and conservation of terp sites in different parts of the Northern Netherlands (see Nicolay 2010).

More information will be found EGA under Adaptation in Archaeology; Human Impacts on Ancient Marine Ecosystems; Maritime Landscapes.

Chapter 26
A Terramare Site on the Po Plain in Italy

Mauro Cremaschi

The "Terramare" are banked and moated villages dating to the Middle and Recent Bronze ages (1600–1150 year BCE), located in the alluvial plain of the Po river, northern Italy. They are witness to a complex society, whose subsistence was based on intensive agriculture, pastoralism, and long-range trade (Barfield 1994). The Terramare people first carried out a radical clearing of the Po plain to provide land for intensive agriculture, and changed the natural drainage by digging canals and ditches to feed moats surrounding the villages and to irrigate the fields in the countryside (Cremaschi et al. 2006). The culture reached its apogee, along with a prolific population, at the beginning of the Recent Bronze age, but at the end of this period suffered a societal collapse that led to the abandonment of the villages in a few generations (Cardarelli 2010).

The Terramare have been a major subject of research by the Italian pioneers of prehistoric archaeology (Pearce 1998), but had been neglected for at least 60 years, and were thought to be almost destroyed by quarrying for soil during the nineteenth century. But at the beginning of the 1970s, geomorphological mapping of the Po plain, using aerial photography, demonstrated that the Terramare had largely survived quarrying. From that period onward, several projects have marked a new stage in their study (Bernabò Brea et al. 1997).

In the framework of this renewed interest, the archaeological excavation of Santa Rosa took on the task of extensively exploring a Terramara village, with the explicit aim of shedding light on its architectural structures and its development over the 400 years that the village lasted. The Santa Rosa site was selected by virtue of its good state of preservation and because it was threatened with destruction by

M. Cremaschi (✉)
Dipartimento di Scienze della Terra 'A. Desio', Università degli Studi di Milano,
via Mangiagalli 34, Milan 20133, Italy
e-mail: mauro.cremaschi@unimi.it

M. Carver et al. (eds.), *Field Archaeology from Around the World*,
SpringerBriefs in Archaeology, DOI 10.1007/978-3-319-09819-7_26

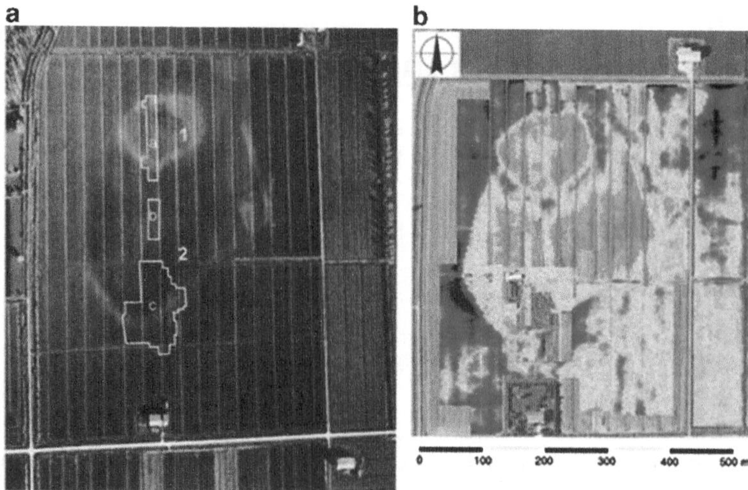

Fig. 26.1 The Terramara Santa Rosa as seen on the aerial photograph (*left*) and on the basis of near-surface geophysical prospection (*right*). Aerial photograph: *1* small village, *2* large village. *Yellow lines* delimitate the areas excavated up to now: *a* area in the small village 1984–1992; *b* area between the two villages 2008–2011; *c* area in the large village and in the moat 1993–2011. Geophysical prospection: *blue colors* indicate conductive media (*clayey deposits*) indicating moat ditches and flood deposits surrounding the site; *yellowish/reddish* colors indicate resistive media (*sandy-silty deposits*) putting in evidence the Terramara shape (Mele et al. 2011)

agricultural work. The site was defined by aerial photography, which revealed its limits in outline (Fig. 26.1 left). Subsequent geophysical survey showed up areas of high and low conductivity, indicating areas dominated by wet and dry features (color coded on Fig. 26.1, right). The interpretation is of two settlements, each surrounded by clay ramparts and moats.

Excavation has been carried out under the aegis of the SoprintendenzaaiBeniArcheologici of Emilia Romagna and the local authority, and performed by a professional team, which also trains archaeology students for the principal research institution (University of Milan). The aims of the excavation are to map the detailed occupation of the larger (7 ha) settlement and explore the relationship between the two. The first 28 seasons have opened an area of 1 ha, revealing the defenses, post-rows of buildings, and numerous wells (Bernabò Brea and Cremaschi 2004; Fig. 26.2). The excavation period is limited to the summer season; during the winter/spring seasons, the water tables rise very close to the ground surface, make digging difficult (Fig. 26.3).

The original settlement was built at the edge of the Po river during the Middle Bronze Age, and consisted of a group of rectangular houses on piles protected by a timber palisade. At the beginning of the Later Bronze age, the Terramara reached its maximum expansion with the construction of the large village. Inside it, the houses were still on piles, but arranged along specific alignments and organized into quarters bounded by roads going through the village and crossing the surrounding moat over

Fig. 26.2 The area excavated in the large village. The buildings, indicated by clusters of post *holes*, are delimited by peripheral moat. Note the high concentration of *circular wells*

wooden bridges thereupon reaching the countryside (Cremaschi and Pizzi 2011). At the end of the Late Bronze Age, the village underwent a radical renovation: the houses were no longer built on piles, but rested on the ground according to the block-house technique. The peripheral wooden fences were replaced by massive earth ramparts.

The region in which the Terramare previously flourished was abandoned for at least five centuries. The Santa Rosa village area became a mound, covered with forest and surrounded by marshes which colonized the former ditches. It was settled again only in the sixth century BCE by Etruscan colonists.

Fig. 26.3 Archaeologists at work in the course of a field season in the Terramara Poviglio Santa Rosa

Chapter 27
Hillfort Investigations in the Czech Republic

Roman Křivánek

The *hillfort* is one of Europe's best known types of pre- and protohistoric monument. Those found in the Czech Republic range in date over the Neolithic, Eneolithic, Bronze Age, Iron Age, Roman, and early medieval periods. Many of these sites have long been familiar in the landscape, but more have been identified or studied during various archaeological survey projects (e.g., Gojda et al. 2004; Křivánek 2004). They vary in size from 0.1–0.5 ha to 100–200 ha. They offer important information on the key roles they performed in each period: military bases, settlement, industry, trade, communications, agriculture, burial, cult, or other activities.

The traditional method of investigating hillforts was the excavated trench, and in this country attention was focused on Slavic and Celtic fortified sites. The new approach places the emphasis on *remote mapping*, making particular use of *aerial survey*, *geophysical survey*, and *surface collection. Geochemical mapping* and *metal detector* surveys have also been used in particular situations. The purpose is to obtain the maximum amount of information about the structure and date range of the site using nondestructive methods, before applying targeted excavation for the solution of particular historical problems. Some examples follow.

The prehistoric hillfort near Zlončice (district Mělník) was first identified from surface collections by an amateur regional archaeologist. Enclosure systems of 12–13 ha on a promontory by the Vltava river confirmed later results of geophysical prospection (Fig. 27.1a). A *magnetometric survey* subsequently revealed an intense level of occupation in the form of numerous pits and seven boundary ditches (Fig. 27.1b). Surface collection of artifacts suggested a Neolithic origin but with some later occupation (Křivánek 2011). Magnetometry also proved very effective at Libice (district Nymburk), an early medieval stronghold of 20 ha in a lowland

R. Křivánek (✉)
Institute of Archaeology of the Academy of Sciences of the Czech Republic,
Prague, Czech Republic
e-mail: krivanek@arup.cas.cz

M. Carver et al. (eds.), *Field Archaeology from Around the World*,
SpringerBriefs in Archaeology, DOI 10.1007/978-3-319-09819-7_27

Fig. 27.1 Zlončice, district Mělník. Combination of (**a**) vertical aerial photography (public web source www.mapy.cz) and (**b**) the result of magnetometric survey of prehistoric hillfort (terrain: plowed field and meadow; surveyed area: approx. 9.5 ha; magnetometric survey: Křivánek 2008–2010)

Fig. 27.2 Prague-Hostivař, district Prague 15. Comparison of old map (stable cadaster 1841, *upper left*), old site plan (Fillip 1949, *upper right*), and magnetometric survey of the Hallstatt hillfort (terrain: park; surveyed area: approx. 4.3 ha, magnetometric survey: Křivánek 2008, *below*)

area on a sand and gravel terrace on the flood plain of a meandering Jizera rives (Křivánek et al. 2009). The Hallstatt hillfort of Prague-Hostivař (district Prague 14) had more or less disappeared from view, but investigators made use of an early map and the cadastral boundary plan to locate the probable location of the fortified enclosure. The extent of occupation and the burnt out defenses were then located by magnetometry (Fig. 27.2).

The La Téne oppidum at Závist in cadaster Lhota (district Prague-west) represents a different type of large hillfort in the Czech landscape, on hilly terrain and now thickly wooded (Fig. 27.3a). This kind of terrain presents a challenge to

Fig. 27.3 Lhota, district Prague-west. Combination of (**a**) aerial documentation (photo by M. Gojda, Inst. of Archaeology, Prague) and (**b**) magnetometric survey of plateau Balda in central part of La Téne oppidum Závist (terrain: hilly forest; surveyed area: approx. 1.1 ha, magnetometric survey: Křivánek 2005)

conventional methods of aerial and geophysical survey. Even so magnetometry was able to map part of the site on the plateau of Balda (Fig. 27.3b), showing ordered settlement, a burnt rampart, and evidence for later plowing (see also *Lidar*, *radar* for other possible approaches, p. 20, p. 36).

The new research initiatives applied to the study of hillforts, both known and previously unknown, in every type of terrain, are providing a systematic basis for understanding their structure and use in different periods. This information leads to proposals for intensive investigation at particular sites for research purposes and at the same time provides an overall inventory to assist in the long-term protection of these cultural (or archaeological) monuments.

Relevant information in EGA may be found under Agrarian Landscapes: Environmental Archaeological Studies; Cultural Heritage Site Damage Assessment; Fortifications, Archaeology of; Heritage Landscapes; Landscape Archaeology; Prospection Methods in Archaeology.

Chapter 28
Excavating Burials in Anglo-Saxon England

Martin Carver

Human burials constitute a major source of evidence for human history. Burials excavated by archaeologists may report on both the individual commemorated and on society more broadly. Human remains may be encountered as burnt bone in containers or in pits (*cremations*), or as skeletons in graves (*inhumations*), or as mixed collections of bones, created by communal deposition (as in European Neolithic long barrows), or by reburial (*charnel*). The state of the remains (and their potential for further research) is dependent on the local terrain and consequent degree of decay (see Chap. 2; that associated with human remains is termed *taphonomy*). In general, acid soils (e.g., sands and gravels) attack bones, while more alkaline soils (chalk) tend to preserve them better. Anaerobic conditions (excluding air) can preserve the soft tissues. Thus *bog burials* (seen in the Scandinavian Iron Age) have preserved skin and inner organs and even the last meal of the deceased, but the acid solution of the bog has nevertheless dissolved the bone (Glob 1969).

The purpose of excavating cemeteries is to gain an insight into the population and thinking of an ancient community and generally involves two lines of inquiry: the study of the burial rites and the study of the skeletal material. The *burial rites* include the form of the grave, its orientation, and the disposition and character of the objects placed in the grave – the *grave goods*. In burial rites, variations in space imply different ranks or families; variations through time may relate to changes in religious or political thinking. *Skeletal material* reveals evidence for basic demography through a study of anatomy: This gives age at death, sex, major diseases, and injuries. The carbon contained in the collagen in the bone (including cremated bone) can be extracted and *radiocarbon*-dated, using the proportions of carbon isotopes. Carbon and nitrogen isotopes present in the bone are also used to assess the emphasis of diet (it will show whether the diet of an individual had a strong or weak marine intake, i.e., fish). Oxygen and strontium isotopes trapped in teeth indicate

M. Carver (✉)
Department of Archaeology, University of York, York, UK
e-mail: martin.carver@york.ac.uk

M. Carver et al. (eds.), *Field Archaeology from Around the World*,
SpringerBriefs in Archaeology, DOI 10.1007/978-3-319-09819-7_28

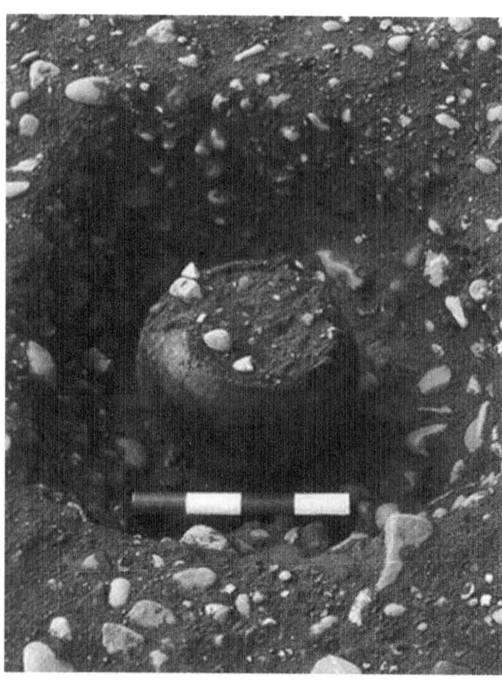

Fig. 28.1 A cremation urn in its pit at Spong Hill, Norfolk

the character of the groundwater where a person grew up. *Ancient DNA* (aDNA) can now be recognized in skeletal material.

The excavation of Anglo-Saxon burials (fifth to seventh century), used here as an example, has generated a notable range of techniques (Williams 2006; Carver 2009, pp. 131–138). The pits containing cremations are exposed on the surface by troweling, and the pot exposed and removed, intact wherever possible, for excavation indoors (Fig. 28.1). The contents of the pot are removed in very small spits to document the association of the fragments of burnt bone with each other and with the fragments of grave goods. The objective is to discover which humans, animals, and grave goods had originally been on the funeral pyre.

Inhumations accompanied by grave goods are commonly encountered in Anglo-Saxon cemeteries (Fig. 28.2). The graves are revealed on the surface by troweling, and the grave fill is then removed in 5- or 10-cm spits against the long axis: This will provide a profile through the grave. The skeleton and all the grave goods (e.g., sword, shield, brooch) are photographed and plotted individually on a grave plan (Fig. 28.3).

An example of a research project at an Anglo-Saxon cemetery is given by Sutton Hoo. A ship burial discovered by chance at the site in 1939 drew attention to its potential. The site was subjected to a 2-year evaluation in the 1980s, with a view to determining what had survived the effects of taphonomy, plowing, and treasure hunting, and a project design was then published. In addition to regional surveys, this design proposed the excavation of 1 ha of the 4 ha site, encompassing 5 of the 18 known burial mounds (and the spaces in between). Several of the mounds contained cremations, two had contained ships, and one contained a young man buried

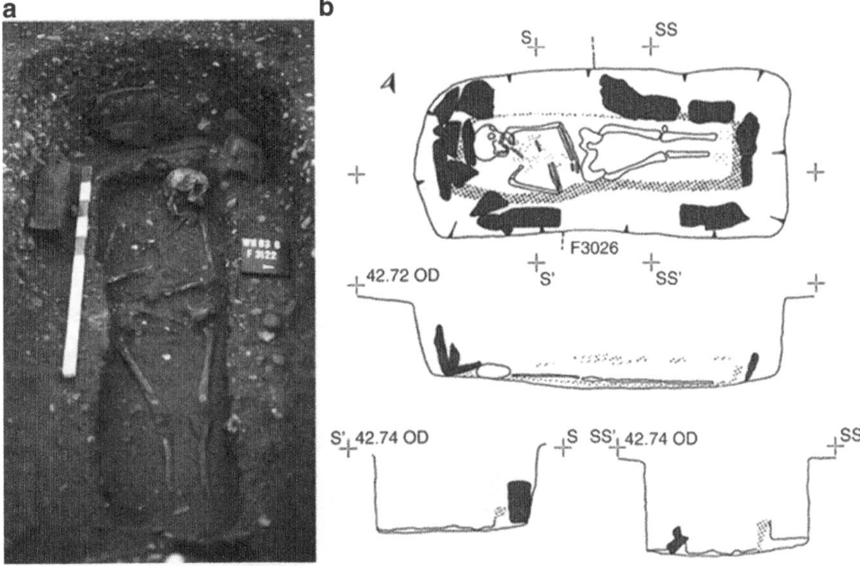

Fig. 28.2 An inhumation with typically poor bone preservation. The stones are part of the burial rite. (**a**) photograph; (**b**) plan and section

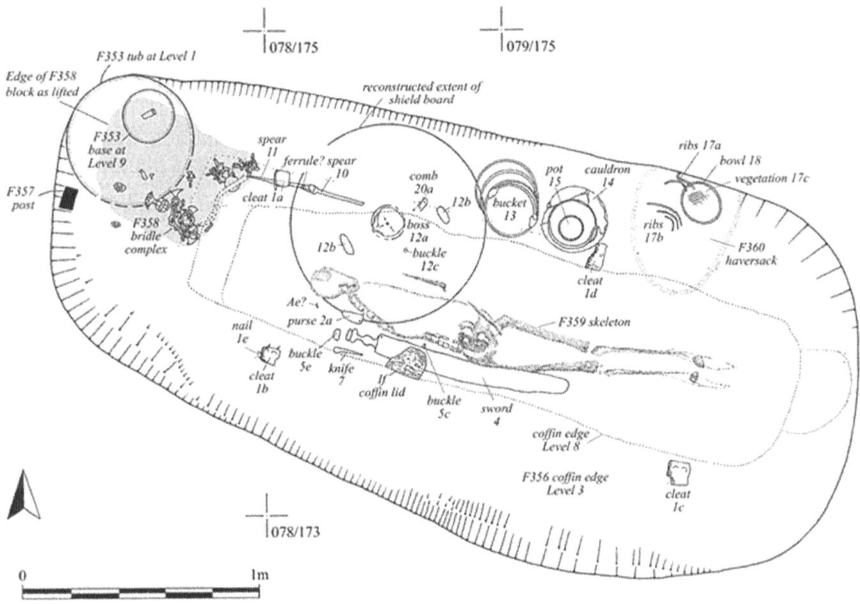

Fig. 28.3 Plan of a furnished inhumation (From Sutton Hoo, Mound 17)

in a coffin (Figs. 28.3 and 28.4). His horse was buried in a separate pit adjacent. In the later Saxon period (eight to eleventh century), this high-ranking pagan cemetery became a place of execution.

Fig. 28.4 The burial under Mound 17 being excavated from a cradle

The ground conditions at Sutton Hoo were hostile, and although fragments of bone were sometimes present, human bodies had decayed markedly in the acid sand, creating "sand fossils" rather than skeletons. The majority of burials, still marked by mounds, had been severely pillaged, scattering bone and objects. The medieval use of the mounds as rabbit warrens had further dispersed the burials.

Nevertheless, the horse and rider burial was undisturbed and could be excavated in precise detail. The execution burials (sand fossils) proved susceptible to excavation in three dimensions, and their shapes were sufficient to show examples that had been killed by hanging or beheading (Fig. 28.5). The chamber in a pillaged mound, Mound 2, was surveyed by intensive chemical mapping, which showed the location of the now vanished body, a copper alloy cauldron, and other grave goods (Fig. 28.6). In spite of the evident battering the cemetery has suffered through the ages, there was sufficient bone to radiocarbon-date the whole sequence, from 580 to 1050, and align it with the typological dates of the rich grave goods from the famous ship burial.

Fig. 28.5 A 'sandman' burial' where the form of the body is preserved (but less so the bone)

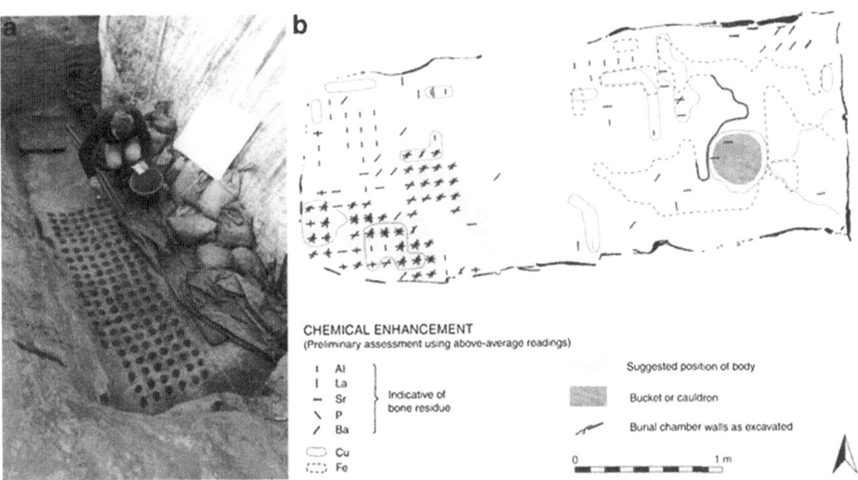

Fig. 28.6 Chemical mapping of the floor of a robbed chamber

More information relevant to this section with be found in EGA under Chemical Survey of Archaeological Sites, Bioarchaeology; Human skeletal remains; Pathological conditions; Taphonomy.

Chapter 29
A Burial Mound Dissection in Sweden

Per H. Ramqvist

In 1949, it was decided to excavate the first of the four Migration Period large mounds in Högom at a cemetery a few kilometers west of Sundsvall in the county of Medelpad, North Sweden. Concentrations of large mounds (>20 m in diameter) in Scandinavia are known at Old Uppsala in Uppland, Bertnem in Trøndelag, and Borre and Snartemo. Often arranged in rows, these are high status burials representing generations of regional leadership. The four mounds in Högom ("mounds") Medelpad north Sweden clearly belonged to this exclusive group. When investigations began in 1949, the site had been largely forgotten and was encumbered by houses, barns and cellars, driveways and threshing places. The National Heritage Board decided to purchase the area, remove the buildings, and restore a cultural landscape around the cemetery. But before restoration, it was decided to investigate the most damaged of the burial mounds (No. 2). The project was one of exceptional innovation.

The mound was 40-m across and at least 4-m high, and in accordance with the excavation methods of the late 1940s, it was initially investigated with a trench. This was placed on the NE side of the mound on the site of a demolished building. Beneath the topsoil, the excavators encountered a cairn, the surface of which was then exposed stone by stone (Fig. 29.1). It proved to be 20 m across, and seen from a tower was clearly no random heap, but the stones had been deliberately sorted by size. To record this information, the whole cairn was carefully planned, stone by stone.

While the stones were being removed, it became apparent that there was a central burial chamber measuring 5×2 m in plan that had been constructed in timber. It had been compressed by the weight of the mound into a compact layer 10-cm thick containing all the wood, the body, and the objects, some of which showed through the matt surface of the compressed wooden roof (Fig. 29.2). Attempts to excavate the chamber

P.H. Ramqvist (✉)
Department of Historical, Philosophical and Religious Studies, Umeå University, Umeå, Sweden
e-mail: per.ramqvist@arke.umu.se

M. Carver et al. (eds.), *Field Archaeology from Around the World*, SpringerBriefs in Archaeology, DOI 10.1007/978-3-319-09819-7_29

Fig. 29.1 Dagmar Selling, excavator (with Sverker Janson) of Högom Mound 2, working on the central cairn (Ramqvist 1992, Fig. 17a)

Fig. 29.2 Metal buttons on the leggings of the buried person showing in the compressed timber roof of the chamber (Ramqvist 1992, Fig. 24)

Fig. 29.3 Metal plates being driven beneath the chamber with jacks (Ramqvist 1992, Fig. 25)

in situ were frustrated by the hardness of the wooden layer; more forceful digging threatened to destroy the objects.

Inspired by the successful lifting of a whale jawbone during the excavation of a Stone Age settlement in Bohuslän (western Sweden) in 1935, it was decided to try and lift the whole chamber in order to excavate it in the laboratory. This much more challenging project was achieved by engineers from the construction firm, Hallström & Nisses of Sundsvall. To provide access, a wide and deep trench was dug around the chamber, making an archaeological record of the layers disturbed. The chamber proved to be resting on silty deposits without a wooden floor. The engineers then built a wooden box around the chamber and drove steel pipes beneath it, with horizontal steel plates jacked into position above them to create a base for the chamber deposit (Fig. 29.3). The wooden box was infilled with plaster to prevent movement of the deposit and the whole encased in a steel frame. It was then lifted and transported to the National Historical Museum in Stockholm.

When unloading the box in Stockholm (Fig. 29.4), it was turned completely upside-down, so that the continuing investigation could take place "from below," with the impenetrable roof now as the base. Before excavation in the laboratory, the entire deposit was X-rayed, producing a set of plates at 1:1 which proved to be an invaluable guide to the indoor excavators (Fig. 29.5). The burial was excavated

Fig. 29.4 The encased burial chamber is unloaded outside the laboratory in Stockholm

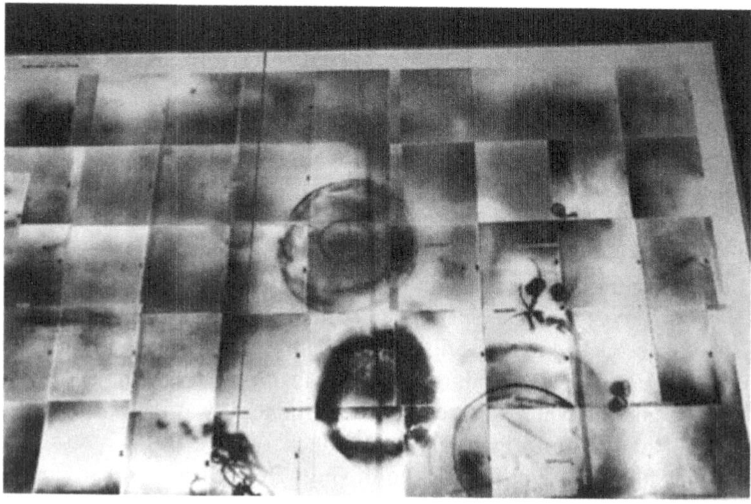

Fig. 29.5 The set of X-ray plates from the eastern part of the chamber showing the bridle and cauldron in position in the laboratory (Ramqvist 1992, Fig. 28b)

in minute detail. Dating to c. 500 CE, it is known as one of the richest and best excavated in the Baltic area.

In 1984, the site was surveyed in detail and the previously unexcavated perimeter around the cairn was examined, revealing large postholes of a building erected before the mound, probably a three-aisled long house. The whole site was eventually published by Ramqvist (1992).

Relevant entries in EGA are Scandinavia/Northern Europe: Historical Archaeology; Trade and Transport in the Ancient Mediterranean.

Chapter 30
Down a Mine at Gavà, Spain

Josep Bosch

Gavà, a village by the sea at the mouth of the Llobregat river in the northeast Iberian Peninsula, is the site of the only known Neolithic mine in Europe extracting *variscite*. This green mineral, similar to turquoise, is found in Neolithic tombs; its color is probably linked symbolically with the regeneration of life. At Gavà it occurs as seams of slate within layers of limestone and dolomite or sealed under clay where it outcrops. The prehistoric miners followed the seams, digging shafts leading to tunnels between 5 and 10 m long and about 2.5 m wide. These later expanded into more complex galleries with chambers, reaching depths of 30 m and more. In general the prehistoric mining cavities had been backfilled with extraction debris, including broken mining tools (stone picks and bone wedges); this saved the labor of transporting it outside the mine. Some of the cavities were reused as graves in Neolithic times (Figs. 30.1 and 30.2).

The first task of archaeological investigation was to make the mining galleries safe. Shoring with metal frames and concrete, as in modern mining, was unsuitable, as it would mask the surface of the rock, where prehistoric tool marks are still visible. Instead, metal anchors are placed on the rock with a resin coating that protects and secures the surface. Cracks and fissures are also filled with resin. The rock surface is impregnated with a product that allows moisture to escape. Humidity and the flow of water inside the mines are controlled with high precision, and warning instruments monitor the stability of the rock.

Excavation to date has focused on the deposits inside the mine. A full stratigraphic record of the strata in the galleries, chambers, and minor cavities is being made, both to define any features such as the graves and to investigate the patterns of extraction and discard noted in the debris. The assemblage includes different kinds of lithics, ceramics, and animal bones. Systematic screening maximizes

J. Bosch (✉)
Gavà Museum, Barcelona, Spain
e-mail: jbosch@gava.cat

M. Carver et al. (eds.), *Field Archaeology from Around the World*,
SpringerBriefs in Archaeology, DOI 10.1007/978-3-319-09819-7_30

Fig. 30.1 The drawing process (Museu de Gavà, Josep Bosch)

Fig. 30.2 Restoration of one of the mines (Museu de Gavà, Benet Solina)

recovery and has allowed the find of a variscite necklace. The date of the mining, from radiocarbon, is between 4100 and 3400 cal. BCE.

After nearly four decades since its discovery, a sizable, but unknown, proportion of the mine has been examined. The mine was declared a site of National Cultural Interest in 1996, and there is a plan to open it to the public once safe access and robust conservation measures are in place (see Parc Arqueologic Mines de Gava n.d.).

Relevant entries in EGA may be found under Conservation and Management of Archaeological Sites; Conservation and Preservation in Archaeology in the Twenty-First Century; Cultural Heritage and the Public; Europe: Mesolithic-Neolithic Transition; Excavation Methods in Archaeology; Field Method in Archaeology: Overview; "Public" and Archaeology; Spain: Archaeological Heritage Management; Western Europe: Historical Archaeology.

Chapter 31
Urban Archaeology at Five Points, New York City

Rebecca Yamin

The construction of a new federal courthouse at Foley Square in Lower Manhattan, New York City, by the General Services Administration (GSA) required a cultural resources investigation as stipulated in Section 106 of the National Historic Preservation Act (amended). The proposed location of the courthouse was on a block that was once part of the infamous Five Points, a neighborhood known as New York City's most notorious, nineteenth-century slum. Historical research conducted by Historic Conservation and Interpretation (HCI), Inc. a New Jersey firm headed by the late Ed Rutsch recommended archaeological testing and excavation before construction of the building began. HCI's report, which was done under contract to Edwards and Kelsey, the engineers for the project, made it clear that any intact remains of the Five Points had the potential to provide a less biased picture of life in the neighborhood than the picture drawn by the yellow journalism of the day.

Before the project began, the site was being used as a parking lot. As is often the case in large cities in the United States, the only open land available for new development is open because buildings that once stood there have been taken down in order to create space for parking. The Courthouse Block was once lined with tenements that faced four streets: Pearl, Park, Chatham, and Baxter. The name, Five Points, derived from the intersection of two of those streets – Baxter and Park – with Worth Street, thus creating five points that emptied into an open area. A lithograph of that open area, dating to 1855, has become the iconic image of Five Points (Fig. 31.1) and was, in great part, the basis for the set of Martin Scorsese's, *Gangs of New York* (2002), a movie based on a book of the same name, published in 1927.

R. Yamin (✉)
John Milner Associates, Inc, West Chester, PA, USA
e-mail: rwyamin@verizon.net

M. Carver et al. (eds.), *Field Archaeology from Around the World*, SpringerBriefs in Archaeology, DOI 10.1007/978-3-319-09819-7_31

Fig. 31.1 Lithograph of Five Points in 1855 (New York State census) (Image: Valentine's Manual, 1855)

A *project design* provided the program for the documentary research, survey, and excavation of the site, and its analysis and publication. When the tenements were taken down in the 1960s, their foundations including basements were left in place and covered with about 10 ft of fill. The site area included 14 historic lots, and excavation began with the mechanical removal of the fill that covered the basement walls and former backyard areas on those lots. Once exposed, the building outlines were compared to a series of fire insurance maps that showed the changing configuration of each lot over time. In addition to the configuration of the structures, the maps, in this case by William Perris, include information on building material, use, and condition. The exposed walls were cleaned by hand (with shovels and trowels), and former backyard areas were cleared in order to locate structural features.

A total of 54 *features* were exposed including privies, cesspools, water closets, sumps, trash pits, at least one cistern, a possible ice pit, and a single bake oven. All were measured and mapped (Fig. 31.2), but only 22 were excavated. The sample included backyard features on lots facing all four street fronts. Features were generally bisected, one-half excavated *stratigraphically*, a profile drawn, and then the second-half was excavated. Catalog (context) numbers were assigned arbitrarily to each provenience (findspot, layer, or *context*) that was removed separately, and all artifacts were bagged by context. With a few exceptions, features were photographed and tied into one of 23 vertical datum points that were located throughout the site area. A few additional excavation units were used to sample the fill that had been deposited before the block was developed for residential use in the late eighteenth–early nineteenth century and to examine underlying strata that were believed to relate to the tanyards that were present on the block before that development.

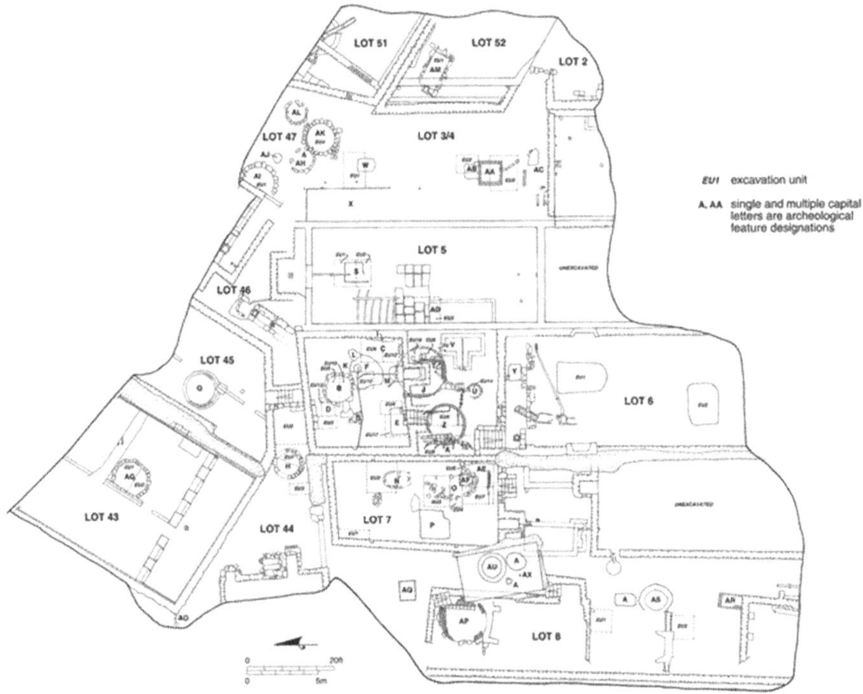

Fig. 31.2 Plan of excavated area

Stratification diagrams were used to model the sequence of contexts and features and deduce phases of occupation – analytical units or AU. Specialists in ceramics, glass, clay pipes, and other objects – together with architectural and faunal remains – used these tentative AUs as an initial guide to grouping artifacts. An effort was made to have all analysts working on, or at least beginning, features at the same time in order to maximize communication. AUs were refined based on cross-mending data, especially from the ceramics, and shared with other analysts. Terminus post quem dates (TPQs) were determined from each artifact category and compared to census and directory data which was being collected by a team of historians at the same time. Artifact and primary historical information were entered into a computerized database, which was available to everyone working on the project. Conservation of fragile materials was conducted in the same laboratory with the artifact analysis. Floral and parasitological analyses were conducted by consultants located elsewhere.

The collaborative approach to analysis provided a stimulating environment in which to consider the research questions posed in the research design and to generate new ones. Artifact analysts used their data, sometimes alone and sometimes in combination with other data, to address predefined general research areas: e.g., family and neighborhood life, work and industry, health and hygiene, the construction of the "slum," and working-class life. In addition to the resulting technical papers, the six-volume report includes a narrative history along with vignettes based on the archaeology, the primary documentary data, an illustrated compendium of smoking pipes, an artifact inventory, and a volume covering conservation (Yamin 2000).

Information relevant to this section will be found in EGA under Urban Dark Earth; Urban landscapes: environmental archaeology; Archaeology as Anthropology; Archival Research and Historical Archaeology; Urban Archaeology in Twenty-First Century Perspective.

Chapter 32
After the Earthquake at Bam, Iran: Archaeological and Social Investigations

Leila P. Yazdi, Omran Garazhian, and Maryam Dezhamkhooy

Bam is a desert city engaged in citrus and palm cultivation, whose residents dwelt in handmade mud-brick houses around an ancient citadel, which is a World Heritage Site (UNESCO 2005). It is located in the southern border of the Lut desert, in south-eastern Iran. Despite this fringe location, it has traditionally served as a center for local trade. On the 26 December 2003, the city was reduced to ruins by an earthquake in only 12 s. Approximately 40,000 people died, 30,000 were injured (Tahmasebi et al. 2005), and 100,000 people made homeless (Mann 2005, p. 3). *Disaster ethnoarchaeology: Bam after the earthquake* was an ethnoarchaeological project aimed at recording this dramatic change (Dezhamkhooy and Papoli 2010; Papoli 2010; Papoli et al. 2011) (Fig. 32.1).

The project, which took place in five seasons from 2004 to 2007, was conducted by 40 archaeologists, 24 women and 16 men, Ph.D. candidates, and M.A. and B.A. students, all familiar with the local and cultural context and supported by the previous directors of the *Bam research foundation*. In the first four seasons, data gathering was based on an *ethnoarchaeological approach*. In the last season (2007), six ruined houses of different status and district were investigated by archaeological excavation. The main mission of the project was to discover the impact of the catastrophe on the intimate lives of the residents. In addition, the project also sought to

L.P. Yazdi (✉)
Neyshabour University, Neyshabour, Iran

Freie Universität Berlin, Berlin, Germany
e-mail: papoli@gmail.com

O. Garazhian
Department of Archaeology, Tehran University, Tehran, Iran
e-mail: papoli@gmail.com

M. Dezhamkhooy
University of Birjand, Birjand, Iran
e-mail: papoli@gmail.com

M. Carver et al. (eds.), *Field Archaeology from Around the World*, SpringerBriefs in Archaeology, DOI 10.1007/978-3-319-09819-7_32

Fig. 32.1 Bam citadel after earthquake

understand from the strata how the settlement had previously been affected by Bam's inhospitable and unstable environment – drought, winds, and frequent earthquakes (see Mahalati 1988).

The lifeways of Bam and its immediate environment were surveyed in five categories: mortuary practices, material culture, population mobility, trade and market patterns, and domestic architecture. Data were gathered through observation and by questionnaires designed to record patterns of life before the earthquake. The recorded changes to everyday life were studied over the short, medium, and long term. Also recorded were accounts of the gradual return to normal conditions.

Recording damaged buildings was a key part of the archaeological inquiry. Bam's domestic architecture was first divided into three general architectural styles: modern (structures built on metal frames), semi-modern (plaster and clay mortar on metal frames), and traditional (made of mud brick). Six hundred and seventy-three houses and 383 destroyed shops (Fig. 32.2) were evaluated during the first three seasons. These buildings were classified by their degree of damage: destruction of decorations, destruction of walls and roofs, or total destruction. The state of the buildings was compared with the socioeconomic status of the occupants, by district. For example, it was shown that most casualties occurred in the traditional type of housing, most vulnerable to earthquake and occupied by the least wealthy.

The excavations of the six houses (Fig. 32.3) showed that most of them had already been searched to discover the remains of the dead and to remove valuable materials. Most of the furniture remained. Divisions recorded within the houses led to information about the use of space and the implied spatial imperatives of gender, class, and wealth. People of higher status had more private spaces such as bedrooms

Fig. 32.2 Buildings for recording (shops)

Fig. 32.3 A store room of the Hafezabadi House under excavation Trench 1

or divided spaces based on gender and age, while the less wealthy had more common spaces, such as one bedroom for all the family. Differences in status were evident in other material culture too. The last moments of the six families were reconstructed from the disposition of the surviving cultural material.

There were interesting differences between the archaeological findings and the statements made on the questionnaires, no doubt through a reluctance to admit to activities of which authorities may have disapproved – such as sexual practices, drinking, or even watching some satellite channels. The earthquake and the subsequent archaeological excavations opened up private spaces such as bedrooms, revealing intimacies of everyday life, love letters, and personal entertainment tools.

Since the investigators were themselves indigenous, their relations with Bam residents developed naturally. But the feelings of the archaeologists were nevertheless strongly affected by the roles they were obliged to adopt. International and national aid initiatives rapidly altered the circumstances, the attitudes, and the decisions of residents. In addition, the changing policies of the Iranian government were determinant, eventually bringing the project to an end.

More information will be found EGA under Cultural Heritage Site Damage Assessment; Disaster Response Planning: Earthquakes.

Chapter 33
Ethnoarchaeology in the Field: Learning from Potters in Gilund

Amrita Sarkar

Ethnoarchaeology is an ever-expanding subdiscipline within archaeology, and pottery undoubtedly gets more than its fair share of attention. But with recent social and economic trends, it can be seen that opportunities of undertaking certain kinds of ethnoarchaeological study are themselves diminishing. By an interesting coincidence, the village of Gilund in Rajasthan, NW India, was host to an important early third millennium BCE, Chalcolithic settlement of Ahar-Banas Complex (Sankalia et al. 1969; Kramer 1997; Shinde 2002; Shinde and Possehl 2005), and at the same time to some of the last indigenous potters still working in the twenty-first century CE (Saraswati and Behura 1966). The modern village of Gilund is located approximately 1.5 km from the archaeological site of Gilund, northeast of the modern village. The potters are locally called *Kumhar*. According to the potters and their family members, use of earthenware or ceramic vessels is no longer profitable because of modernization and the popularity of stainless steel vessels. None of their children have taken up this tradition, which is therefore likely to disappear with the present generation of adults. These potters will be the last to practice, and in this respect ethnoarchaeology is itself under threat (Fig. 33.1).

All the potters in Gilund obtain clay from the same source, named Soniana, which lies approximately 8 km to the northwest of the village. On rare occasions, usually for emergency purposes when demand is higher than expected, the potters get clay from a location much closer to the village named *taknivali nadi*. In this case, the clay is transported to their homes by donkey which is owned by them. Pottery produced in Gilund is customarily ornamented with red and white pigment. The red pigment locally called *harmachh* and the white pigment locally called *Khadi* are brought from a market in Gangapur, which is approximately 25 km from Gilund. The potters purchase 1 year's worth of pigment at a time.

A. Sarkar (✉)
Department of Archaeology, Deccan College Postgraduate & Research Institute, Deemed University, Pune 411006, India
e-mail: amritjoy@gmail.com

M. Carver et al. (eds.), *Field Archaeology from Around the World*, SpringerBriefs in Archaeology, DOI 10.1007/978-3-319-09819-7_33

Fig. 33.1 Women carrying both earthen ware vessels and steel vessels during a marriage ceremony in Gilund village (Sarkar 2011)

Potters in Gilund usually prepare their clay 2–3 h before they plan to make vessels. The raw clay is first pounded to reach to a finer consistency and then sometimes sieved in order to remove large impurities. Water is then added to the crushed clay and wedged until it has a sticky yet elastic consistency. Some potters add ash or dried donkey dung to their clay as tempering material. After a vessel is shaped on the wheel and dried to leather-hard condition, it is then carefully beaten to achieve the required shape by using a marble dabber – *pindi* in the local Mewari dialect – and the other implement used is a wooden tool called *thapa,* which looks like a table tennis bat.

After the vessel is made on the wheel and then beaten to its required shape, the outer surface is rolled in ash, locally called *bani.* Once dried in the sun, the vessel is then dipped into a liquid of dissolved red pigment. The most common surface treatment is painting. The pots are painted in both geometric and naturalistic designs. These include straight and wavy lines, dots, and leaf and peacock designs. Most of the surface treatment and design is done by women of the family, both old and young, using a paint brush of donkey tail hair. Pots are open fired in fields close to the potters' houses or in the workshops themselves. Generally, cow dung, wood, and twigs are used as fuels.

The modern pottery of Gilund village (Sarkar 2011) can be classified into types used for storage, cooking and food processing, eating and drinking, ceremonial, and miscellaneous, following the typology designed by Dr Malti Nagar at Parla (Nagar 1967). *Storage and cooking vessels* include the *matka*, a big globular pot with broad mouth, round belly, and base. It is used for fetching water and for liquid storage, particularly for water and butter milk. *Matki* is a smaller version of the matka with the same function. *Pauni* is a *tawa* (slightly concave disk-shaped griddle) for making *chapatti* (flat bread made of whole wheat flour). A *Kelaria* is similar to a *pauni* but comparatively deeper. *Kala handi* or *munho* is narrow-mouthed carinated cooking pot mostly used for making butter milk. They are burnished on the outer surface. *Chuklio* and *nani chuklio* are small globular pots used for drinking water or transferring water from larger pot.

Ceremonial vessels include *dhupania* which are incense stands used in worship and in rituals. *Karva* are small globular spouted pots used by married Hindu women during *Karvachaut* (a festival celebrated by Hindu married women where they keep fast that ensures the well-being, prosperity, and longevity of their husbands). *Dela* is similar to *karva* without the spout and is used by the Hindus to proffer offerings in death rituals. A similar vessel is used by Muslims in the village to drink water. *Bijora*, *dhakno*, *dhakni*, and *dhankan* take the form of small goblets with narrow mouths and pointed bases. *Miscellaneous vessels* include the *gurga* – a stand. A handi-like vessel is made first; it is then separated along the line of carination. The upper part is used as stand for seating cooking vessels over chulhas, and the lower portion is used as tawa. A *galla* is a coin box, for collecting money. *Deepak* are lamps.

The prehistoric Chalcolithic people at Gilund seem to have used narrow-mouthed and wide-mouthed globular jars in coarse red ware and thick red slipped ware which are very similar to modern *matka* and *matki* (Mishra 2007, 2008). Similarly, the carinated wide-mouthed cooking vessels in gray ware recall present-day *handi* produced in Gilund Village (Fig. 33.2).

Another remarkable resemblance is found between the present-day *dhupania*, which are incense stands used in worship, with dishes-on-stands and bowls-on-stands retrieved from Ahar-Banas Complex sites (Sankalia et al. 1969) (Fig. 33.3).

Further striking similarity may be noted between a vessel from the Ahar excavation described as "crucible-like with slightly sloping sides, bulbous at the belly, rimless" to that of the vessel in which *lassi* (butter milk) is sold on trains in Rajasthan. There is even similarity in the painted decorations. Present-day potters in Gilund village use painted motifs such as groups of straight or wavy lines, dots, and hatched

Fig. 33.2 (*Left*) Chalcolithic, narrow-mouthed, globular pot in thick *red* slipped ware from Gilund; (*right*) modern day matka (Sarkar 2011)

Fig. 33.3 (*Left*) Modern day dhupania manufactured in Gilund village; (*right*) Chalcolithic bowl-on-stand reported from Ahar (Courtesy of Deccan College) (Sarkar 2011)

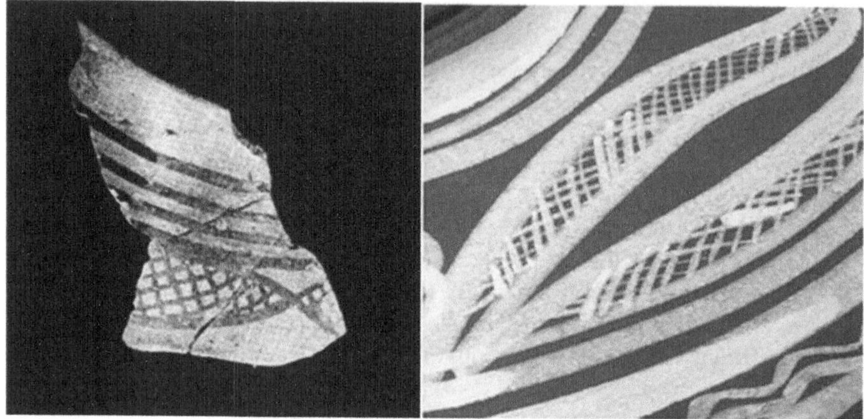

Fig. 33.4 (*Left*) Example of Chalcolithic painting on buff ware reported from Ahar; (*right*) similar painting executed on present-day pots in Gilund (Sarkar 2011)

diamonds, which parallel Chalcolithic buff ware and BRW's groups of straight or wavy lines, spirals, dots, hatched diamonds, concentric circles, and chevrons filled with dots and circles (Sankalia et al. 1969, pp. 88–98) (Fig. 33.4).

Thus, ethnographic data gathered from the present village potters of Gilund has been able to throw some light on the Chalcolithic pottery of Ahar-Banas Complex including likely methods of manufacture and the possible functions of certain ancient vessel forms. This shows that ethnographic data helps us in providing insights into the technology and behavior of prehistoric people.

More information will be found in EGA under Ethnoarchaeology; Ethnoarchaeology: Building Frames of Reference for Research.

Part III
Traditions

Chapter 34
America

David M. Carballo

The Americanist tradition of archaeology is defined by comparatively oriented research that draws heavily on an innovative tradition of regional-scale fieldwork (Willey and Sabloff 1980; Willey and Phillips 2001[1958]). Many early pioneers worked in multiple culture areas of the Americas, seeking direct connections between the archaeological record and living or historical indigenous peoples and fostering close ties with anthropology as a result. This brief outline covers seminal developments in stratigraphic excavation, regional survey, and other field methods within their historical and geographic context.

Stratigraphic excavation in the Americas began nearly two decades after its initial development in Europe, but then quickly became part of standard archaeological practice. The stratigraphy of the Emeryville Shellmound, near San Francisco, was explored by the German archaeologist Max Uhle in 1902 and by the American Nels Nelson in 1906 (Uhle 1907; Nelson 1909). The Mexican archaeologist Manuel Gamio, together with Franz Boas – his graduate advisor at Columbia University and generally acknowledged "father" of American Anthropology – initiated a chronological sequence for Central Mexico in 1911 (Gamio et al. 1921). This work involved ceramic collections at six sites surrounding Mexico City and Gamio's excavation of nearly 6 m of superimposed cultural layers at Azcapotzalco. Two years later, Nelson participated in stratigraphic excavations at the Paleolithic cave site Cueva de El Castillo, Spain, and returned to New Mexico convinced of the importance of the methodologies he learned there, which he then applied to Southwestern archaeology through his work in the Galisteo Basin (Nelson 1914). The pace of stratigraphic work in these culture areas accelerated rapidly and spread elsewhere. Direct successors within these two regions include George Vaillant's excavations of nine Central Mexican sites, while a curator at the American Museum

D.M. Carballo (✉)
Department of Archaeology, Boston University, Boston, MA, USA
e-mail: carballo@bu.ed

M. Carver et al. (eds.), *Field Archaeology from Around the World*,
SpringerBriefs in Archaeology, DOI 10.1007/978-3-319-09819-7_34

Fig. 34.1 WPA trowelmen at work, Thompson Village Site, Tennessee (Image courtesy of the McClung Museum of Natural History and Culture (62HY5[B]))

of Natural History, and Alfred Kidder's 15 years of investigations at Pecos Pueblo, sponsored by the Peabody Museum of Harvard University and of Phillips Academy (e.g., Kidder 1924; Vaillant 1937). Both projects were critical to establishing cultural sequences and served as benchmarks for future excavations in Mesoamerica and the Southwest.

Part of Franklin D. Roosevelt's New Deal put Americans back to work during the Great Depression by offering jobs as laborers on archaeological survey and excavation crews led by trained professionals (Lyon 1996; Fagette 2008). This boon to US archaeological research resulted in investigations in 36 states and included the widespread adoption of methods such as excavation by horizontal stripping, spraying sediments for better visibility of features and strata, plotting the post molds and pit features of perishable structures (Fig. 34.1), and the circulation of manuals on field and lab methods. New Deal archaeology also saw the professionalization of historical archaeology in the USA. Whereas earlier excavations had focused primarily on architectural restoration, J. C. Harrington's 1934–1941 investigations at Jamestown, Virginia, included excavations targeted especially at areas lacking architecture, in order to document the ditches and fence lines that defined property boundaries, and the collection of all artifacts with special attention to context (e.g., Harrington 1955).

Gordon Willey (Fig. 34.2 launched the field of regional archaeology (aka landscape archaeology) with his 1946 survey of Peru's Virú Valley while working for the Smithsonian Institutions' Bureau of American Ethnology (Willey 1953). Willey followed this project with over two decades of settlement research in Central America and Mesoamerica. His work transformed global archaeology by demonstrating that sites cannot be understood in isolation, nor should archaeologists focus exclusively on large or architecturally conspicuous sites; rather, sites must be viewed holistically, as parts of ecological and cultural landscapes.

Fig. 34.2 Gordon Willey at Tula, Mexico (Gordon Willey Slide Archive, courtesy of William L. Fash)

Field methods in the Virú Valley included the production of site maps from aerial photos, "ground truthing" these maps in the field using a compass and measuring chains, recording details of site setting and architecture, and plotting all sites on a valley map made by the geographer F. W. McBryde. In North America, Willey's long-time collaborator Philip Phillips developed a similar approach during his 1940–1947 survey of the Lower Mississippi Valley, undertaken with James Griffin and James Ford, the latter of whom worked with Willey in Virú (Phillips et al. 1951). The greater use of test pits in the Mississippi Valley reflects the differences in surface cover and visibility between the arid coast of Peru and temperate woodlands of the eastern USA. Full test pits or shovel test pits are much more common in surveys of densely vegetated regions of the Americas such as the Eastern Woodlands, Maya Lowlands, and Amazon Basin, compared to drier regions of western North America, and the highlands of Mesoamerica and the Andes.

The regionally oriented and stratigraphically deep research of Stuart Struever in the Lower Illinois Valley during the 1960s was highly influential for its use of multiscalar sampling strategies (within sites, ecozones, and regions) and of flotation as a means of recovering small ecofacts and artifacts (e.g., Struever 1968, 1971). Field sampling methods were further developed by projects such as the Chevelon Archaeological Research Project, directed by Fred Plog (1974); the New Survey of the Southwest Archaeological Expedition of the Field Museum (e.g., Hanson and Schiffer 1975); and the Prehistory and Human Ecology in the Valley of Oaxaca Project, directed by Kent Flannery (1976). These projects emphasized the importance of some element of randomness in the placement of test units in order to minimize biases based on initial assumptions of the patterning of subsurface remains and to derive statistically significant samples upon which to build social interpretations.

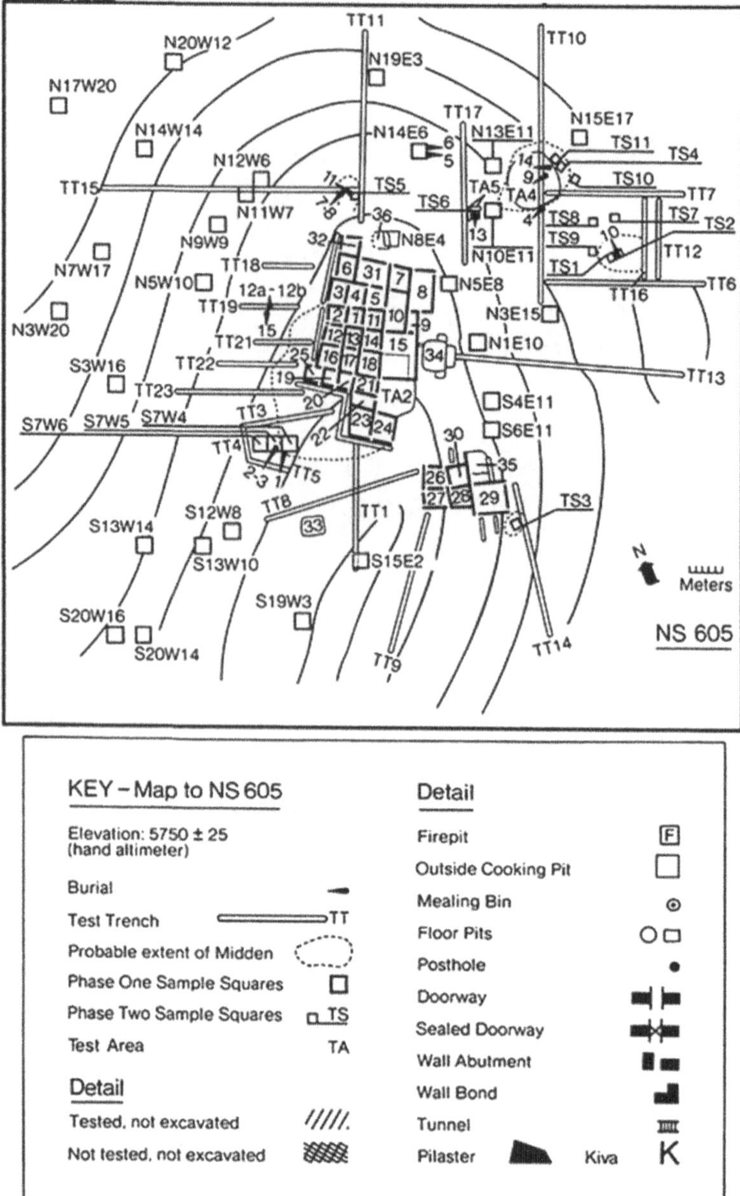

Fig. 34.3 Site sampling by *squares* and *trenches* at the Joint Site Pueblo, Arizona (Hanson and Schiffer 1975: Fig. 5) (Image courtesy of the Field Museum)

The choice of squares or trenches as sample units might be determined by the depth of deposits – as was done by Flannery and colleagues, who found trenches to be more efficient for deep sites in Oaxaca, thereby avoiding "telephone booth" style pits – or the strategies could be integrated at the same site, as was done by Hanson and Schiffer at the Joint Site Pueblo (Fig. 34.3).

The Americanist tradition of cross-cultural comparison drawing on regional archaeological datasets is exemplified by work such as Flannery's and by Robert McC. Adams's (1966) comparative study of urbanization in Mesopotamia and Mesoamerica. Building on this base of pioneering researchers, methods in American archaeology continue to develop, today increasingly incorporating new spatial technologies and material sciences in the field. This is not only true of archaeology sponsored by universities and museums but also of Cultural Resource Management (CRM), which is currently the public face of archaeology and largest employer of archaeologists in the USA.

More information will be found in EGA under Binford, Lewis R. (Theory); Cultural Heritage Management and Native Americans; Early Excavations Around the Globe; Flannery, Kent Vaughn; Gamio Martínez, Manuel; Historic Jamestowne; Indigenous Archaeologies: North American Perspective; Native American Graves Protection and Repatriation Act (NAGPRA), USA; Schiffer, Michael Brian (Theory); Society for American Archaeology (SAA); Surface Survey: Method and Strategies; US National Park Service and World Heritage; Uhle, Friedrich Max; Willey, Gordon Randolph.

Chapter 35
Poland

Przemysław Urbańczyk

In Poland, as elsewhere, excavations in the nineteenth century were conducted unsystematically and hastily, with the aim of acquiring interesting finds. Exceptional was Kalikst Jagmin's dig of 1873 at Łęgonice (central Poland) where a large barrow was sectioned along a W-E axis in order "…to uncover the very base of the mound and to expose a section which, showing the layout and quality of layers, would produce a visible proof of the manner in which this grave-mound was raised" (Jagmin 1876, p. 83). This isolated experiment produced one of the world's earliest examples of the relatively detailed observation and documentation of stratigraphy (Fig. 35.1). The first excavation manual published in Poland stressed that when digging multilayered mounds, "it is necessary to recognize… the height of every layer above ground level" (Majewski 1902, p. 195). Innovatory was Leon Kozłowski's method of excavating cemetery in Iwanowice by sequentially opening squares of 10×10 m (Kozlowski 1917, p. 2). Careful stratigraphic analysis is testified by multi-strata profiles of a cave site published by Stefan Krukowski (1921, pp. 3–5 and Figs. 3, 4).

In 1928 and 1930, Józef Kostrzewski explored a stronghold in Jedwabne with two small trenches. There he discerned nine layers which served to build the first relative chronology of medieval pottery (Kostrzewski 1931, p. 6, Fig. 2a, b). At Biskupin ca 3,000 m^2 were uncovered during the 1934 and 1935 seasons, and the five identified culture layers were defined using small tools only (Kostrzewski 1936, p. 11). Soil was sieved and overhead photography (from planes and balloons) was employed. Experimentally, finds from a limited surface were all recorded three dimensionally (Kostrzewski 1950, pp. 5, 12). In 1936–1937, another 3,400 m^2 were excavated using 10 cm thick arbitrary layers (spits) which were recorded on plans at

P. Urbańczyk (✉)
Institute of Archaeology and Ethnology, Polish Academy of Sciences, Warsaw, Poland
e-mail: uprzemek@iaepan.edu.pl

M. Carver et al. (eds.), *Field Archaeology from Around the World*,
SpringerBriefs in Archaeology, DOI 10.1007/978-3-319-09819-7_35

Fig. 35.1 A profile cut by Kalikst Jagmin in 1873 across a barrow in Łęgonice

1:10. on which all important finds were marked. A geologist analyzed 80 m of profiles (Kostrzewski 1938, pp. 4, 9, 69, 132–139, Tables LXIX and LXX). This promising development was halted in 1939.

The handful of archaeologists who survived the War were confronted with the practical and theoretical problems posed by vast areas that the war destruction suddenly "opened" for archaeological investigation. The theoretical dilemma and the rapid development of unusually sophisticated responses are recorded in the dialogue between the two innovative archaeologists Tadeusz R. Żurowski and Włodzimierz Hołubowicz. In 1947, Hołubowicz stated the principle that "during excavation there are no less or more valuable layers, they are all equally important" (Holubowicz 1947, p. 37). Digging and recording of a multilayer site must be based on a system of contiguous squares, so that "…it should be possible to reconstruct the system of layers with every item precisely localized…" (Holubowicz 1947, p. 34). Żurowski had already written down many of his ideas in 1939, but they were not to appear in print until after the war. He maintained that a "culture layer is also a monument of the past (*zabytek*), even when it does not contain any finds of the material culture" (Żurowski 1949). He emphasized that "naturally formed layers may be interlaced with culture layers" (Żurowski 1947, p. 138) and thus urged the sampling of "every cultural and geological layer" (Żurowski 1947, p. 140) in order "to execute detailed geological, palaeobotanical, palaeontological, anthropological and other analyses" (Żurowski 1947, p. 137). He also believed that "topography is best reflected by contour-lines," the principle of his "topographico-stratigraphic" method of excavating and recording that was to ensure "reconstruction of the configuration of the surface in the moment of starting the excavation and of the every lower layer in sequence – period after period backwards" (Żurowski 1947, p. 137). "This means that we will always be able to show three-dimensionally or by contour-lines a given surface in its shape before so and so many thousand years" and "from the layout of contour-lines we can cut sections in any directions and we can draw profiles" (Żurowski 1947, p. 138). If we note also that all finds must be recorded "according to precise instrumental measurements" (Żurowski 1947, p. 137) and that "the interrelation of characteristic points at a drawing must be precise enough to make possible, even after several years, to impose the same measurement system and to achieve the same results in an unquestionable way" (Żurowski 1947, p. 137), we can see that there was a powerful guide to excavation method.

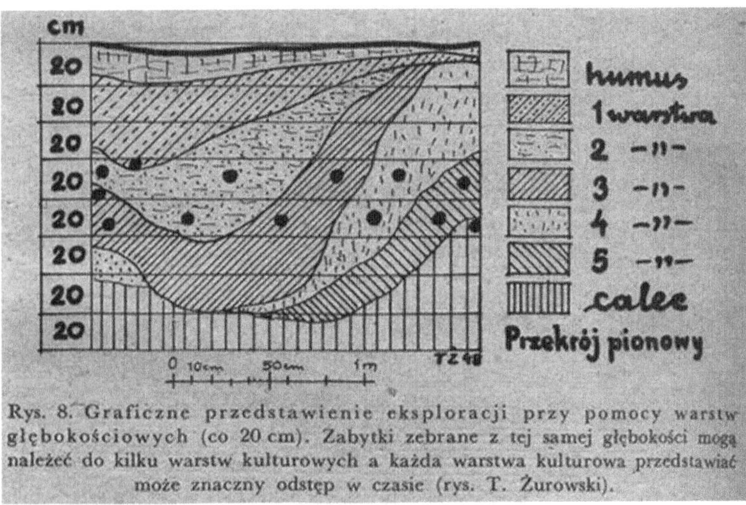

Fig. 35.2 Graphic presentation of the fallacy of the exploration of complex stratigraphy by arbitrary levels (Żurowski 1949, Fig. 8)

Hołubowicz in turn published an attack on the technique of "arbitrary levels" (spits) for exploring complex stratigraphic structures, which may be "...studied correctly only by defining cultural layers" (Holubowicz 1948, pp. 38, 40). Żurowski criticized Hołubowicz's zealotry but he made it clear that "exploration by arbitrary layers without discerning culture layers may lead to serious mistakes... because finds from very recent and very old culture layers may fall in the same arbitrary layer" (Żurowski 1949, p. 427). He illustrated this with clear drawings (Fig. 35.2) showing the fallacy of what he called "the most primitive method" (Żurowski 1949, p. 462). He argued that "all finds must be localised in relation to a culture layer and not an arbitrary layer" (Żurowski 1949, p. 458). Such an attitude imposed treatment of every part of a site with equal piety, reinforced by the fact that the site "usually undergoes total destruction" (Żurowski 1949, p. 413).

Unfortunately, this promising "brain storm" died out quickly because almost all Polish archaeological "manpower" became engaged in the extensive "millennial" program which preceded celebrations of the millennial anniversary of the origins of Polish state in 1966. Numerous medieval towns and strongholds were excavated (c. 25 large sites a year), and the results were studied by multidisciplinary teams of archaeologists, architects, ethnographers and historians, which was called the "history of material culture." There was simply no time for discussions that did not offer immediate solutions to daily problems. Polish archaeologists became again very "practical," which meant that effectiveness counted higher than methodological rigor. Methods of excavation and recording that seemed too sophisticated were openly questioned (e.g., Dembińska 1954, p. 97). Very few archaeologists tried to follow the standards that had been set during the postwar decade, and Poland's important contribution to excavation methodology remains largely obscure despite

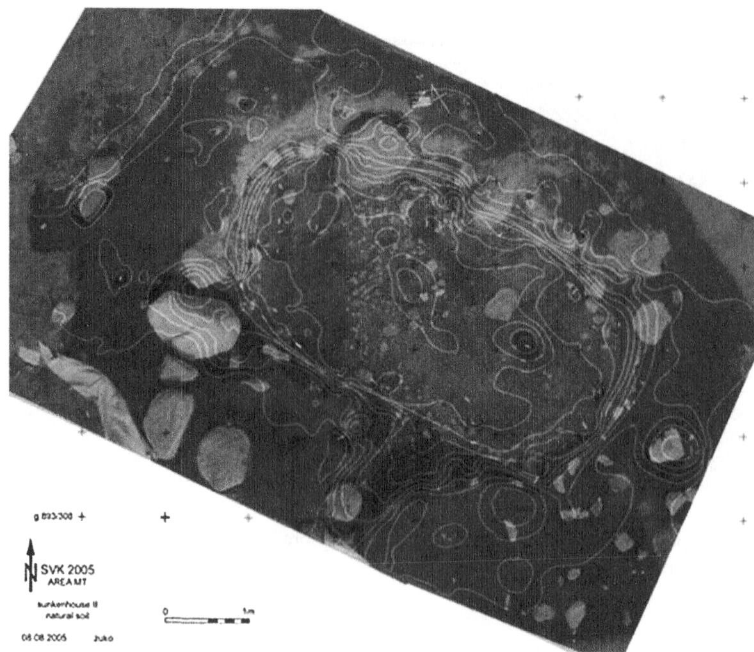

Fig. 35.3 Orthophoto map of a sunken house excavated by P. Urbańczyk in North-East Iceland in 2002–2005

attempts at its promotion (e.g., Urbańczyk 1999, 2004). The lack of theoretical discussion and of progressive methodology promotion resulted in stagnation. Digging in arbitrary levels found common acceptance (e.g., Mazurowski 1996, p. 4) and dominates until today.

Quick economic development after the political transformation of 1989 resulted in extensive investments in production and transport infrastructure, which made necessary to excavate huge areas. Again town centers and hectares of fields have been being excavated to free space for factories, habitation quarters, highways, and pipelines. Only some outsiders lucky to have a chance to dig slowly (usually abroad) have experimented, for example, with new methods of electronic recording (e.g., Urbańczyk 2002, 2011) (Fig. 35.3). Thus, 65 years later, we may recall Żurowski's bitter observation that "some prehistorians consider excavation technique too easy to learn it. Such attitudes, based on ignorance, inhibit progress…" (Żurowski 1947, p. 136).

More information will be found in EGA under Stratigraphy in Archaeology: A Brief History.

Chapter 36
Britain

Timothy Darvill

From its antiquarian origins, the development of field method in Britain reflects attempts by archaeologists to balance the merits of survey against excavation, research against rescue, and empiricism against theorized interpretation. While early methods lacked consistency, most were based on a modified form of empiricism known as inductivism: observations in the field gathered together to create interpretative statements (Marsden 1983). Richard Colt Hoare (1758–1838), excavator of more than 500 sites in the early 1800s, memorably summed up the position by declaring that "We speak from facts not theory" as the epigraph to *Ancient Wiltshire* published between 1812 and 1820. Importantly, a community of practice emerged to foster a network of amenity societies.

The late nineteenth century was a watershed in the development of archaeological fieldwork. Positivism strengthened as the preferred philosophy, suiting archaeology well by perpetuating distinctions between *facts* as things that could be observed and *laws* or *interpretations* as statements making sense of the facts. Maintaining the integrity of the facts therefore became important, and one of the main steps toward achieving this involved structuring investigation methods and recording systems. Leading this field was General Pitt Rivers (1827–1900) whose interests in social evolution carried through to developing a method of excavation that charted sequences of activity at particular sites. In practice, this meant recording every object so it could be replaced accurately in its findspot through the use of plans and section drawings – essentially three-dimensional recording of finds. A generation later, Mortimer Wheeler (1890–1976) added the need to record strata (every layer) three dimensionally as well. To achieve this, he developed an excavation method that still bears his name – the Wheeler system – in which the area of investigation was divided into squares with balks between. Each square was separately excavated, and the plans and four sections of each carefully drawn (Wheeler 1954).

T. Darvill (✉)
School of Applied Sciences, Bournemouth University, Bournemouth, Dorset, UK
e-mail: tdarvill@bournemouth.ac.uk

M. Carver et al. (eds.), *Field Archaeology from Around the World*,
SpringerBriefs in Archaeology, DOI 10.1007/978-3-319-09819-7_36

Continental methods of *open-area excavation* were meanwhile imported into Britain, notably by Gerhard Bersu (1889–1964) at Little Woodbury, Wiltshire, in 1938–1939. This approach to excavation and recording had far-reaching consequences after the Second World War, but even during the war, a small team of archaeologists led by W.F. Grimes (1905–1988) recorded sites in this way before they were destroyed by the construction of military installations. Noteworthy was Grimes' rigorous open-plan excavation of the Burn Ground long barrow, Gloucestershire, in 1940–1941, where he planned every stone in the mound. After the war, rebuilding programs coupled with industrial expansion, agricultural extensification, urban regeneration, and infrastructure renewal created many opportunities for archaeological investigation. Subsequent changes in methodology can be gauged from six successive textbooks on the subject by Richard Atkinson (1946), John Coles (1972), Philip Barker (1977), Ian Hodder (1999), Steve Roskams (2001), and Martin Carver (2009).

Operationally, work has expanded into hitherto under-investigated environments such as occupied towns, wetlands, uplands, agricultural land, and coastlands, often with rich rewards. Practically, there was much experimentation with the shape and size of excavation trenches, including uses of quadrant methods, *planum* systems, and large-scale open-area excavation taken from continental innovations. However, in Britain, attention remained focused on the removal of individual layers or *contexts* as they became widely known, in the reverse stratigraphic order to deposition. Teasing apart complicated sequences, finding natural construction or erosional surfaces, positive and negative features, deposits, and cuts became a technical as well as an intellectual challenge. Finds were associated with contexts as the basic unit of recovery, and the application of archaeological site science promoted systematic sampling for ecofacts and artifacts down to microscopic levels as well as the recovery of environmental indicators and chemical characterization.

In field survey, the tradition based on the idea of cultural property and monuments promoted by Pitt Rivers was continued for much of the twentieth century by government-sponsored *Royal Commissions* which had the remit of recording everything visible on the surface (Crawford 1960). Aerial photography was adopted for archaeology immediately after World War 1 and exported to the countries of the then British Empire. The postwar period saw the development of *landscape archaeology*, a set of more sophisticated and analytical approaches that focused on wide geographical areas and assumed that the land was regularly overwritten by successive generations to form a *palimpsest* (Darvill 2001). Aerial photography, remote sensing, ground surveys, place-name studies, and past cartography were among the many primary sources used to create landscape regression models – snapshots of a landscape as it might have been at a particular period. Uniquely, in England, where treasure hunting on private property remains legal, a new voluntary scheme has encouraged the reporting of objects found by metal detectorists. The *Portable Antiquities Scheme* has produced an immense harvest of reported finds, creating a rich geographical database of dated artifacts, the majority of metal.

From the 1960s, representatives from museums, universities, local and national archaeological societies, local authorities, and the government agencies began working together to meet the needs of *rescue archaeology* in their locality (RCHM 1960). While the rescue of archaeological sites in Britain is not obligated by law, in 1990, its justification was embedded in Planning Policy Guidance Note 16 (=PPG16 *Archaeology and Planning*) for England, with similar statements for other parts of Britain, and these have remained the basis for the funding of archaeological intervention by the private sector. In excess of 4,800 investigations a year were being undertaken in England alone by the year 2000. This has coincided with a revolution in IT, resulting in innovative approaches to on-site data capture and the subsequent production and processing of plans, sections, photographs, and descriptive records. Compiled in *client reports*, these are presented to the commercial sponsors of the work in fulfillment of contact.

More than 95 % of archaeological fieldwork in Britain is now prompted by planned commercial development. It comprises predetermination work such as desk-based assessments, field evaluations, and environmental impact assessments, and post-determination work that focuses on mitigating impact, implementing conservation measures, recording buildings, and investigating deposits faced with destruction through a range of techniques that include both trenching and open-area excavation. Conceptually, the *archaeological resource* of the 1970s and 1980s, *heritage* as it was called in the 1990s, has now been redefined as *historic environment assets*. Large-scale projects remain common, including, for example, the high-speed railway line from London to the Channel Tunnel and Terminal 5 at London's Heathrow Airport. But size is less important than quality. Since revisions to the planning system in 2010 and the gathering strength of *localism* as a political philosophy, integrating archaeology with local communities and using the knowledge generated to create public value have taken center stage.

Economic instability and the global recession are having an effect on archaeological fieldwork traditions in Britain at the time of writing (early 2012). The profession has already scaled back, and more cuts are anticipated in order to meet lower demand for archaeological services (Aitchison 2010). On the brighter side, current conditions allow the chance to take stock of achievements over the past 20 years: to rebalance the scope and aims of fieldwork, reconcile positivist and relativist approaches under the rubrics of creative science and community engagement, promote academic recognition and definitions of the discipline, and integrate opportunities offered by development-driven research with the power of problem-orientated research – in fact, a twenty-first-century version of the agenda faced 300 years ago by the founders of Britain's fieldwork traditions.

See also the entry in EGA for Landscape Archaeology, Aitken (Martin), Hall (E T), Evans (Arthur), Wheeler (Mortimer),

Chapter 37
Scandinavia

Stefan Larsson

Scandinavian archaeology has been influenced by three important factors: its embrace by the state, its terrain, and its methodological innovations. The position of Scandinavian archaeology within the state administration descends from the frequent, long, and bloody conflicts between Denmark-Norway and Sweden-Finland. The number of monuments that could be claimed was instrumental in the diplomatic game of the day: the most venerable history gave a higher ranking at peace negotiations. In short, Scandinavian archaeology is the offspring of an "antiquarian arms race." The Danish legal tradition goes back as far as medieval times: all "treasure" found is the property of the King, while in the Swedish tradition, which has been a reference for both the Norwegian and Finnish legislation, sites and monuments belong to the state. Sites and monuments are to be protected or, if this not being possible, recorded professionally, thus making it a public responsibility to maintain a body of archaeologists. The overwhelming majority of excavations are performed within this legal administration, resulting in large-scale archaeological projects, today aided by digital recording (Fig. 37.1).

Archaeological deposits in Scandinavia vary from Paleolithic deposits and large Mesolithic dwelling sites of the Ertebølle culture, to the heaped clay Bronze Age burial mounds of Jutland ("the mound people," Glob 1974), to large-scale settlements, votive deposits in bogs, ship burials, shipwrecks, and large-scale central places of the Iron Age to early trading and manufacturing centers of the Viking Age. In upland areas, settlements and burial mounds remain visible above ground level. In lowland areas, they have been located by intensive surveys (Welinder 2009).

Scandinavian innovations include the development of typology, large-scale survey, and different approaches to excavation. Typology became something of a Scandinavian speciality, starting with C.J. Thomsen's (1788–1865) presentation of

S. Larsson (✉)
Swedish National Heritage Board, Lund, Sweden
e-mail: stefan.larsson@raa.se

M. Carver et al. (eds.), *Field Archaeology from Around the World*,
SpringerBriefs in Archaeology, DOI 10.1007/978-3-319-09819-7_37

Fig. 37.1 A large-scale excavation of the medieval village of Örja, just outside Landskrona, Sweden (Photo by Thomas Hansson, Swedish National Heritage Board)

the "three-age system," i.e., the division of prehistory into the Stone, Bronze, and Iron Ages, which was developed indirectly from the taxonomy developed by C. Linnaeus and his disciples. The system was gradually refined during the course of the nineteenth century by, among others, J.J Worsaæ (1821–1885), S. Müller (1846–1934), and B.E. Hildebrand (1806–1884). Particularly influential was the concept of chronological evolution to explain the changing forms of artifacts by O. Montelius (1843–1921) (Fig. 37.2).

Since all archaeological remains were (and are) regarded as the cultural property of the state, large-scale surveys pursued the goal of total record. This has empowered geographical methods of historical analysis, such as Bjørn Myhre's early medieval kingdoms in Norway, drawn by Thiessen polygons from hierarchies of burials, ship-sheds, and hill forts (1987), and Åke Hyenstrand's use of Sweden's Ancient Monuments Register for tracing regions and socioeconomical systems (Hyenstrand 1984).

In excavation, Scandinavian archaeologists have been influenced by both the German approach, which divides a deposit into horizontal and vertical slices ("schnitt"), and the British, which gives primacy to the stratification. However, it was the pioneering work of Gudmund Hatt and C.J. Becker in the 1930s and 1940s that led to the development of large-scale open area excavations. These were applied in particular to prehistoric and medieval settlements where survival may be little more than postholes and ribbons of small stones left by turf and timber buildings. These techniques were taken up in Britain and spread widely in Europe. On site pioneering methodologies by Scandinavian archaeologists include the excavation of huge preserved timber ships and their contents from mounds at Gokstad and Oseberg (see Gansum 2004), the recovery and analysis of bog bodies (Asingh and Lynnerup 2007), and the lifting of an entire *burial chamber* at Medelpad, Sweden, in 1952 (p. 169). Modern pioneers have been contributing in particular to the development of methods of electronic *remote mapping*.

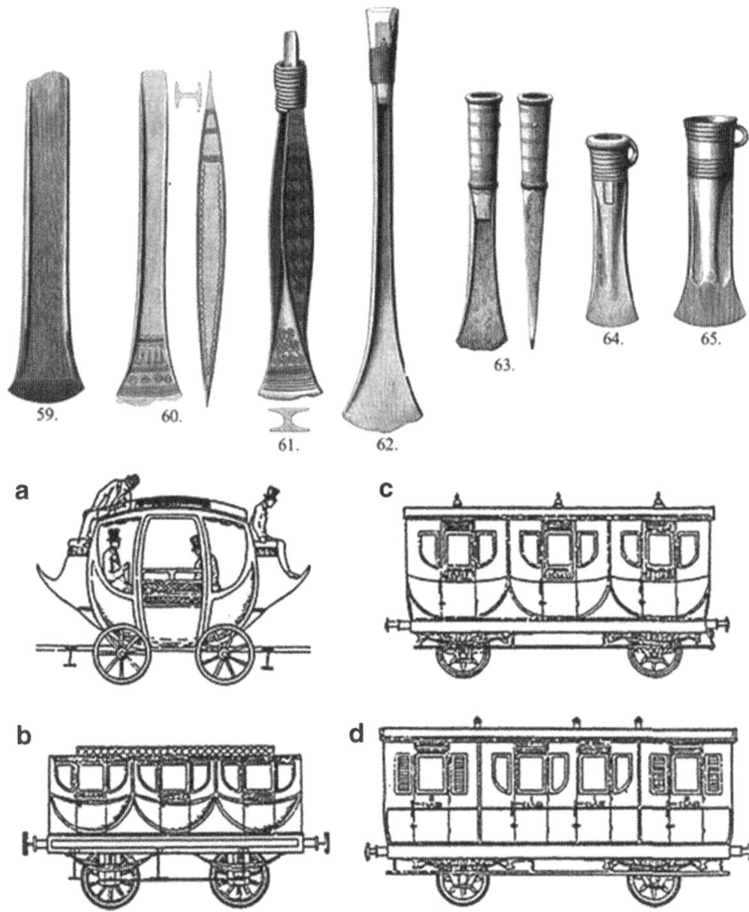

Fig. 37.2 Oscar Montelius (1843–1921) used the evolution of carriages, from horse drawn to railway, to illustrate how artifacts develop through time. The method allows an artifact type, and assemblages of artifacts, to be assigned to a particular period

Information relevant to this section will be found in EGA under Scandinavia and the Baltic Sea Region; Scandinavia/Northern Europe: Historical Archaeology.

Chapter 38
France

Nathan Schlanger

It was through the innovative application of sound field methods that Jacques Boucher de Perthes (1788–1868), a customs official in northern France, contributed decisively to the establishment of human antiquity. He argued that proof of an object's antiquity resided first and foremost in "its surrounding [*entourage*] and the place where it is encountered" (Boucher de Perthes 1847, pp. 34, 178, 181). By insisting on such principles of stratigraphic position and integrity, Boucher de Perthes could argue that the artificially shaped flint *haches* he found beneath meters of undisturbed gravels in association with fossil bones of extinct species were therefore of infinitely ancient age, long before the Biblical Flood (thus *antediluvian*). While these claims had met with skepticism, a dramatic reversal of fortune occurred in 1859 with the visit to the region of two English scientists, the wine merchant and geologist Joseph Prestwich (1812–1896) and the paper manufacturer and numismatist John Evans (1823–1908). Besides conducting a thorough audit of the context of discovery, the visitors also took the unprecedented step of having a photograph taken, on the 27th April 1859, of an in situ hand axe embedded in a quarry section at Saint-Acheul (Fig. 38.1). This very first use of the photographic medium for stratigraphic demonstration not only confirmed human antiquity but also served to shift the onus of archaeological demonstration from rhetoric and personal reputation to methodically documented observation (Gamble and Kruszynski 2009).

Meanwhile in the South of France, cave sites were being explored by Édouard Lartet (1801–1871), a lawyer and paleontologist from Sarlat. The *Reliquiae Aquitanicae* he published together with banker Henry Christy in the mid-1860s highlighted the rich potential of these caves, with their well-preserved faunal remains as well as flint and bone tools, for establishing a sequence of periods when

N. Schlanger (✉)
Trajectoires, Maison Archéologie & Ethnologie (MAE), 21 Allée de l'Université, Nanterre 92023, France
e-mail: schlanger1@gmail.com

M. Carver et al. (eds.), *Field Archaeology from Around the World*, SpringerBriefs in Archaeology, DOI 10.1007/978-3-319-09819-7_38

Fig. 38.1 A quarry worker showing the location of an in situ hand axe, Saint-Acheul, 27th April 1859 (Photograph by C. Pinsard, albuminated paper. Courtesy of Bibliothèques d'Amiens Métropole, Ms 1370.f.33)

rhinoceros, mammoth, and reindeer roamed. This research was soon brought together at the newly created *Musée des antiquités nationales* by the engineer and curator Gabriel de Mortillet (1821–1898). By means of their association with geological strata and fauna, de Mortillet defined the artifacts themselves as fossil types, so establishing the succession of Acheulean, Mousterian, Solutrean, and Magdalenian periods, named after the French sites where they were defined. While undergoing many revisions and expansions over the years, this classificatory system still remains today as the cornerstone of Paleolithic archaeology.

This development of vertical investigation in France was followed in the 1960s by the development of the horizontal (*décapage*) method of excavation pioneered by the ethnologist, technologist, and prehistorian André Leroi-Gourhan (1911–1986. See Courbin 1987; Audouze and Schlanger 2004). It was not of course without precedents. In the loess plains of Central and Eastern Europe, from Dolní Věstonice in Moravia to Kostenki in Russia, Upper Paleolithic habitations and mammoth-bone huts had long been identified and excavated through investigations in open area. Fluent in Russian, Leroi-Gourhan was well aware of these studies, though not necessarily of their historical materialist underpinnings. Drawing on his own paleontological and anatomical expertise, he himself had undertaken since the 1940s (e.g., at Les Furtins) the meticulous recording of human burials, in their sequence of inhumation and deposition, thus pioneering the subfield of funerary archaeology.

These initiatives converged in 1964, at the excavation of an extremely well-preserved hunter-gatherer occupation site in the sand quarries of Pincevent, south of Paris. This series of Magdalenian camps (c. 12,500 BP) represent the seasonal halts

Fig. 38.2 On-site briefing in front of a *décapage* at Pincevent. From *left*: André Leroi-Gourhan, Michèle Julien, Claudine Karlin, and Michel Brézillon (©: Centre archéologique de Pincevent)

of reindeer hunters, next to a ford on the R. Seine (Bodu et al. 2006). The dedicated excavation methodology deployed there by Leroi-Gourhan and his team included the meticulous exposure and millimetric stripping (sometimes with dental tools) of vast surfaces of finds and features, left for as long as possible in situ to be drawn, recorded, photographed, and thoroughly documented, square meter by square meter (Fig. 38.2). This small-scale plotting of the distribution of the finds – flint and bone remains – made it possible to map the functional and spatial relations between such features as hearths, tents, butchery areas, knapping areas, and dumps and led to the identification of vanished structures. Moreover, the extensive refitting of flint débitage and tools at Pincevent (and subsequently at other sites in the region) not only served to retrace the spatial and functional biographies of tools and thus grasp "precise moments in the remote past" – they also made it possible to reconstruct the technical processes of Upper Paleolithic flint tool production and use, thus contributing decisively to the development and demonstration of the *chaîne opératoire* approach in prehistoric archaeology.

Leroi-Gourhan's concern with the minutiae of "prehistoric ethnology" led subsequently to ongoing comparative research in Arctic areas – where it was to converge with ethnoarchaeological studies by Lewis Binford and others on hunter-gatherer campsites in Alaska, as well as Australia and Southern Africa.

Entries in EGA relevant to this section will be found in EGA at France: Promotion of Archaeological Heritage; Europe: Early Upper Paleolithic; Lithic Technology, Paleolithic.

Chapter 39
China

Liangren Zhang

Although the study of ancient artifacts has a long history in China, the modern science of archaeology was brought to China only in the late nineteenth century by foreign explorers and archaeologists. Since the 1920s, however, as the Nationalist government curbed foreigners' field activities in its land, native archaeologists, mostly Western-trained, from a few institutions (the Cenozoic Research Laboratory of the Geological Survey of China, the Institute of History and Philology of Academic Sinica and the Society for Historical Studies of National Beiping Academy) began to play the major role (Chen 1997, p. 87). The political fragility and economic feebleness of the time, however, did not allow science to develop significantly. Although much progress was made in excavation techniques, including the division of strata and typological analysis of artifacts (Chen 1997, pp. 145–162, 227–249, 310–329), only a modest number of sites had been excavated and a small group of archaeologists had been trained by 1949, the year when the Communist Party took over the mainland China.

Dramatic changes came about after 1949. Having unified the country, the communist government set out to modernize its industry, science, and education. And having decided to dissect its relations with the West and sided with the Soviet Union, it urged the academic community to learn the "advanced experience" of the Soviet science. The archaeologists and their students, who were trained in the West or educated in the pro-West Nationalist Era, had little choice but to study Soviet theories and methods (Zhang 2011, p. 1052). Archaeology, which now received lavish state support, continued to be cast as a subdiscipline of history as in the Nationalist Era, but it was now imposed upon a new paradigm: Marxist dialectical materialism and historical materialism. While dialectical materialism introduces the concept of social evolution, historical materialism brings the subjects of social

L. Zhang (✉)
School of Cultural Heritage, Northwest University, Xi'an City, Shaanxi Province, China
e-mail: xianjuman@gmail.com

M. Carver et al. (eds.), *Field Archaeology from Around the World*,
SpringerBriefs in Archaeology, DOI 10.1007/978-3-319-09819-7_39

relations, economy, and technology to archaeology (Xia 1952, pp. 81–84). The Soviet archaeology also demands that archaeologists devote themselves to the life of the subject and down-trodden people, as a counterforce to their natural instinct, that is, to excavate tombs and monuments of the social elites. It does not follow, however, that Chinese archaeologists give priority to settlements and tombs of the common people. In fact, apart from a few exemplary Neolithic settlements that were dug to fulfill the Marxist mandate, they continue to favor large urban centers, such as Erlitou, Anyang, Luoyang, and Chang'an, and monumental tombs for the purpose of uncovering treasures and wonders to illustrate the grandeur of Chinese history and civilizations (Zhang 2011, p. 1052).

Chinese archaeologists translated many Soviet publications to avail themselves not only of ready-made models of integrating the Marxist theories into archaeological interpretation, but also of "advanced" fieldwork methodologies. As a result, they began their fieldwork with systematic survey, thereby acquiring the basic information of the location, chronology, and cultural definition of a single site as well as informing questions such as the geographic distribution and the ecological environment of a culture (Xia 1958, p. 2). In addition, Chinese archaeologists innovatively adopted the "Luoyang Spade," a coring device which local treasure hunters had developed to discover tombs, as a prospecting tool. Skilled hands were trained to identify various types of features (tombs, architectural foundations, trash pits, riverbeds) from the soil samples taken from underground. Thanks to its efficiency and low cost, the tool is still popular today; one can often use it to get a good idea of the layout as well as stratigraphy of a site without excavation.

When Chinese archaeologists excavate a settlement, they usually lay out box pits of 2×2 m, which they replicate to expose large areas (Fig. 39.1). This method is very helpful because many settlements in China comprise feature long habitation history and complex cultural deposit. Although it had also been used in the West, they were obliged by the ideology of the time to attribute the credit of inspiration to the Soviet archaeologist T. S. Passek (1903–1968). While earlier excavators were unable to discover houses at the Tripoly'e settlement because they had only opened narrow trenches and small areas, in the 1930s, Passek successfully discovered structures of 100–120 m^2 in dimension with the box excavation. In a country blessed with long history and thick cultural deposit, this method appears to be very useful, as it provides a better stratigraphic control and a better understanding of a settlement: division of space and episodes of reconstruction (Yan 1994, p. 252). Dubbed by Chinese archaeologists as "small excavation units but large-scale exposure," it was put to good use at the model Neolithic settlement of Banpo near Xi'an and Jiangzhai (Zhongguo Kexueyuan Kaogu Yanjiusuo 1963, p. 6; Banpo Museum, Shaanxi Institute of Archaeology, and Lintong County Museum 1988, pp. 3–5). While the size of the unit is often adjusted to the specific circumstances and objectives of an excavation (it is now usually 5×5 m or 10×10 m), the box-pit excavation remains the standard operational method today (Shi 1982, pp. 18–19).

Ancient cities, especially those of the proto-historic and historical periods, demand a different approach. Following the Soviet guidelines, Chinese archaeologists first study historical documents to address questions about material production, social relations, and the spiritual life of the population. They can then turn to other questions

Fig. 39.1 The 'small unit/large exposure' (box system) in action on an excavation in advance of road building at Boatou, Inner Mongolia in 2006 (China, State Administration 2007, p. 165)

such as spatial division, public amenities, and external economic connections. Since cities are much larger and more sophisticated than Neolithic settlements, it is unrealistic to implement the full-coverage excavation; small excavation units are instead deployed at particular sections to address particular questions, such as layout and chronology. Three phases of deposit are generally investigated to define their chronology: those formed during construction, those formed during occupation, and those after abandonment. This set of methods was effectively applied to the excavation of Chang'an, a capital of the Western Han Dynasty (206 BCE–9 CE), near the present-day city of Xi'an. Together with the method of dividing cultural strata by soil content and color, it is still cherished as a working principle today (Zhang 1983, p. 62).

Regional Genealogy and Variations

The intense learning of the Soviet archaeology came to a halt after the breakup of the Sino-Soviet brotherhood in the 1960s. Having turned away from the West in 1949, Chinese archaeologists were now secluded from the development of archaeological theories and methods over the world. Without external inspiration, they were left to move forward from what they had inherited from the Nationalist Era and learned from the Soviet. In the volatile political atmosphere that lingered from the 1950s through to the 1980s, however, theoretical thinking, even in the name of Marxist theories, was a life-threatening venture. Hence, no middle-range theories and methodologies were developed to extrapolate the Marxist subjects of social relations, economy, and technology; discussion of these subjects was little more than filling fresh data into the old pigeonholes of Marxist theories. It was the typology and culture-historical paradigm inherited from the Nationalist Era, safeguarded by the sustained nationalism, that had the chance of further development in the subsequent decades.

It was Su Bingqi (1909–1997), a courageous thinker for his time, who held the beacon for theoretical development in China. He began his theoretical venture in the 1930s when he attempted to work out a chronology for the cemetery at Doujitai in Baoji, Shaanxi Province. Employing Montelius' typology but tempering it with his own interpretation, he selected the diagnostic ceramic ware li-tripod as the subjects of typological analysis, divided them into four types, and traced each type's evolutionary path (Su 1948[1984]). Since the 1950s, the division of *xing* (type), and *shi*, which stands for the chronological subtype, became the standard method in Chinese typology (Su 1959[1984], 1965). This method was further refined to fit the ever-growing excavation materials by Su Bingqi himself and his disciples. In his endeavor to set up chronologies for the Shang urban centers of Zhengzhou and Anyang, Zou Heng (1956, 1964) innovatively correlated stratigraphic and typological sequences of ceramic wares from these sites.

Su Bingqi's creativity did not end up at the typological analysis. He further developed a theory, namely, the "regional cultural genealogy and variations (quxileixing)," that offers a handy framework for organizing and explaining them (Su and Yin 1981, 1982). In this general and flexible formulation, the archaeological cultures that had been discovered by the 1970s were grouped into six macroscopic cultural-historical regions; each region comprises of a few micro-regions, whose cultures are lined up from the Paleolithic Age through to the Bronze Age. Rejecting the conventional assumption that Central China was the cradle of Chinese civilizations lifting the outlying regions from backwardness, he emphasized instead that it was the outlying regions that outshined and enlightened Central China in the Prehistoric periods. Believing in the historicity of traditional texts, he further linked some of the regional cultures with early ethnic groups recorded in these texts (Su and Yin 1981, 1982).

New Development

The typological analysis and the "regional cultural genealogy and variations" theory were imbued into a national fieldwork manual issued in 1984 (Ministry of Culture 1984). Su Bingqi and his disciplines, all prominent figures in Chinese archaeology, frequently traveled across the nation to deliver them to his fellow colleagues, and urged them to mend up the gaps of the cultural lineages of their regions. Blessed by the growing excavations since the 1970s, each province was able to write its cultural history, more or less complete, from the Paleolithic Age well into the historical periods (Wenwu Editorial Committee 1979, 1991). They nevertheless brought much harm to Chinese archaeology in the meantime. Emphasizing on the importance of deposit strata and ceramic typology, they ignored many of other questions, such as the settlement pattern, and subsistence economy, as well as many types of data, such as soil, food residue, and botanical and faunal remains.

Since the late 1970s, however, China reopened itself to the World, and once again appreciated foreign archaeological theories and methods, mostly of the West and Japan. In 2005, the SACH commissioned the Archaeology Department of Beijing University, the leading institution in China, a major revision of the 1984 manual to catch up with the current development in archaeology over the globe. From manuals of Britain and Japan, the new manual, which was issued in 2009, adopts the social archaeology of the West and the research subjects of settlement pattern, subsistence economy, craft production, and social organization. It asks excavators to pay attention not only to stratigraphy, but also to spatial organization and formation process of a site. It inserts sifting and flotation facilities into the excavation process so as to gather tiny animal bones, plant seeds, and artifacts for future analysis. In addition, it demands on-site conservation for the purpose of protecting fragile artifacts and features (China, State Administration of Cultural Heritage 2009). In line with the new standards, an excavation project is no longer targeted at narrow subjects such as chronology and culture definition, but becomes a platform for multidisciplinary cooperation; it is no longer a closed domain for the excavators alone, but an open territory for many specialists who examine various types of materials. In this way, Chinese archaeology will surely interact with the world communities more actively in the future.

Information relevant to this section will be found in EGA under China: Cultural Heritage Management; China: Managing Cultural Heritage and the World Heritage List; China: Museums; China: New Approaches to Heritage Administration; Banpocun, Archaeology of; Histories of the Archaeological Discipline: Issues to Consider; Multicultural Archaeology; Nationalism and Archaeology.

Chapter 40
Japan

Yumiko Nakanishi

Principles

The basis for archaeological intervention in Japan is the *Law for the Protection of Cultural Properties* inaugurated in 1950 and updated regularly since. Archaeological resources underground are designated as "buried cultural properties (*Maizou Bunkazai*)." Since then every excavation has to be notified to the responsible government department, traditionally the Board of Education. Most archaeological fieldwork takes the form of *rescue excavation* (CRM) in advance of development rather than research projects. Universities do undertake excavations for academic purposes, but these are overwhelmingly exceeded by rescue work, both in number and budget. Academics are required to obtain permission to excavate from the local authority (who may not give it).

On the principle that it is better for buried cultural properties to be preserved underground than to be destroyed, the initiator of the development is required to pay for excavation of archaeological deposits in advance of their destruction. This principle was challenged in the courts in the late 1970s and the early 1980s, when private development companies sued for the losses caused by covering these costs. But the High Court of Tokyo found in favor of government and ruled that developers should cover the cost of excavation but with the condition that there should be the limit defined by an "appropriate level of investigation." Not all remains of the past are eligible for record: according to government advice dated 1998, only remains dating back to the Middle Ages and earlier are mandatorily subject to investigation.

Y. Nakanishi (✉)
Osaka Prefectural Government, Osaka, Japan
e-mail: yn218@gaia.eonet.ne.jp

M. Carver et al. (eds.), *Field Archaeology from Around the World*,
SpringerBriefs in Archaeology, DOI 10.1007/978-3-319-09819-7_40

Methods

Nondestructive field methods may be used at the evaluation stage, although rescue archaeology mostly uses *test pits* to determine and estimate the depth of cultural layers, as well as the anticipated structures and their likely date. This information also allows an estimation of the cost and duration of the intervention, which is then fed into the *project design*. The project design forms the basis for negotiation with the developers. Once fixed, archaeological contractors tender for the work, comprising the necessary equipment and the required labor force. Payment is usually calculated according to the volume of soil to be removed or the numbers of workdays required.

A mechanical excavator ("jumbo") is used to remove top layers, and then digging switches to human labor using hoes and the other tools. Narrow trenches are first dug at the edges of the area to be excavated to reveal sections through the deposit. These trenches provide drainage, and their sections are used as a guide to the excavators, who peel back from them, layer by layer. Excavators use a versatile trowel hoe on a long handle, which can pick, cut, slice, and create a smooth surface (p. 46). The spoil is removed using electrically driven belt conveyors (Fig. 40.1). When the surface of the layer is clean, those features showing in it are recorded by photography and drawing. Features and collected artifacts are located in three dimensions using a grid system connected to the national and world geodesic systems. A new departure is the recording of excavations using overhead photography from a helicopter or a crane supporting a cage. The photographs are used to generate measured drawings, which are then checked on site.

Once excavations are complete, all artifacts will be washed and marked with a serial number to identify date and location of discovery. Broken pieces are refitted, drawn, and photographed. This is often done by part-time workers. Comprehensive excavation reports are prepared containing all the information collected during the excavation. The public are invited to view the excavations' open days. This usually includes a safe route overlooking the excavated and a few tents, one for reception and others for exhibiting artifacts.

Archaeological work in advance of development is big business. A recent example of a large-scale urban project is the 2nd Keihan Highway project, which involved a national expressway and a bypass about 27 km in length (Naniwa n.d.). The section crossing Osaka was about 16.1 km and had 18 potential sites ("areas known to contain cultural properties"). Agreement for trial excavations was negotiated between the different agencies and authorization given to the contractor, in this case the Osaka Center for Cultural Heritage (OCCH), a nonprofit foundation partly invested by Osaka Prefectural Government. After completing trial excavations in 1996, the area in need of excavation was estimated as about 450,000 m^2. In 2000, the full-scale excavations started at Tsudajo site in Hirakata City, and all excavations were completed in January 2010.

Fig. 40.1 Excavations in progress: use of conveyor (By courtesy of Nara National Research Institute for Cultural Properties)

Reflections

Privatized contract work needs appropriate surveillance, or it can simply become "the cheapest option." This must be avoided: to record sites properly requires the application of a certain standard, for example, by the issue of licenses, which has been under discussion for the past few years. A second concern is the usage of the new knowledge that is being generated. Many reports are not well researched nor accessible to the public. Some have been kept long in the archive without ever being consulted. We also need to rethink the role of archaeologists in the public sector. It is probably a good moment to discuss opening up field archaeology in Japan to wider involvement.

More information about archaeology in Japan today will be found in EGA at Japan: Cultural Heritage Management; Japan: Indigenous Occupation; Japan World Heritage; Japanese Archaeological Museums.

Chapter 41
Australia

Kylie Lower-Eskelson

Australia's first archaeological observations were made by early explorers and colonists or noted by observers primarily working in other disciplines (Smith and Burke 2007, p. 1). The first excavation in Australia was undertaken by the governors of the Colony of New South Wales with a focus on human burials (Horton 1991, pp. 3–5), while the first to employ the method of stratigraphic analysis were anthropologists Herbert Hale and Norman Tindale, who undertook archaeological excavations at Devon Downs in 1929 (Hale and Tindale 1930).

Formal archaeological work in Australia began in the 1950s when John Mulvaney returned from courses at Cambridge University and introduced archaeological study into the Australian curriculum (Mulvaney 2011). Mulvaney began work on a number of archaeological excavations around Australia and instructed and mentored a number of students who would become leaders in the field, including Isabel McBryde, Jim Allen, and Ian Glover.

In the 1970s, a series of political circumstances spurred by a confluence between the Aboriginal land rights movement and public environmental concerns led to the creation of state heritage legislation, After this, the amount of archaeological work conducted in Australia dramatically increased, both with development of heritage surveys required by legislation and in academic circles, with several universities opening archaeology departments.

While Australia's first department of archaeology had been instituted at the University of Sydney in 1948, the focus was not specific to Australian archaeology. Later, archaeologists with an Australian focus arrived at the university, with Vincent Megaw and Richard Wright arriving in 1961 and Rhys Jones in 1963. John Mulvaney was appointed to the History Department University of Melbourne in 1953, later moving to ANU. Isabel McBryde took up the first titled position in Prehistory and

K. Lower-Eskelson (✉)
Department of Archaeology, Flinders University, Adelaide, SA, Australia
e-mail: kylielowereskelson@yahoo.com

M. Carver et al. (eds.), *Field Archaeology from Around the World*,
SpringerBriefs in Archaeology, DOI 10.1007/978-3-319-09819-7_41

Ancient History at the University of New England, Armidale, in 1960, while Jack Golson was appointed to the Anthropology Department at Australian National University in 1961, which was then just moving into the field of archaeology.

Since this time, Australia has grown a thriving discipline covering a range of research topics. The nature and timing of human settlement in the continent has been a long standing topic of interest in Australian archaeology, with the first estimate being made in 1884 by Reverend Peter MacPherson, who postulated an age of 400 years BP for human arrival on the basis of his excavations in Victoria (Horton 1991, pp. 34–43). This date was quickly superseded with the commonly accepted date of human arrival in Australia now being an estimated 50,000 years BP (see Hiscock 2008, p. 1). The archaeology of the periods of European contact and industrialization has developed into a major field.

The first Australian book dedicated to an overview of archaeological field methods was written in 1983 by Graham Connah (see Connah 1983), which was followed by a more detailed treatment of field methods and related topics by Heather Burke and Claire Smith (see Burke and Smith 2004). The method of ethnographic analogy has often been employed in Australian archaeology and in many cases has served to inform our interpretation of the past (Hiscock 2008, pp. 268–285).

One of Australia's strengths in archaeology has been its analysis of sociopolitical issues, particularly the reflexive analysis of its relationship as a discipline with Aboriginal people (see Burke et al. 1994). This has evolved from simple consultation in the early days to numerous community-based research projects, informed, and sometimes initiated by Indigenous people (Greer et al. 2002). This has begun to transform archaeology in Australia from a field that studied the history of indigenous people to one that cannot only learn more about the past but also benefit contemporary peoples. Employment in cultural heritage management increased dramatically in the early twenty-first century, in response to the legislative requirements of a mining boom in Australia. In 2012, there were over 1,000 members of the Australian Archaeological Association.

More information on Australian archaeology can be found in EGA under Australasian Historical Archaeology, Australia: Cultural Heritage Management Education, Australia: Domestic Archaeological Heritage Management Law, Australia: Indigenous Cultural Property Return; and on Australian archaeologists at Allen (Jim), Burke (Heather), Golson (Jack), Jones (Rhys Maengwyn), McBryde (Isabel), Mulvaney, John) and Smith (Claire).

References

Adams, R. M. (1966). *The evolution of urban society: Early Mesopotamia and Prehispanic Mexico*. Chicago: Aldine.

Aitchison, K. (2010). United Kingdom archaeology in economic crisis. In N. Schlanger & K. Aitchinson (Eds.), *Archaeology and the global economic crisis. Multiple impacts and possible solutions* (pp. 25–30). Tervuren: Culture Lab Editions. Available at: http://ace-archaeology.eu/fichiers/25Archaeology-and-the-crisis.pdf. Accessed 10 Jan 2012.

Alcock, S. E., & Cherry, J. F. (2004). *Side-by-side survey: Comparative regional studies in the Mediterranean world*. Oxford: Oxbow.

Andrews, G., & Thomas, R. (1995). The management of archaeological projects: Theory and practice in the UK. In M. Cooper, A. Firth, J. Carman, & D. Wheatley (Eds.), *Managing archaeology* (pp. 184–202). London: Taylor and Francis.

Asingh, P., & Lynnerup, N. (Eds.). (2007). *Grauballe man. An Iron Age bog body revisited*. Højbjerg: Jutland Archaeological Society & Moesgaard Museum.

Aspinall, A., Gaffney, C., & Schmidt, A. (2008). *Magnetometry for archaeologists*. Lanham: AltaMira.

Aston, M., & Rowley, T. (1974). *Landscape archaeology: An introduction to fieldwork techniques on post-Roman landscapes*. Newton Abbot: David and Charles.

Atkinson, R. J. C. (1946). *Field archaeology*. London: Methuen.

Audouze, F., & Schlanger, N. (Eds.). (2004). *Autour de l'homme: Contexte et actualité d'André Leroi-Gourhan*. Antibes: Editions APDCA.

Bailey, G. (Ed.). (1997). *Klithi: Palaeolithic settlement and Quaternary landscapes in northwest Greece*. Cambridge: The McDonald Institute for Archaeological Research.

Bailey, G., & Galanidou, N. (2009). Caves, palimpsests and dwellings places: Examples from southeast Europe. *World Archaeology, 41*(2), 215–241.

Bailey, G., Cadbury, T., Galanidou, N., & Kotjabopoulou, E. (1997). Rockshelters and open-air sites: Survey strategies and regional site distributions. In G. Bailey (Ed.), *Klithi: Palaeolithic settlement and Quaternary landscapes in northwest Greece* (Volume 2: Klithi in its local and regional setting, pp. 521–536). Cambridge: MacDonald Institute for Archaeological Research.

Banpo Museum, Shaanxi Institute of Archaeology, Lintong County Museum. (1988). *Jiangzhai-a report on the excavation of a Neolithic site*. Beijing: Wenwu.

Bar-Matthews, M., Marean, C. W., Jacobs, Z., Karkanas, P., Fisher, E. C., Herries, A. I. R., Brown, K., Williams, H. M., Bernatchez, J., Ayalon, A., & Nilssen, P. J. (2010). A high resolution and continuous isotopic speleothem record of paleoclimate and paleoenvironment from 90 to 53 ka from Pinnacle Point on the south coast of South Africa. *Quarternary Science Review, 29*, 2131–2145.

M. Carver et al. (eds.), *Field Archaeology from Around the World*, SpringerBriefs in Archaeology, DOI 10.1007/978-3-319-09819-7

Barfield, L. (1994). The Bronze Age of northern Italy: Recent work and social interpretation. In C. Mathers & S. Stoddart (Eds.), *Development and decline in the Mediterranean Bronze Age* (Sheffield Archaeological Monographs 8, pp. 129–144). Sheffield: Collis J.R. Publications.

Barker, P. (1977). *Techniques of archaeological excavation*. London: Batsford.

Becker, H. (2009). Caesium-magnetometry for landscape archaeology. In S. Campana & S. Piro (Eds.), *Seeing the unseen – geophysics and landscape archaeology* (pp. 129–165). London: CRC.

Becker, K., Armit, I., & Swindles, G. (2010). From data to knowledge – the new Irish Iron Age. *Archaeology Ireland, 24*(3), 13.

Bellwood, P., Chambers, G., Ross, M., & Hung, H. C. (2011). Are 'cultures' inherited? Multidisciplinary perspectives on the origins and migrations of Austronesian-speaking peoples prior to 1000 BC. In B. W. Roberts & M. Van der Linden (Eds.), *Investigating archaeological cultures: Material culture, variability, and transmission* (pp. 321–354). New York: Springer.

Bernabò Brea, M., & Cremaschi, M. (2004). La terramara di Santa Rosa di Poviglio nel corso del Bronzo Recente. *Atti del Convegno L'età del Bronzo Recente in Italia, Lido di Camaiore 26–29 ottobre 2000*, pp. 101–111.

Bernabò Brea, M., Cardarelli, A., & Cremaschi, M. (Eds.). (1997). *Le terramare. La più antica civiltà padana*. Milano: Electa.

Bernatchez, J. A. (2010). Taphonomic implications of orientation of plotted finds from Pinnacle Point 13B (Mossel Bay, Western Cape Province, South Africa). *Journal of Human Evolution, 59*, 274–288.

Bernatchez, J. A., & Marean, C. W. (2011). Total station archaeology and the use of digital photography. *SAA Archaeological Record, 11*(3), 16–21.

Besteman, J. C., Bos, J. M., Gerrets, D. A., Heidinga, H. A., & de Koning, J. (Eds.). (1999). *The excavations at Wijnaldum* (Reports on Frisia in Roman and Medieval Times 1). Rotterdam/Brookfield: Taylor & Francis.

Bewley, R., & Rączkowski, W. (Eds.). (2002). *Aerial archaeology. Developing future practice*. Amsterdam: IOS.

Bewley, R. H., Crutchley, S. P., & Shell, C. A. (2005). New light on an ancient landscape: Lidar survey in the Stonehenge World Heritage Site. *Antiquity, 79*, 636–647.

Binford, L. (1978). *Nunamiut ethnoarchaeology*. New York: Academic.

Binford, L. (1987). *Bones: Ancient men and modern myths*. New York: Academic.

Bintliff, J. (2000). Beyond dots on the map: Future directions for surface artefact survey in Greece. In J. Bintliff, M. Kuna, & N. Venclov (Eds.), *The future of surface artefact survey in Europe* (Sheffield Archaeological Monographs 13, pp. 3–20). Sheffield: Sheffield Academic.

Bintliff, J., & Snodgrass, A. (1988). Off-site pottery distributions: A regional and interregional perspective. *Current Anthropology, 29*(3), 506–513.

Bird, D. W., Bliege Bird, R., & Codding, B. F. (2009). In pursuit of mobile prey: Martu hunting strategies and archaeofaunal interpretation. *American Antiquity, 74*, 3–29.

Bodu, P., Debout, G., Julien, M., & Valentin, B. (Eds.). (2006). Un dernier hiver à Pincevent: les Magdaléniens du niveau IV-0. *Gallia-Préhistoire, 48*, 19–35.

Bogaard, A., Krause, R., & Strien, H.-C. (2011). Towards a social geography of cultivation and plant use in an early farming community: Vaihingen an der Enz, south-west Germany. *Antiquity, 85*, 395–416.

Boucher de Perthes, J. (1847). *Antiquités celtiques et anté-dilluviennes. Mémoire sur l'industrie primitive et les arts à leur origine* (Vol. 1). Paris: Treuttel & Würtz.

Brophy, K., & Cowley, D. (Eds.). (2005). *From the air: Understanding aerial archaeology*. Stroud: Tempus.

Brown, D. H. (2007). *Archaeological archives: A guide to best practice in creation, compilation, transfer and curation*. London: Institute of Field Archaeologists.

Brown, K. S., Marean, C. W., Herries, A. I. R., Jacobs, Z., Tribolo, C., Braun, D., Roberts, D. L., Meyer, M. C., & Bernatchez, J. (2009). Fire as an engineering tool of early modern humans. *Science, 325*, 859–862.

Buck, C. E. (2001). Applications of the Bayesian statistical paradigm. In D. R. Brothwell & A. M. Pollard (Eds.), *Handbook of archaeological sciences* (pp. 695–702). New York: Wiley.

Bullinger, J., Leesch, D., & Plumettaz, N. (2006). *Le site magdalénien de Monruz, 1. Premiers éléments pour l'analyse d'un habitat de plein air* (Archéologie neuchâteloise 33). Neuchâtel: Service et Musée cantonal d'archéologie.

Burke, H., & Smith, C. (2004). *The archaeologists field handbook*. Crows Nest: Allen and Unwin.

Burke, H., Lovell-Jones, C., & Smith, C. (1994). Beyond the looking-glass: Some thoughts on sociopolitics and reflexivity in Australian archaeology. *Australian Archaeology, 38*, 13–22.

Cardarelli, A. (2010). The collapse of the Terramare culture and growth of new economic and social systems during the Bronze Age in Italy. *Scienze dell'Antichità. Storia, Archeologia, Antropologia, 15*, 449–520.

Carson, M. T. (2011). Palaeohabitat of first settlement sites 1500-1000 B.C. in Guam, Mariana Islands, western Pacific. *Journal of Archaeological Science, 38*, 2207–2221.

Carver, M. O. H. (2005). *Sutton Hoo. A seventh-century princely burial ground and its context*. London: British Museum.

Carver, M. O. H. (2009). *Archaeological investigation*. Boca Raton: Taylor & Francis.

Carver, M. O. H. (2011). *Making archaeology happen*. Walnut Creek: Left Coast.

Carver, M. O. H., Hills, C., & Scheschkewicz, J. (2009). *Wasperton. a Roman, British and Anglo-Saxon Community in Central England*. Woodbridge: Boydell.

Cavers, G., & Crone, A. (2010). Galloway crannogs: An interim report on work at Cults Loch and Dorman's Island by the Scottish Wetland Archaeology Programme. *Transactions of the Dumfriesshire and Galloway Natural History and Antiquarian Society, 84*, 11–18.

Cavers, G., & Henderson, J. (2005). Underwater excavation at Ederline crannog, Loch Awe, Argyll, Scotland. *International Journal of Nautical Archaeology, 34*, 282–298.

Cavers, G., Crone, A., Engl, R., Fouracre, L., Hunter, F., Robertson, J., & Thoms, J. (2011). Excavations at Dorman's island, Whitefield Loch: An Iron Age crannog in SW Scotland. *Journal of Wetland Archaeology, 10*, 71–108.

Chapman, J. (1990). Social inequality on Bulgarian tells and the Varna problem. In R. Samson (Ed.), *The social archaeology of houses* (pp. 49–92). Edinburgh: Edinburgh University Press.

Charlton, T. H., & Nichols, D. L. (2005). Settlement pattern archaeology in the Teotihuacan Valley and the adjacent northeastern Basin of Mexico: A.P. (after Parsons). In R. E. Blanton (Ed.), *Settlement, subsistence, and social complexity: Essays honoring the legacy of Jeffrey R. Parsons* (pp. 43–62). Los Angeles: Cotsen Institute of Archaeology, University of California.

Chen, X. (1997). *Zhongguo Shiqian Kaoguxueshi Yanjiu 1895–1949*. Beijing: Sanlian Shudian.

Cherry, J. F. (2003). Archaeology beyond the site: Regional survey and its future. In J. K. Papadopoulos & R. M. Leventhal (Eds.), *Theory and practice in Mediterranean archaeology Old World and New World perspectives* (pp. 137–160). Los Angeles: Cotsen Institute of Archaeology, University of California.

Cherry, J. F., Davis, J. L., Mantzourani, E., & Whitelaw, T. M. (1991). The survey methods. In J. F. Cherry, J. L. Davis, & E. Mantzourani (Eds.), *Landscape archaeology as long-term history: Northern Keos in the Cycladic Islands from earliest settlement until modern times* (Monumenta Archaeologica 16, pp. 13–35). Los Angeles: Institute of Archaeology, University of California.

China, Ministry of Culture. (1984). *Manual of archaeological fieldwork*. (Reprinted by the Experimental Teaching Center of Archaeology and Anthropology of Xiamen University, 2007).

China, State Administration of Cultural Heritage. (2009). *Manual of archaeological fieldwork*. Beijing: Wenwu.

Coles, J. (1972). *Field archaeology*. London: Methuen.

Connah, G. (1983). *Australian field archaeology: A guide to techniques*. Canberra: Australian Institute of Aboriginal Studies.

Conyers, L. B. (2004). *Ground-penetrating radar for archaeology*. Walnut Creek: AltaMira.

Courbin, P. (1987). André Leroi-Gourhan et la technique des fouilles. *Bulletin de la Société Préhistorique Française, 84*(10–12), 328–334.

Crawford, O. G. S. (1923). Air survey and archaeology. *The Geographical Journal, 61*, 342–360.

Crawford, O. G. S. (1960). *Archaeology in the field*. London: Phoenix.

Cremaschi, M. & Pizzi, C. (2011). Exploiting water resource in the Bronze Age villages (terramare) of the Po plain (northern Italy). Recent investigation in the terramara Santa Rosa of

Poviglio. *Antiquity Project Gallery, 85* (327). Available at: http://antiquity.ac.uk/projgall/cremaschi327/

Cremaschi, M., Pizzi, C., & Valsecchi, V. (2006). Water management and land use in the terramare and a possible climatic co-factor in their collapse. The case study of the Terramara S. Rosa (northern Italy). *Quaternary International, 151*, 87–98.

Crone, B. A. (2000). *The history of a Scottish lowland crannog: Excavations at Buiston, Ayrshire 1989-90* (STAR Monograph series 4). Edinburgh: Scottish Trust for Archaeological Research.

Crutchley, S., & Crow, P. (2009). *The light fantastic: Using airborne laser scanning in archaeological survey*. Swindon: English Heritage.

Dallas, R. (Ed.). (2003). *Measured survey and building recording for historic buildings and structures* (Guide for Practitioners 4). Edinburgh: Historic Scotland.

Darvill, T. (2001). Traditions of landscape archaeology in Britain: Issues of time and scale. In T. Darvill & M. Gojda (Eds.), *One land, many landscapes. Papers from a session held at the European Association of Archaeologists fifth annual meeting in Bournemouth 1999* (British Archaeological Reports International series 987, pp. 33–46). Oxford: Archaeopress.

David, N., & Kramer, C. (2001). *Ethnoarchaeology in action*. Cambridge: Cambridge University Press.

David, N., Sterner, A., & Gauva, K. B. (1988). Why pots are decorated. *Current Anthropology, 29*, 365–389.

Dean, M., Ferrari, B., Oxley, I., Redknap, M., & Watson, K. (Eds.). (1992). *Archaeology underwater: The NAS guide to principles and practice*. London: Nautical Archaeology Society, Archetype Press.

DeBoer, W. (1974). Ceramic longevity and archaeological interpretation: An example of the Upper Ucayali, Peru. *American Antiquity, 39*, 335–343.

Deevy, M. B., & Murphy, D. (2009). *Places along the way. First findings on the M3* (NRA Scheme Monographs 5). Dublin: NRA.

Dembińska, M. (1954). Dyskusja w sprawie metody wykopaliskowej. *Wiadomości Archeologiczne, 20*(1), 97–98.

Devereux, B. J., Amable, G. S., Crow, P., & Cliff, A. D. (2005). The potential of airborne lidar for detection of archaeological features under woodland canopies. *Antiquity, 79*, 648–660.

Dezhamkhooy, M., & Papoli, L. (2010). The archaeology of last night… what happened in Bam (Iran) on 25–6 December 2003. *World Archaeology (Archaeology and Contemporary Society), 42*(3), 341–354.

Dibble, H., Marean, C. W., & McPherron, S. P. (2007). The use of barcodes in excavation projects. *SAA Archaeological Record, 7*, 33–38.

Dixon, N. (2004). *The crannogs of Scotland: An underwater archaeology*. Stroud: Tempus.

Dodson, J., Fullagar, R., & Head, L. (1992). Dynamics of environment and people in forested crescents of temperate Australia. In J. Dodson (Ed.), *The naive lands: Prehistory and environmental change in Australia and the South-West Pacific* (pp. 115–192). Melbourne: Longman Cheshire.

Doneus, M., & Briese, C. (2011). Airborne laser scanning in forested areas – potential and limitations of an archaeological prospection technique. In D. Cowley (Ed.), *Remote sensing for archaeological heritage management* (pp. 59–76). Brussel: Archaeolingua.

Douglass, M. J., Holdaway, S. J., Fanning, P. C., & Shiner, J. I. (2008). An assessment and archaeological application of cortex measurement in lithic assemblages. *American Antiquity, 73*, 513–526.

Fagette, P. (2008). *Digging for dollars: American archaeology and the New Deal*. Albuquerque: University of New Mexico Press.

Fanning, P., Holdaway, S. J., & Rhodes, E. (2008). A new geoarchaeology of Aboriginal artefact deposits in western NSW, Australia: Establishing spatial and temporal geomorphic controls on the surface archaeological record. *Geomorphology, 101*, 524–532.

Fanning, P. C., Holdaway, S. J., & Bryant, T. (2009). The surface archaeological record in arid Australia: Geomorphic controls on preservation, exposure and visibility. *Geoarchaeology, 24*, 121–146.

Fewster, F. (2001). The responsibilities of ethnoarchaeologists. In M. Pluciennik (Ed.), *The responsibilities of archaeologists: Archaeology and ethics* (British Archaeological Reports International series 981, pp. 65–73). Oxford: Archaeopress.

Fisher, E. C., Bar-Matthews, M., Jerardino, A., & Marean, C. W. (2010). Middle and late Pleistocene paleoscape modeling along the southern coast of South Africa. *Quaternary Science Reviews, 29*, 1382–1398.

Flannery, K. V. (Ed.). (1976). *The early Mesoamerican village*. New York: Academic.

Forsén, B., & Tikkala, E. (Eds.). (2011). *Thesprotia expedition II environment and settlement patterns* (Papers and Monographs of the Finnish Institute at Athens XVI). Helsinki: Foundation of the Finnish Institute at Athens.

Fortin, M., & Aurenche, O. (Eds.). (1998). *Espace naturel, espace habité en Syrie du Nord (10e-2e millénaires av. J-C.), Natural space, inhabited space in northern Syria (10th-2nd millennium B.C.)*. Québec and Lyon: Canadian Society for Mesopotamian Studies and Maison de l'Orient Méditerranéen Lyon.

Gaffney, C. F., & Gater, J. (2003). *Revealing the buried past: Geophysics for archaeologists*. Stroud: Tempus Publishing.

Gamble, C., & Kruszynski, R. (2009). John Evans, Joseph Prestwich and the stone that shattered the time barrier. *Antiquity, 83*, 461–475.

Gamio, M., Best, A., & Boas, F. (1921). *Álbum de colecciones arqueológicas*. Mexico City: Museo Nacional de Arqueología, Historia y Etnografía.

Gansum, T. (2004). *Hauger som konstruksjoner – arkeologiske forventninger gjennom 200 år* (GOTARC Series B, Gothenburg Archaeological Theses). Gothenburg: Gothenburg University.

Garrow, D., Beadsmoore, E., & Knight, M. (2005). Pit clusters and the temporality of occupation: An earlier Neolithic pit site at Kilverstone, Thetford, Norfolk. *Proceedings of the Prehistoric Society, 71*, 139–158.

Gerster, G. (2003). *The past from above*. London: Frances Lincoln.

Glob, P. V. (1969). *The bog people*. London: Faber & Faber.

Glob, P. V. (1974). *The mound people. Danish Bronze-Age man preserved*. London: Faber & Faber.

Gojda, M., et al. (2004). *Ancient landscape, settlement dynamics and non-destructive archaeology – Czech research project 1997–2002*. Praha: Academia.

Goldberg, P., & Macphail, R. I. (2006). *Practical and theoretical geoarchaeology*. Malden: Wiley-Blackwell.

Gonzalez Ruibal, A. (2009). De la etnoarqueología a la arqueología del presente. In *Mundos Tribales. Una visión etnoarqueológica* (pp. 16–27). Madrid.

Gosselain, O. (2000). Materializing identities. An African perspective. *Journal of Archaeological Methods and Theory, 7*, 187–218.

Greaves, R. (2006). Use and residential landscape. Foragers organization. In F. Sellers, R. Greaves, & P.-L. Yu (Eds.), *Archaeology and ethnoarchaeology of mobility* (pp. 127–152). Gainesville: University Press of Florida.

Greer, S., Harrison, R., & McIntyre-Tamwoy, S. (2002). Community-based archaeology in Australia. *World Archaeology, 34*(2), 265–287.

Hale, H. M., & Tindale, N. B. (1930). Notes on some human remains in the Lower Murray Valley, SA. *Records of the South Australian Museum, 4*, 145–218.

Hanson, J. A., & Schiffer, M. B. (1975). The Joint Site – a preliminary report. Chapters in the prehistory of eastern Arizona, IV. *Fieldiana Anthropology, 65*, 47–91.

Harrington, J. C. (1955). Archeology as an auxiliary science to American history. *American Anthropologist, 57*, 1121–1130.

Harris, E. C. (1989). *Principles of archaeological stratigraphy*. London: Academic.

Hebsgaard, M. B., Gilbert, M. T. P., Arneborg, J., Heyn, P., Allentoft, M. E., Bunce, M., Munch, K., Schweger, C., & Willeslev, E. (2009). 'The farm beneath the sand' – an archaeological case study on ancient 'dirt' DNA. *Antiquity, 83*, 430–444.

Hedges, R. E. M. (2001). Overview – dating in archaeology: Past, present and future. In D. R. Brothwell & A. M. Pollard (Eds.), *Handbook of archaeological sciences* (pp. 3–8). New York: Wiley.

Herries, A. I. R., & Fisher, E. C. (2010). Multidimensional GIS modeling of magnetic mineralogy as a proxy for fire use and spatial patterning: evidence from the Middle Stone Age Bearing Sea cave of Pinnacle Point 13B (Western Cape, South Africa). *Journal of Human Evolution, 59*, 306–320.

Hesse, A., Jolivet, A., & Tabbagh, A. (1986). New prospects in shallow depth electrical surveying for archaeological and pedological applications. *Geophysics, 51*(3), 585–594.

Hester, T. R., Shafer, H. J., & Feder, K. L. (1997). *Field methods in archaeology* (7th ed.). Mountain View: Mayfield Publishing.

Hiscock, P. (2008). *Archaeology of ancient Australia*. London/New York: Routledge.

Hodder, I. (1982). *The present past: An introduction to anthropology for archaeologists*. London: Batsford.

Hodder, I. (1997). 'Always momentary, fluid and flexible': Towards a reflexive excavation methodology. *Antiquity, 71*, 691–700.

Hodder, I. (1999). *The archaeological process. An introduction*. Oxford: Blackwell.

Holdaway, S. J., & Fanning, P. (2008). Developing a landscape history as part of a survey strategy: A critique of current settlement system approaches based on case studies from western New South Wales, Australia. *Journal of Archaeological Method and Theory, 15*, 167–189.

Holdaway, S. J., Fanning, P., & Rhodes, E. (2008). Challenging intensification: human – environment interactions in the Holocene geoarchaeological record from western New South Wales, Australia. *The Holocene, 18*, 403–412.

Holubowicz, W. (1947). O metodzie badania grodów. *Z Otchłani Wieków, 16*(3–4), 33–37.

Holubowicz, W. (1948). *Studia nad metodami badań warstw kulturowych w prehistorii polskiej* [Studies on methods of culture layers studying in Polish prehistory]. Toruń.

Horton, D. R. (1991). *Recovering the tracks: The story of Australian archaeology*. Canberra: Aboriginal Studies.

Hyenstrand, Å. (1984). *Fasta fornlämningar och arkeologiska regioner*. Stockholm: Riksantikvarieämbetet (in Swedish).

Jacobs, Z. (2010). An OSL chronology for the sedimentary deposits from Pinnacle Point Cave 13B - a punctuated presence. *Journal of Human Evolution, 59*, 289–305.

Jagmin, K. (1876). Opis mogiły (kurhanu) pod Łęgonicami i wydobytych z niej przedmiotów. *Wiadomości Archeologiczne, 3*, 83–94.

Jerardino, A., & Marean, C. W. (2010). Shellfish gathering, marine paleoecology and modern human behavior: Perspectives from cave PP13B, Pinnacle Point, South Africa. *Journal of Human Evolution, 59*, 412–424.

Karkanas, P., & Goldberg, P. (2010). Site formation processes at Pinnacle Point Cave 13B (Mossel Bay, Western Cape Province, South Africa): Resolving stratigraphic and depositional complexities with micromorphology. *Journal of Human Evolution, 59*, 256–273.

Kelly, R., Poyer, L., & Ticker, B. (2006). Mobility and houses in southwestern Madagascar. Ethnoarchaeology among the Mikea and their neighbors. In F. Sellers, R. Greaves, & P.-L. Yu (Eds.), *Archaeology and ethnoarchaeology of mobility* (pp. 75–107). Gainesville: University Press of Florida.

Kidder, A. V. (1924). *An introduction to the study of southwestern archaeology with a preliminary account of the excavations at Pecos and a summary of southwestern archaeology today*. New Haven: Yale University Press; Andover: Phillips Academy.

Kobyliński, Z., & Moszczyński, W. A. (1992). Conjoinable sherds and stratification processes: An example from Wyszogród, Poland. *Archaeologia Polona, 30*, 109–126.

Kostrzewski, J. (Ed.). (1936). *Osada bagienna w Biskupinie w pow. Żnińskim*. Poznań.

Kostrzewski, J. (1938). *Gród prasłowiański w Biskupinie w pow. Żnińskim*. Poznań.

Kostrzewski, J. (1950). *III sprawozdanie z prac wykopaliskowych w grodzie kultury łużyckiej w Biskupinie w pow. Żnińskim za lata 1938-1939 i 1946-1948*. Poznań.

Kostrzewski, J. (1931). Grodzisko w Jedwabnie w pow. toruńskim. Przyczynek do relatywnej chronologii ceramiki pomorskiej okresu wczesnohistorycznego. *Slavia Occidentalis, 10*, 244–273.

Kowalewski, S. (2008). Regional settlement pattern studies. *Journal of Archaeological Research, 16*, 225–285.

Kozlowski, L. (1917). *Badania archeologiczne na górze Klin w Iwanowicach, powiatu Miechowskiego*. Warszawa.

Kramer, C. (1982). *Village ethnoarchaeology: Rural Iran in archaeological perspective*. New York: Academic.

Kramer, C. (1997). *Pottery in Rajasthan: Ethnoarchaeology in two Indian cities*. Washington, DC: Smithsonian Institution Press.

Křivánek, R. (2004). Geophysical survey in the archaeologically uninvestigated parts of Czech oppida. *Antiquity Project Gallery*. Available at: http://antiquity.ac.uk/ProjGall/krivanek/index.html

Křivánek, R. (2011). Contribution of geophysical surveys to changes of archaeological interpretation on examples of various enclosed sites in Bohemia. In M. Drahor & M. Berge (Eds.), *Archaeological prospection* (pp. 136–139). Izmir: Archaeology and Art Publications.

Křivánek, R., Mařík, J., & Mařík, J. (2009). Early medieval stronghold Libice nad Cidlinou. An example of use of geophysical methods in systematic non-destructive archaeological project. *ArcheoSciences, revue d'archéométrie, 33*, 93–95.

Krukowski, S. (1921). Badania jaskiń pasma Krakowsko-Wieluńskiego w 1914 r. *Archiwum Nauk Antropologicznych, 1*(1).

Kuniholm, P. I. (2001). Dendrochronology and other applications of tree-ring studies in archaeology. In D. R. Brothwell & A. M. Pollard (Eds.), *Handbook of archaeological sciences* (pp. 35–46). New York: Wiley.

Leesch, D., & Bullinger, J. (2012). Identifying dwellings in Upper Palaeolithic open-air sites: the Magdalenian site at Monruz and its contribution to analysing palimpsests. In M. Niekus, R. Barton, M. Street, & T. Terberger (Eds.), *A mind set on flint. Studies in honour of Dick Stapert* (Groningen Archaeological Studies 16, pp. 165–181). Groningen: Barkhuis.

Lourandos, H. (1985). Intensification and Australian prehistory. In T. D. Price & J. A. Brown (Eds.), *Prehistoric hunter-gatherers: The emergence of cultural complexity* (pp. 385–423). New York: Academic.

Lucas, G. (2012). *Understanding the archaeological record*. Cambridge: Cambridge University Press.

Lucy, S. (2000). *The Anglo-Saxon way of death*. Stroud: Sutton.

Lupo, K., & O'Connell, J. (2002). Cut and tooth mark distribution on large animal bones: Ethnoarchaeological data from the Hadza and their implications for current ideas about early human carnivory. *Journal of Archaeological Science, 29*, 85109.

Lyon, E. A. (1996). *A new deal for southeastern archaeology*. Tuscaloosa: University of Alabama Press.

Mahalati, M. (1988). *Bam geography*. Kerman: Tolou Azadi (in Persian).

Majewski, E. (1902). Jak rozkopywać kurhany? *Światowit, 4*, 193–200.

Malm, G. (Ed.). (2001). *Archaeology and buildings* (British Archaeological Reports International Series 930). Oxford: Archaeopress.

Mann, P. (Ed.). (2005). *Active tectonics and seismic hazards of Puerto Rico, the Virgin Islands, and offshore areas* (Geological Society of America Special Paper 385). Washington, DC: Geological Society of America.

Marean, C. W., Bar-Matthews, M., Fisher, E., Goldberg, P., Herries, A., Karkanas, P., Nilssen, P. J., & Thompson, E. (2010). The stratigraphy of the Middle Stone Age sediments at Pinnacle Point Cave 13B (Mossel Bay, Western Cape Province, South Africa). *Journal of Human Evolution, 59*, 234–255.

Marean, C. W., Nilssen, P. J., Brown, K., Jerardino, A., & Stynder, D. (2004). Paleoanthropological investigations of Middle Stone Age sites at Pinnacle Point, Mossel Bay (South Africa): Archaeology and hominid remains from the 2000 field season. *PaleoAnthropology, 5*, 14–83.

Marean, C. W., Bar-Matthews, M., Bernatchez, J., Fisher, E., Goldberg, P., Herries, A. I. R., Jacobs, Z., Jerardino, A., Karkanas, P., Minichillo, T., Nilssen, P. J., Thompson, E., Watts, I., & Williams, H. M. (2007). Early human use of marine resources and pigment in South Africa during the Middle Pleistocene. *Nature, 449*, 905–908.

Marsden, B. (1983). *Pioneers of prehistory. Leaders and landmarks in English archaeology (1500–1900)*. Ormskirk: Hesketh.

Matthews, R. (Ed.). (2003). *Excavations at Tell Brak, Volume 4: Exploring an Upper Mesopotamian regional centre, 1994-1996*. Cambridge: The McDonald Institute for Archaeological Research and The British School of Archaeology in Iraq.

Mazurowski, R. (1996). *Założenia i wskazówki metodyczne dla archeologicznych badań ratowniczych wzdłuż Trasy gazociągu tranzytowego*. Poznań: EuRoPol GAZ s.a.

McPherron, S., & Holdaway, S. J. (1996). Entrer Trois. In H. Dibble & S. McPherron (Eds.), *A multimedia companion to the Middle Paleolithic site of Combe-Capelle Bas (France)*. CD-ROM. Philadelphia: The University Museum.

Mele, M., Cremaschi, M., Giudici, M., Bassi, A., Pizzi, C., & Lozej, A. (2011). Near-surface geophysical prospection to reveal the hidden structure of the Terramara Santa Rosa, Poviglio (Italy). Abstract in *Epitome*, p. 339.

Menotti, F., Baubonis, Z., Brazaitis, D., Higham, T., Kvedaravicius, M., Lewis, H., Motuzaite, G., & Pranckenaite, E. (2005). The first lake-dwellers of Lithuania: Late Bronze Age pile settlements on Lake Luokesas. *Oxford Journal of Archaeology, 24*(4), 381–403.

Milek, K. B. (2006). Houses and households in early Icelandic society: Geoarchaeology and the interpretation of social space. Unpublished PhD dissertation, University of Cambridge.

Milek, K. B. (2012a). Floor formation processes and the interpretation of site activity areas: An ethnoarchaeological study of turf buildings at Thverá, northeast Iceland. *Journal of Anthropological Archaeology, 31*, 119–137.

Milek, K. B. (2012b). Roles of pit houses and gendered spaces on Viking Age farmsteads in Iceland. *Medieval Archaeology, 56*, 85–130.

Mishra, V. N. (2007). *Rajasthan: Prehistoric and early historic foundations*. New Delhi: Aryan Books International.

Mishra, A. (2008). *Beyond pots and pans: A study of Chalcolithic Balathal*. New Delhi: IGRMS & Aryan Books International.

Morriss, R. K. (2000). *The archaeology of buildings*. Stroud: Tempus.

Mulvaney, D. J. (2011). *Digging up the past*. Sydney: University of New South Wales Press.

Museum of London Archaeology Service (MoLAS). (1994). *Archaeological site manual* (3rd ed.). London: MoLAS. Available at http://www.museumoflondonarchaeology.org.uk/NR/rdonlyres/056B4AFD-AB5F-45AF-9097-5A53FFDC1F94/0/MoLASManual94.pdf.

Myhre, B. (1987). Chieftain's graves and chiefdom territories in South Norway in the migration period. *Studien zur Sachsenforschung, 6*, 169–187.

Nagar, M. (1967). The Ahar culture: An archaeological and ethnographic study. Unpublished PhD dissertation, Poona University.

Naniwa. (n.d.). Available at: http://www.kkr.mlit.go.jp/naniwa/03/04.html

Nelson, N. C. (1909). Shellmounds of the San Francisco Bay region. *University of California Publications in American Archaeology and Ethnology, 7*, 319–348.

Nelson, N. C. (1914). *Pueblo ruins of the Galisteo Basin* (Anthropological Papers of the American Museum of Natural History 15). New York: American Museum of Natural History.

Neubauer, W. (2004). GIS in archaeology – the interface between prospection and excavation. *Archaeological Prospection, 11*, 159–166.

Neumann, T. W., & Sanford, R. M. (2001). *Cultural resources archaeology: An introduction*. Walnut Creek: AltaMira.

Nicolay, J. A. W. (Ed.). (2010). *Terpbewoning in oostelijk Friesland. Twee opgravingen in het voormalige kweldergebied van Oostergo* (Groningen Archaeological Studies 10). Groningen: Barkhuis Publishing and the Groningen University Library.

O'Connell, J. (1987). Alyawara site structure and its archaeological implications. *American Antiquity, 52*, 74–108.
O'Sullivan, J., & Stanley, M. (Eds.). (2008). *Roads, rediscovery and research. Proceedings of a public seminar on archaeological discoveries on national road schemes, August 2007*. Dublin: NRA.
Oates, D., Oates, J., & MacDonald, H. (Eds.). (2001). *Excavations at Tell Brak, Volume 2: Nagar in the third millennium BC*. Cambridge: The McDonald Institute for Archaeological Research and the British School of Archaeology in Iraq.
Oonk, S., Slomp, C. P., & Huisman, D. J. (2009). Geochemistry as an aid in archaeological prospection and site interpretation: Current issues and research directions. *Archaeological Prospection, 16*, 35–51.
Papoli, L. (2010). Public and private lives in Iran: An introduction to the archaeology of the 2003 Bam earthquake. *Archaeologies: Journal of the World Archaeological Congress, 6*, 29–47.
Papoli, L. O., Garazhian, O., & Dezhamkhooy, M. (2011). Exchange system patterns in Bam southeastern Iran after the earthquake (December 2003): An ethnoarchaeological study. *Ethnoarchaeology, 3*, 29–61.
Parc Arqueològic Mines de Gavà. (n.d.). Available at: http://www.parcarqueologic.cat/cat/imgpcn/m.asp
Parcak, S. H. (2009). *Satellite remote sensing for archaeology*. London: Routledge.
Parron-Kontis, I., & Reveyron, N. (Eds.). (2005). *Archéologie du bâti*. Paris: Editions Errance.
Pavel, C. (2010). *Describing and interpreting the past: European and American approaches to the written record of the excavation*. Bucharest: Bucharest University Editions.
Pearce, M. (1998). New research on the terramare of northern Italy. *Antiquity, 72*, 743–746.
Phillips, P., Ford, J. A., & Griffin, J. B. (1951). *Archaeological survey in the Lower Mississippi Alluvial Valley, 1940-47* (Papers of the Peabody Museum 25). Cambridge, MA: Peabody Museum.
Philip, G., Bradbury, J., & Jabbur, F. (2011). The archaeology of the Homs basalt, Syria, the main site types. *Studia Orontica, 9*, 38–55.
Pitulko, V. V. (2008). Principal excavation techniques under permafrost conditions (based on Zhokhov and Yana Sites, northern Yakutia). *Archaeology, Ethnology and Anthropology of Eurasia, 34*(2), 26–33.
Pitulko, V. V., & Pavlova, E. Y. (2010). *Geoarchaeology and radiocarbon chronology of the Stone Age of the North-East Asia*. Saint Petersburg: Nauka.
Plog, F. T. (1974). *The study of prehistoric change*. New York: Academic.
Politis, G. (2007). *Nukak. ethnoarchaeology of an Amazonian people*. (University College London Institute of Archaeology Publications). Walnut Creek: Left Coast.
Powlesland, D. (2012). The Landscape Research Centre Digital Atlas of Archaeological Research in the Vale of Pickering. An online resource employing Google Earth to publish primary data and time linked interpretive overlays covering the LRC core remote sensing dataset. Available at: http://www.landscaperesearchcentre.org/atlas/LRC_Atlas.html
Powlesland, D. J., Haughton, C. A., & Hanson, J. H. (1986). Excavations at Heslerton, North Yorkshire 1978-82. *Archaeological Journal, 143*, 53–173.
Powlesland, D., Lyall, J., & Donoghue, D. (1997). Enhancing the record through remote sensing: the application and integration of multi-sensor, non-invasive remote sensing techniques for the enhancement of the Sites and Monuments Record, Heslerton Parish Project, N. Yorkshire, England. *Internet Archaeology, 2*. Available at: http://intarch.ac.uk/journal/issue2/pld/index.html.
Py, M. (Ed.). (1997). *SYSLAT 3.1. Système d'information archéologique: manuel de référence (Lattara 10)*. Lattes: Association pour la recherche archéologique en Languedoc oriental.
Ramqvist, P. H. (1992). *Högom. Part 1. The excavations 1949-1984* (Archaeology and Environment 13). Umeå: Umeå University.
RCHM. (1960). *A matter of time: An archaeological survey*. London: HMSO.
Reynolds, N., & Barber, J. (1984). Analytical excavation. *Antiquity, 58*, 95–102.
Robin, C. (2012). *Chan: An ancient Maya farming community*. Gainesville: University Press of Florida.
Roskams, S. (2001). *Excavation* (Cambridge Manuals in Archaeology). Cambridge: Cambridge University Press.

Roux, V. (2007). Ethnoarchaeology: A non-historical science of reference necessary for interpreting the past. *Journal of Archaeological Method and Theory, 14*(2), 153–178.

Rye, O. S. (1981). *Pottery technology: Principles and reconstruction* (Manuals on Archeology 4). Washington, DC: Taraxacum.

Sankalia, H. D., Deo, S. B., & Ansari, Z. D. (1969). *Excavation at Ahar (Tambavati)*. Pune: Deccan College.

Saraswati, B., & Behura, N. K. (1966). *Pottery techniques in peasant India* (Anthropological Survey of India Memoir 13). Calcutta: Anthropological Survey of India.

Sarkar, A. (2011). Chalcolithic and modern potting at Gilund, Rajasthan: A cautionary tale. *Antiquity, 85*, 994–1007.

Schalich, J. (1988). Boden- und Landschaftsgeschichte. In U. Boelicke, D. von Brandt, J. Lüning, P. Stehli, & A. Zimmermann (Eds.), *Der bandkeramische Siedlungsplatz Langweiler 8, Gemeinde Aldenhoven, Kreis Düren* (pp. 17–29). Köln: Rheinland Verlag.

Schiffer, M. (1987). *Formation processes of the archaeological record*. Albuquerque: University of New Mexico Press.

Schuller, M. (2002). *Monuments & sites VII: Building archaeology*. Munich: ICOMOS.

Scollar, I., Tabbagh, A., Hesse, A., & Herzog, I. (1990). *Archaeological prospecting and remote sensing*. Cambridge: Cambridge University Press.

Sease, C. (1994). *A conservation manual for the field archaeologist* (Archaeological Research Tools 4). Los Angeles: Cotsen Institute of Archaeology, University of California.

Shi, X. (1982). Tianye kaogu fangfa – diaocha, faju eyu zhengli. In W. Yin (Ed.), *Kaogu Gongzuo Shouce* (pp. 1–92). Beijing: Wenwu.

Shinde, V. (2002). The emergence, development and spread of agricultural communities in South Asia. In Y. Yasuda (Ed.), *The origins of pottery and agriculture* (pp. 89–115). New Delhi: Roli Books.

Shinde, V., & Possehl, G. L. (2005). A report on the excavations at Gilund. In C. Jarrige & V. Lefèvre (Eds.), *South Asian archaeology, 2001: Proceedings of the 16th international conference of the European Association of South Asian Archaeologists held in College de France, Paris, 2–6 July 2001* (pp. 292–302). Paris: Recherche sur les Civilisations.

Smith, C., & Burke, H. (2007). *Digging it up down under: A practical guide to doing archaeology in Australia*. New York: Springer.

Stehli, P. (1994). Chronologie der Bandkeramik im Merzbachtal. In J. Lüning & P. Stehli (Eds.), *Die Bandkeramik im Merzbachtal auf der Aldenhovener Platte* (Rheinische Ausgrabungen Band 36, pp. 79–191). Köln: Rheinland Verlag.

Stein, J. K. (1987). Deposits for archaeologists. *Advances in Archaeological Method and Theory, 11*, 337–395.

Struever, S. (1968). Flotation techniques for the recovery of small-scale archaeological remains. *American Antiquity, 33*, 353–362.

Struever, S. (1971). Comments on archaeological data requirements and research strategy. *American Antiquity, 36*, 9–19.

Su, B. (1948[1984]). Doujitai goudongqu muzang (excerpt). In *Su Bingqi Kaoguxue Lunshu Xuanji*, pp. 3–58. Beijing: Wenwu.

Su, B. (1959[1984]). Jieyu, in Zhongguo Kexueyuan Kaogu Yanjiusuo (Ed.), *Luoyang Zhongzhoulu (xigongduan)*. Reprinted in *Su Bingqi Kaoguxue Lunshu Xuanji*, pp. 65–87. Beijing: Wenwu.

Su, B. (1965). Guanyu Yangshao wenhua de ruogan wenti. *Kaogu Xuebao, 1*, 51–82.

Su, B., & Yin, W. (1981). Guanyu kaoguxue wenhua de quxi leixing wenti. *Wenwu, 5*, 10–17.

Su, B., & Yin, W. (1982). Dicengxue yu qiwuxingtaixue. *Wenwu, 4*, 1–7.

SWAP (Ed.). (2007). *Archaeology from the wetlands: Recent perspectives. Proceedings of the 11th WARP conference, Edinburgh 2005*. Edinburgh: Society of Antiquaries of Scotland.

Tahmasebi, M., et al. (2005). Musculoskeletal injuries associated with earthquake: A report of injuries of Iran's December 26, 2003 Bam earthquake casualties managed in tertiary referral centers. *Journal of Injury, 36*(1), 27–32.

Tassie, G. J., & Owens, L. S. (2010). *Standards of archaeological excavation: A fieldguide* (Egyptian Cultural Heritage Organisation Monograph 1). London: Golden House Publications.

Taylor, R. E. (2001). Radiocarbon dating. In D. R. Brothwell & A. M. Pollard (Eds.), *Handbook of archaeological sciences* (pp. 23–34). New York: Wiley.
Terrenato, N. (2004). Sample size matters! The paradox of global trends and local surveys. In S. E. Alcock & J. Cherry (Eds.), *Side-by-side survey. Comparative regional studies in the Mediterranean world* (pp. 36–48). Oxford: Oxbow.
Thompson, E., Williams, H. M., & Minichillo, T. (2010). Middle and late Pleistocene Middle Stone Age lithic technology from Pinnacle Point 13B (Mossel Bay, Western Cape Province, South Africa). *Journal of Human Evolution, 59*, 358–377.
Uhle, M. (1907). *The Emeryville shellmound* (University of California Publications in American Archaeology and Ethnography 7). Berkeley: The University Press.
UNESCO. (2005). *Bam Citadel (Iran)*. (UNESCO report 1208). Available at: http://whc.unesco.org/archive/advisory_body_evaluation/1208.pdf
Ur, J. A. (2003). CORONA satellite photography and ancient road networks: A northern Mesopotamian case study. *Antiquity, 77*, 102–115.
Ur, J. A. (Ed.). (2010). *Urbanism and cultural landscapes in northeastern Syria: The Tell Hamoukar Survey 1999-2001*. Chicago: The Oriental Institute of the University of Chicago.
Urbańczyk, P. (1999). Teoria i praktyka badań wykopaliskowych Tadeusza R. Żurowskiego [Tadeusz R. Żurowski's theory and practice of excavations]. In Z. Kobyliński & J. Wysocki (Eds.), *Tadeusz R. Żurowski i konserwatorstwo archeologiczne w Polsce XX wieku*. Warszawa: "SNAP".
Urbańczyk, P. (2002). Sveigakot 2001. Area T – pit house. In O. Vesteinsson (Ed.), *Archaeological investigations at Sveigakot 2001* (pp. 29–49). Reykjavik: The Icelandic Institute of Archaeology.
Urbańczyk, P. (2004). Excavation methodology in post-war Poland: The forgotten revolution. In G. Carver (Ed.), *Digging in the dirt* (pp. 111–114). Oxford: Tempus.
Urbańczyk, P. (2011). Skonsvika and experiments with digitalised recording system. In B. Olsen, C. Amundsen, & P. Urbańczyk (Eds.), *Hybrid spaces. Medieval Finnmark and the archaeology of multi-room houses* (pp. 169–177). Tromsø: IFSK.
Vaillant, G. C. (1937). History and stratigraphy in the Valley of Mexico. *Scientific Monthly, 44*, 307–324.
Wallace, G. E. (2000). Microscopic views of Swiss lake villages. *Antiquity, 74*, 283–284.
Watson, P., & Todeschini, C. (2007). *The Medici conspiracy*. New York: PublicAffairs.
Watts, I. (2010). The pigments from Pinnacle Point Cave 13B, Western Cape, South Africa. *Journal of Human Evolution, 59*, 392–411.
Welinder, S. (2009). *Sveriges Historia. 13000 f.Kr. – 600 e.Kr.* Stockholm: Norstedts.
Wenwu Editorial Committee (Ed.). (1979). *Wenwu Kaogu Gongzuo Sanshinian*. Beijing: Wenwu.
Wenwu Editorial Committee (Ed.). (1991). *Wenwu Kaogu Gongzuo Shinian*. Beijing: Wenwu.
Wheeler, M. (1954). *Archaeology from the earth*. Oxford: Clarendon.
Whitmore, C. L. (2007). Landscape, time, topology: An archaeological account of the southern Argolid, Greece. In D. Hicks, D. Hicks, L. McAtackney, & G. Fairclough (Eds.), *Envisioning landscape: Situations and standpoints in archaeology and heritage* (pp. 194–225). Walnut Creek: Left Coast.
Wilkinson, T. J. (2003). *Archaeological landscapes of the Near East*. Tucson: The University of Arizona Press.
Willey, G. R. (1953). *Prehistoric settlement patterns in the Virú Valley, Peru* (Bureau of American Ethnology Bulletin 155). Washington, DC: Bureau of American Ethnology.
Willey, G. R., & Sabloff, J. A. (1980). *A history of American archaeology* (2nd ed.). San Francisco: W.H. Freeman.
Willey, G. R. & Phillips, P. (2001[1958]). *Method and theory in American archaeology* (R. L. Lyman & M. J. O'Brien (Eds.). Tuscaloosa: University of Alabama Press.
Williams, H. (2006). *Death and memory in early medieval Britain*. Cambridge: Cambridge University Press.
Wilson, D. R. (1982). *Air photo interpretation for archaeologists*. London: Batsford.

Wiseman, J., & Zachos, K. (Eds.). (2003). *Landscape archaeology in southern Epirus, Greece I* (Hesperia Supplement 32). Athens: The American School of Classical Studies at Athens.

Wolfhechel Jensen, O. (Ed.). (2012). *Histories of archaeological practices: Reflections on methods, strategies and social organisation in past fieldwork* (Stockholm Studies 20). Stockholm: National Historical Museum.

Wood, J. (Ed.). (1994). *Buildings archaeology: Applications in practice* (Oxbow Monograph 43). Oxford: Oxbow Books.

Wood, J. (2006). Historic buildings. In J. Hunter & I. Ralston (Eds.), *Archaeological resource management in the UK: An introduction* (2nd ed., pp. 97–109). Stroud: Sutton.

Xia, N. (1952). Tianye kaogu xulun. *Wenwu Cankao Ziliao, 4*, 81–90.

Xia, N. (1958). Kaogu gongzuo de jinxi–liangtiao luxian de duibi. *Kaogu Tongxun, 2*, 1–4.

Yamin, R. (Ed.). (2000). *Tales of Five Points:Working-class life in nineteenth-century New York*, Volumes I–VI. (Edwards and Kelcey Engineers, Inc. and General Services Administration, Region 2). West Chester: John Milner Associates.

Yan, W. (1994). Kaogu yizhi de fajue fangfa. In *Kaoguxue Yanjiu* (Vol. 2, pp. 249–266). Beijing: Beijing Daxue.

Yellen, J. E. (1977). *Archaeological approaches to the present*. New York: Academic.

Zhang, Z. (1983). Dicengxue yu leixingxue de ruogan wenti. *Wenwu, 5*, 60–69.

Zhang, L. (2011). Soviet inspiration in Chinese archaeology. *Antiquity, 85*(329), 1049–1059.

Zhongguo Kexueyuan Kaogu Yanjiusuo. (1963). *Xi'an Banpo*. Beijing: Wenwu.

Zimmermann, A., Meuers-Balke, J., & Kalis, A. (2005). Das Neolithikum im Rheinland. *Bonner Jahrbücher, 205*, 1–63.

Zou, H. (1956). Shilun Zhengzhou xin faxian de Yin Shang wenhua yizhi. *Kaogu Xuebao, 3*, 77–103.

Zou, H. (1964). Shilun Yinxu wenhua fenqi. *Beijing Daxue Xuebao*, Renwen kexue ban *4*, 77–103; *5*, 63–90.

Żurowski, T. (1947). Pomiar w technice wykopaliskowej [Surveying in excavation technique]. *Z otchłani wieków, 16*(5–6), 136–141.

Żurowski, T. (1949). Uwagi na marginesie 'Studiów nad metodami badań warstw kulturowych w prehistorii polskiej' Włodzimierza Hołubowicza [Remarks on studies on methods of culture layers studying in Polish prehistory" by Włodzimierz Hołubowicz]. *Światowit, 20*, 411–480.

Index

M. Carver et al. (eds.), *Field Archaeology from Around the World*, SpringerBriefs in Archaeology, DOI 10.1007/978-3-319-09819-7

T

Lightning Source UK Ltd.
Milton Keynes UK
UKOW07f2356280115

245270UK00003B/9/P

9 783319 098180